On a
Shoestring
Series

MW01146340

Needs
Assessment
on a Shoestring

Kelly L. Jones
Jody N. Lumsden

PRESS

Alexandria, VA

ATD Press is an internationally renowned source of insightful and practical information on talent development, training, and professional development.

ATD Press
1640 King Street
Alexandria, VA 22314 USA

Ordering information: Books published by ATD Press can be purchased by visiting ATD's website at td.org/books or by calling 800.628.2783 or 703.683.8100.

Library of Congress Control Number: 2023940473

ISBN-10: 1-95394-693-3
ISBN-13: 978-1-953946-93-5
e-ISBN: 978-1-95715-708-5

ATD Press Editorial Staff
Director: Sarah Halgas
Manager: Melissa Jones
Content Manager, Learning and Development: Jes Thompson
Developmental Editor: Jack Harlow
Production Editor: Katy Wiley Stewts
Text and Cover Designer: Shirley E.M. Raybuck

Printed by BR Printers, San Jose, CA

Contents

ABOUT THE
ON A
SHOESTRING
SERIES

ATD's On a Shoestring series helps professionals successfully execute core topics in training and talent development when facing limitations of time, money, staff, and other resources. This series was designed for practitioners who work as a department of one, for new or "accidental" trainers, instructional designers, and learning managers who need fast, inexpensive access to practical strategies that work, and for those who work for small organizations or in industries that have limited training and development resources. This book will help you whether you're new to needs assessments or have a lot of experience but now must conduct needs assessments with less time, support, and budget.

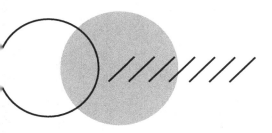

Dedication and Acknowledgments

We dedicate this book to each other. Jody has always enjoyed having Kelly as her supporter, sounding board, and learning theory guru. Kelly has always appreciated Jody's creativity, energy, and curiosity. Life got more exciting when our paths intersected and eventually led to this book. Here's to many more years of being learning friends and co-authors.

To Eliza Blanchard, former content manager and now operations manager for Talent Leader Consortiums, ATD: Thank you for giving us the opportunity to write this book!

To Jack Harlow, senior acquisition and development editor, ATD Press: Thank you for guiding us through drafting and editing. Your work made our work better, and we greatly appreciate your patience and insight.

Kelly would also like to thank the Unicorn Tribunal—Lani, Patty, Jen, and Cinnamon—for your never-ending support and all-around awesomeness. For the grad school angels—Jolly, Jennifer, Susie, and Bonnie—after 13 years, longitudinal data suggest y'all are delightful. For Noelle, there aren't enough words. I can't wait to watch you open a box of these books. For Joshua, you continue to be my favorite child. Thank you for always making me laugh.

Jody would also like to thank the non-book-club book club—Molly Ebel, Laura Russel, and Angie Rybacki—for unyielding support; work buddies Jamie Vanderhyden, Stephanie Hardy, and Naomi Pusch, who encourage me to dream big while getting the work done; and last but not least, Greg Lumsden, Winston, and Whitman who are my favorite people on the planet. The sweetest moments in my life have been shared with you.

Introduction

You can learn a lot about needs assessments through mystery stories. Sherlock Holmes leveraged observational skills and deductive reasoning to solve crimes. Velma Dinkley sought rational explanations for each conundrum she faced with the Scooby gang. Angus MacGyver employed ingenuity to defeat different problems using simple, readily available tools. Hercule Poirot relied on psychology and a knowledge of human tendencies to figure out every puzzle. These detectives didn't have large teams, unlimited budgets, or a bottomless well of resources to work with, but they succeeded by identifying *who*, *where*, and *how* to solve the problems that no one else could solve. ("It was Professor Plum, in the library, with the candlestick!")

Talent development practitioners have many job titles and serve many capacities. We wear many hats, including instructional designer, content developer, e-learning specialist, trainer, facilitator, teacher, coach, learning manager, project manager, performance improvement specialist, researcher, analyst, problem solver, and change agent. To conduct an effective needs assessment, you'll add one more role to your professional repertoire, and for that, you need a detective hat.

There are many parallels between a detective's role in leading an investigation and your role in leading a needs assessment. Detectives don't have answers when they start a case, and it's important for them not to jump to conclusions. Through the process of investigation, they ask questions, conduct interviews, make observations, collect evidence, evaluate findings, and eventually solve the case. When you conduct a needs assessment, you'll follow a strategic analysis process to uncover real problems, root causes, and viable solutions.

There's not one right way to conduct a needs assessment, but conducting one is always the right way to begin a training, organization development, or change management project. Ultimately, your job is to provide analysis and solutions, and you can't do that without understanding employees, the contexts in which they work, the organization and its goals, and the real problems that need to be addressed. During a needs assessment, you'll investigate and uncover everything you can about the key problem to be solved—without immediately jumping to solutions. To solve a business need, think like a detective.

Conducting a Needs Assessment— Even on a Shoestring

No matter what talent development problem you're tackling, we have one piece of advice for you: Always start with a needs assessment.

This book will help you build, borrow, and buy your way through a successful needs assessment. The work may feel intimidating, overwhelming, or impossible, especially if you're part of a small team or operating as a department of one. You may be new to the process and unsure of how to begin. You may face expectations from stakeholders who don't understand the importance of needs assessments, demand training when training may not be the right solution, or expect deliverables with accelerated deadlines. You may think that needs assessments make sense in theory, but in practice, completing one requires more time and resources than you have available.

If you struggle in any of these ways, this is the book for you. Regardless of the scope of the project, the constraints of the business problem, or how you get the job done, the steps associated with needs assessments are flexible enough to scale up or down. In other words, you don't need months, thousands of dollars, or a large staff to conduct an effective needs assessment. Needs assessments can be complex and challenging, but with a good strategy, the work can be broken down into manageable pieces, and many tasks can be completed simultaneously or iteratively. You can save time, effort, and costs without cutting corners on quality.

We have each been a "department of one" with limited resources, and we understand the challenges of meeting expectations and delivering results while operating on a shoestring budget. We wrote this book so that you can learn how to conduct a needs assessment with confidence and efficiency—two of the best things you can have when you're operating with limited resources.

Jody has worked as a graduate teaching assistant, graphic designer, instructor, learning designer, media developer, digital instructional designer, and learning technology consultant. She now works as a senior consultant, guiding organizations through large-scale change management strategies and workforce upskilling efforts. Kelly has worked as a learning technology specialist, instructional designer, curriculum developer, instructor, consultant, and leader for higher education, nonprofit, and corporate organizations. She's currently the director of learning and development for a rapidly growing startup, leading efforts to educate and empower thousands of employees in almost 200 locations across the country.

In each of our professional roles, we've conducted various types of needs assessments and encountered challenges and failures when solutions were implemented without one. We advocate for needs assessments because we learned their value the hard way. Through trial and error, diverse experiences, challenges, and successes, we've developed practical strategies for designing and conducting needs assessments in a reasonable amount of time, without a lot of help, and with small budgets. Our goal is to give you the strategies you need to efficiently identify needs, collect and analyze data, and make informed recommendations.

Work Backward: Needs Assessment Overview

What is a needs assessment? A needs assessment is a contextual, investigative process of identifying and addressing gaps between a current state and a goal state. When you conduct a needs assessment, you begin by determining the end goal and then identifying what is needed to reach that goal. The *gaps* you identify are the *needs*—the things that must change so that an organization can reach its goal. This process includes analyzing the current state and the goal state within the context of the organization and identifying the gaps, root causes, challenges, opportunities, roadblocks, and solutions that must be addressed to solve problems.

It Doesn't Always End With Training

A needs assessment should be intentionally broad in scope. A training needs assessment can be part of a broader needs assessment but should not be the initial focus—the right solution may or may not be training. If the need is identified as a gap in skills, behaviors, or knowledge, then it makes sense to expand the project to include a training-specific needs assessment. Other needs require different solutions such as new processes, organizational practices, resource allocation, or change management initiatives. Training is not always the answer.

Training is expensive—it costs time and money to build, deliver, evaluate, and maintain training programs, and employees' time away from work is expensive as well. According to ATD's *2022 State of the Industry*, the direct learning expenditure per employee was $1,280 in 2021. By ensuring that training is only leveraged as a solution when the need is a knowledge or skills gap, and that when training solutions are built, they are effective, talent development professionals can make positive contributions to their organization's bottom line and build trusted partnerships with organizational leaders.

It's important to recognize the risk of not doing a needs assessment. Training can be misunderstood as a miracle cure that will fix all performance issues, productivity challenges, communication gaps, and more. Training can also be minimized as a check-the-box step and be overlooked in new technology rollouts, process improvements, and other change initiatives.

If business needs are not correctly identified, you can end up with scope creep, multiple rounds of revisions, lack of performance metrics, ineffective solutions, unrealized return on investment (ROI), frustrated learners, and leaders who question the value of training initiatives. If the gaps you identify are knowledge or skill needs, then a training needs assessment is the first step of the instructional design work required to address the training need. Training isn't a magic bullet, but when it's done right and addresses real needs, it can be a significant contributor to organizational success.

DEEPER DIVE
Instructional Design on a Shoestring

Want to learn more about designing effective training and learning solutions? Check out *Instructional Design on a Shoestring* by Brian Washburn.

The Purpose of Needs Assessments

A needs assessment focuses on real business problems and answers the question: "What needs to change?" If you need to change behavior, increase knowledge or conceptual understanding, shift organizational culture or practices, improve processes, allocate resources, or enhance performance, you must understand both the current state *and* the goal state to accurately identify the problem, root cause, and needs. Almost all training, process, resource, and organizational goals can be analyzed in terms of change and addressed through an effective needs assessment, but you must start broad and work backward to identify which solutions will best address the true needs.

Why Work Backward?

To solve the right problem, you must have a clear picture of the end goal and then identify what is needed to reach that goal within the context of the organization's present reality. By starting with the end goal and working backward, an effective needs assessment allows you to make a real impact while saving time, effort, and money.

Working backward—analyzing the gaps between the ideal future state and the current state—allows you to understand the big picture, including business goals, needs, root causes, priorities, resources, and constraints. This big picture perspective will allow you to:

- Set realistic expectations with your stakeholders, clients, leaders, participants, team, and the employees you serve.
- Accurately identify needs.
- Design solutions that will meet those needs.
- Plan the metrics for measuring the success of solutions.

To conduct an effective needs assessment, you must have the right contextual understanding, ask the right questions, observe the right things, gather accurate data, analyze data effectively, and build actionable recommendations. It can be tough to identify needs, especially when you're sorting through conflicting opinions, asked to be reactive instead of proactive, pressured by the urgent needs and demands of other departments and company leaders, and trying to demonstrate the ROI of your work.

The strategies in this book will help you accurately identify needs, collect and analyze data, and align recommendations with strategic goals so that you can solve the right problems and bring value to your organizations through efficient, cost-effective, time-saving solutions.

Build, Borrow, or Buy: How to Use This Book

This book offers guidance and strategies to support talent development professionals in identifying and addressing organizational needs. It's a field guide designed for savvy practitioners who may not have enough time or resources available but want to conduct high-quality needs assessments. This book will also be helpful for graduate students, talent development teams who want to design their own professional development paths through a shared book study, or a book club discussion for professional association chapter members or communities of practice. This book is designed to help you find the information, strategies, and resources you need as quickly and easily as possible. It's organized into three parts:

- **Build.** Part 1 provides a comprehensive overview of needs assessments methodology and describes processes and strategies you can use even when facing time and resource constraints. You'll learn how to build a needs assessment strategy (chapter 1), build insight through data collection (chapter 2) and analysis (chapter 3), and build effective solution recommendations (chapter 4). For most needs assessments, especially when you're working on a shoestring, you'll likely build more than you'll borrow or buy, so this part of the book is the longest.
- **Borrow.** Part 2 provides solutions for borrowing existing information, talent, and resources. You'll learn how to identify and use relevant data that already exists within your organization (chapter 5), and how to best leverage the time, talent, and perspectives of your subject matter experts and stakeholders (chapter 6).
- **Buy.** Part 3 provides resource management strategies for conducting needs assessments, including ways to gain buy-in from leadership and stakeholders. You'll learn ways to budget the time needed to conduct a needs assessment and strategies for managing your time effectively (chapter 7). You'll also find suggestions for free or cost-effective tools and resources that are worth spending money on (chapter 8), along with strategies for advocating for more time and resources when needed (chapter 9).

Recurring Elements

Throughout this book, you'll see icons marking four recurring elements:

 Time Saver: This is a strategy for shaving time off a best practice.

 On the Cheap: These are free or low-cost ideas and tools or suggestions for how to get funding.

 Deeper Dive: These callouts say something like, "Did this whet your appetite? Here's a resource to deepen your knowledge."

 Tool: This is a job aid, tool, or checklist to help you put ideas into action. You'll find them throughout the text and complete versions in appendix A.

In addition to the tools, in chapter 1 we introduce you to a needs assessment case study based on a customer service scenario. In appendix B, you'll find the complete worked example for this scenario. This worked example will walk you through the team's journey from start to finish, and you'll see samples of their strategy plan, data collection and analysis methods, findings, conclusions, recommendations, and results report.

PART 1
BUILD

When you're operating on a shoestring, you'll most likely build more than you borrow and borrow more than you buy. Part 1 of this book provides a comprehensive overview of needs assessment methodology. The following chapters include many suggestions, tools, and examples to help you understand the big-picture view of the needs assessment strategy so you can invest your time wisely, work backward to start with the end goal, and build the strategy you need to get there as quickly and easily as possible.

In this part of the book, you'll learn how to build:

- A needs assessment strategy
- Insight through data collection and analysis
- Recommendations based on your findings and conclusions to effectively share the results of a needs assessment

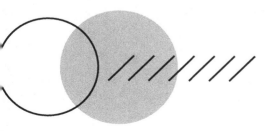

1
Building the Strategy

What do a detective and a needs assessment practitioner have in common? They're both under pressure to solve problems quickly and thoroughly, often with limited resources and in challenging situations. They both need insight and a strong strategy to leverage the best research tactics. And if you're a gumshoe operating on a shoestring, you need techniques that will save you time, effort, and money while still getting the job done right.

A needs assessment is a contextual, investigative process of identifying and addressing gaps (or needs) between a current state and a goal state. The purpose of a needs assessment is to answer the question: "What needs to change?" Conducting a needs assessment is the best way to set yourself and your stakeholders up for success *before* you invest in designing training, workshops, programs, or other organizational initiatives.

Data-driven needs assessments are critical for organizational success. As the Indeed.com Editorial Team (2019) explains, "A needs assessment removes uncertainty by exploring the company's specific needs and the actions it can take to attain them." Start with a needs assessment to ensure that you've identified the right problem and have the right data to address it. Organizational challenges that can benefit from an effective needs assessment include:
- Training requests
- New technology or process rollouts
- New products or product updates
- Declining employee performance or revised performance standards
- Increasing employee turnover rates
- Modified budget allocations
- Low customer satisfaction rates

- Loss of profitability or productivity
- New laws, regulations, or compliance requirements

Needs assessments can help provide strategic focus during volatility, reduce uncertainty, create clarity from ambiguity, and solve complex problems. This chapter will walk you through the entire needs assessment process, give you tools you can begin using immediately, and help you identify each step of building a successful needs assessment strategy.

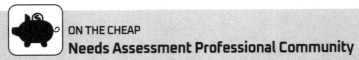

ON THE CHEAP
Needs Assessment Professional Community

Jody and Kelly are active members of ATD (the Association for Talent Development) and AEA (the American Evaluation Association). You can purchase membership to either organization (at td.org or eval.org) to gain access to resources that will help you conduct needs assessments. Each organization also publishes a blog that you can access for free:

- ATD Blog: td.org/insights
- AEA365 Blog: aea365.org/blog

You can also learn more about the AEA Needs Assessment Topic Interest Group at comm.eval.org/needsassessment/home to connect with other practitioners who are tackling the work of conducting needs assessments on a shoestring.

Be Sure You're Solving the Right Problem

Many training projects and other organizational initiatives begin with a manager requesting an immediate solution that they believe will solve an urgent problem. However, the problem is often more complex than they realize, caused by something they haven't accounted for, or requires a different solution than originally imagined. Consider this customer service scenario:

> Over the last year, the turnover rate for customer service employees has increased by 7 percent. High employee turnover is causing serious performance problems. When the customer service director learns that the customer satisfaction rate has fallen to 68 percent, he contacts the functional training team and insists they start work right

away on a new onboarding training course. He believes new employees' lack of knowledge is driving the performance declines.

The functional training team's instructional designer pauses her current projects to meet this urgent need. She interviews the customer support director to determine key skills for new hires, revises the current onboarding materials, and spends three weeks developing a new, interactive, mobile-friendly e-learning course.

For the next six months, all new customer service employees complete the course during their first few days on the job, but performance metrics don't improve and the turnover rate continues to rise. The customer service director now blames the instructional designer—he believes the new onboarding course isn't effective.

The instructional designer feels defeated. Learner satisfaction scores in the course are high, the content is engaging, and the course functionality works well. She's not sure what went wrong. She didn't know that employee turnover had been a critical issue for the last two years, and that the director had already tried a financial intervention—merit increases, key performance indicator (KPI) incentives, and signing bonuses—with no resulting improvements in retention. If she had known, she would have approached his training request very differently. This situation calls for a needs assessment.

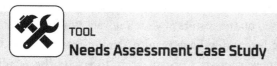

TOOL
Needs Assessment Case Study

In appendix B, you'll find a worked example of a needs assessment case study based on this customer service scenario. The worked example will walk you through the team's journey from start to finish, and you'll see samples of their strategy plan, data collection and analysis methods, findings, conclusions, recommendations, and results report. The details and explanations provided in this example will help you connect the concepts presented in this book to a realistic needs assessment project conducted by a team of one.

Talent development teams receive many urgent requests for training, and urgency can often overshadow the true cause of performance problems. Many talent development professionals go into this field of work because they want to help others succeed. Because they are often departments of one or few, tasked with managing all training and professional development efforts on a shoestring budget, they try to meet requests quickly to add value to their organization. To truly make a positive impact, however, you must identify the real need at the heart of the issue you're being asked to address *before* delivering a solution. To do that, work backward to build a strong needs assessment strategy.

The Needs Assessment Process

The needs assessment process is both an art and a science. With experience, you will refine your own needs assessment methodology and adjust as needed to serve the project you're working on. In general, though, the needs assessment process has three parts: building the strategy, building the case, and building the recommendations.

First, build your needs assessment process strategy—this is your investigation plan. Think of your strategy as the iconic magnifying glass; it's the way you'll unravel the complex mystery of business needs. Building your strategy is the discovery work of identifying the key problem, current state, goal state, gaps (needs) between those states, key stakeholders, research questions, and the success metrics needed to evaluate solutions.

Once your strategy is in place, you'll build your case through data collection and analysis. Building your case is the work of critical, creative thinking that leads to actionable insights. Once your data case is established, you'll build recommendations based on the results of your analysis. Building recommendations is the work of leveraging your results, demonstrating value to your stakeholders, and empowering your organization to act on the results of your needs assessment. This chapter will walk you through building your needs assessment process strategy. Chapters 2 and 3 will take you through building your case by collecting and analyzing data. Chapter 4 will guide you through the process of building recommendations based on your data analysis and sharing the results of the needs assessment.

A great way to start is by envisioning the results of your needs assessment so that you can account for and manage expectations and focus on the right things. The questions in the Future Debrief time saver are a great resource for working backward and starting strong.

TIME SAVER
Future Debrief

Before launching a needs assessment, it can be helpful to envision the *results* of the project. Pretend that you are debriefing your CEO on the results of the needs assessment and summarizing your key findings and recommended solutions. The following questions create a framework for planning your needs assessment strategy. Consider the data you will need to collect, the people you will need to include, and the insight you will need to gain to answer these questions at the end of the needs assessment:

- What was the key problem?
- How did you know this was the right problem to solve?
- What was the current state of this problem?
- What was the goal state of this problem?
- Which stakeholders participated in this needs assessment?
- What data did you collect and analyze to assess needs and build recommendations?
- What solutions did you recommend, and why?
- What resources are needed to implement those solutions?
- If implemented, how will the solutions be evaluated?
- What value did this needs assessment provide to your organization?

A Strategic Approach

Before you solve an organizational problem, you must verify that you've identified the *right* problem. It sounds obvious, but this first step will make or break your needs assessment and it's easy to overlook key considerations After all, you don't yet know what you don't yet know. Strategically planning your needs assessment approach, in collaboration with your stakeholders, is the best way to gain the insights needed for meaningful, measurable results (Figure 1-1).

Figure 1-1. Needs Assessment Methodology: Build the Strategy

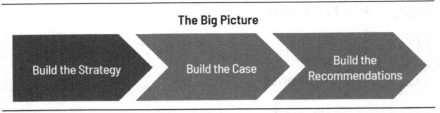

For example, Jody worked on a project that focused on the localization of an enterprise-backed training program. Prior to doing the work, she considered what she needed, when it was due, and how she could get the work done. She decided that during the limited project timeframe, she wanted to understand the local employees' needs. This was the highest value work because it helped with implementation, communication strategies, and company knowledge. She identified the best opportunity through strategy planning.

Kelly conducted a needs assessment for an industry-specific leadership development program and wanted to conduct multiple focus groups with dozens of potential program participants and participating companies' CEOs. The project timeline absolutely did not allow for that work. Instead, she opted for interviews with 10 members of the client's board of directors. Not only did that approach save valuable time, but it also helped gain buy-in from board members who would later support and promote the program. Kelly's strategic plan for this project helped her focus on the most important information she needed to collect (industry leaders' perspectives) and identify resources for data collection (members of the board of directors).

10 Needs Assessment Strategy Components

Building a strong strategy is especially important when you are operating on a shoestring. You don't want to waste time, money, or resources, so start by building a strategy plan that will help you focus on the work that brings the most value to your project.

The top 10 components of your needs assessment strategy are:

1. The primary problem to be solved
2. The business impact of the problem
3. The current state and goal state of the problem, and known gaps

4. The stakeholders

5. The research methodology (research questions, data collection, and analysis plan)

6. The project scope (expectations, timeline, budget, and available resources)

7. Plans for sharing the results of the needs assessment

8. Constraints (limitations and delimitations)

9. Success measures to evaluate recommendations

10. Value measures for the needs assessment

If you're thinking, "Wait! I'm a team of one and working without a budget! How am I supposed to build a strategy with 10 parts?" Hang tight. These components are important, but you can build a solid plan with less. Table 1-1 shows a shoestring version of our top 10 list.

Table 1-1. Categorizing the 10 Components of a Needs Assessment Strategy

Must Have	• The primary problem to be solved • The business impact of the problem • The current state and goal state of the problem, and known gaps • The stakeholders • The research methodology (research questions, data collection, and analysis plan)
Should Have	• The project scope (expectations, timeline, budget, and available resources) • Plans for sharing the results of the needs assessment
Nice to Have	• Constraints (limitations and delimitations) • Success measures to evaluate recommendations • Value measures for the needs assessment

We'll discuss each of these components in order of importance and share pointers to help you plan your needs assessment strategy on a shoestring.

In addition, we've included a summary at the beginning of each component section designed to help you determine the value of that component for your project. You can skip or revisit these sections as needed to design strategy plans for different types of needs assessment projects. To save you time, effort, and frustration, we also created worksheets to help you build your needs assessment strategy (appendix A) and a worked example of how to use them (appendix B).

▶ **Why is this important for your strategy plan?** A quick summary of why you should consider including this component

▶ **When can you skip it?** Reasonable considerations for when this component may not be required for your project

▶ **What's the minimal viable product (MVP)?** The realistic requirements for completing your project with usable results

TOOL
Needs Assessment Strategy Worksheet

In appendix A, you'll find a worksheet you can adopt or adapt for your own needs assessment projects. It captures all the elements covered in this chapter from problem statement to after-action review and lessons learned.

Now let's dive into the components, starting with the most important: identifying the real problem that needs to be solved.

Identifying the Problem

▶ **Why is this important for your strategy plan?** The problem is the reason for the needs assessment; it is the issue, challenge, or opportunity to be solved. If you don't know the real problem, you can't assess needs.

▶ **When can you skip it?** Never. You can't build a strategy until you identify the real problem. A perfectly executed needs assessment that solves the wrong problem doesn't help anyone and will end up costing you time, effort, money, relationship capital, and credibility.

▶ **What's the MVP?** It will include clear descriptions of:
  • The key problem to be solved
  • The business impact of the problem
  • The current state of the problem
  • The goal state
  • The gaps between the current state and the goal state

Needs assessment projects may come to you in several ways. You may be directly assigned a needs assessment by your manager or by a leader at your organization. You may need to conduct a needs assessment in response to a training request. You may have a client who hires you to conduct a needs assessment, or a client who doesn't realize that they need a needs assessment. In any case, the first step is to capture the reason for the needs assessment.

The heart of a needs assessment is identifying the key problem to be solved, the business impact of the problem, the current state, the goal state, and the gaps that exist between the current and goal states. Aim for quantifiable, measurable descriptions of each element; specificity will set the parameters of the needs assessment and provide metrics needed to evaluate the business impact and the feasibility of recommendations. You might be wondering what each of these terms means and why they are essential to address at the beginning of a needs assessment. Let's define our terms.

Problem

A problem is a business need. The problem is the reason for the needs assessment; it is the issue, challenge, or opportunity to be solved. You'll most likely hear the problem expressed in need statements:

- "We need training! Our employees don't know how to use our systems."
- "We need to hire more employees. The workload is too much for our staff."
- "We need to improve the accounts payable process. We're falling behind on payments."
- "We need better software. This system just doesn't work."

Identifying the problem can be challenging. It's human nature to jump to solutions as soon as we see a problem—notice that each of the examples actually expresses needs in terms of solutions. Also, notice that none of these problem statements include metrics; they aren't yet quantifiable. You'll need to work with stakeholders to identify and quantify the problem as early as possible to plan an effective needs assessment.

During the intake discussion (the first conversation you have with a sponsor about a needs assessment project), make sure to ask two critical questions:

1. When did this problem start?
2. What has already been tried to solve it?

A needs assessment should focus on only one problem at a time. Today's workplace challenges are complex, and complex problems require in-depth assessment. Key problems usually affect profitability, productivity, strategic goals, employee retention, and organizational performance. If you identify multiple key problems, you will need to work with senior leaders and stakeholders to prioritize needs assessment projects to address each one.

Current State

The current state of the problem is a measurable description of reality as it is today. You can start to identify the current state by listening to stakeholders' rationale of needs. In the previous examples, the follow-up statements—the takeholder's expression of *why* the solution is needed—are possible indications of the current state:

- "Our employees don't know how to use our systems."
- "The workload is too much for our staff."
- "We're falling behind on payments."
- "This system just doesn't work."

Just like with the problem, you will work with stakeholders to identify and quantify the current state and validate with data. Sometimes, conducting a needs assessment requires you to collect and analyze data about the current state *before* you can accurately determine needs.

Goal State

The goal state is the desired outcome of change—the future results of solving today's problem. Just like the problem and current state, it's important to quantify the goal state so that recommendations can be made and metrics can be identified to evaluate solutions. A goal state like "improve employee retention" isn't quantifiable, so stakeholders may have different expectations of the needs assessment and recommended solutions. A goal statement like "increase employee retention by 15 percent over the next six months and maintain a retention rate of 85 percent or greater" is measurable, and the quantifiable outcomes can be used to determine project priority, value measures for the needs assessment, and solutions evaluation. Notice, however, that the goal "increase employee retention by 15 percent over the next six months" requires you to identify the current employee retention rate. You can't measure improvement without a current baseline.

Known Gaps

Gaps are the differences between the current state and the goal state. Identify a gap, and you've identified a business need. Gaps (needs) emerge during a needs assessment, and some gaps are known or can be identified and measured as soon as the problem, current state, and future state are identified and quantified.

Business Impact

The business impact tells us why this problem is worth solving, how the problem is affecting the organization's performance, and how urgently the problem needs to be solved. If the business impact is high, the problem's priority should also be high.

Crafting the Problem Statement

It can be helpful to draft several versions of the problem statement and refine it as you define the current state, goal state, known gaps, and business impact. Be as precise and concise as possible.

Clearly defining the problem, current state, goal state, and business impact is more difficult than it sounds. When trying to accurately describe the current state, for example, you may face a lack of current data or documentation, limited access to interviews and observations, lack of access to or limited time with subject matter experts, or employees who are reluctant to complain or tell you about skill or knowledge gaps. Or, when attempting to define the goal state, you may face unrealistic expectations, budget constraints, workforce gaps, technology and system challenges, or deadlines that are either too soon or set too far in the future.

Your job in these conversations is to ask questions; learn the landscape of the problem; holistically understand the current state, goal state, and business impact; collect data to verify the problem's current state and business impact; and help leaders identify measurable objectives for the goal state. Stakeholders may disagree about the problem and the business impact. By asking a lot of questions, you can compare stakeholders' responses and then compare their responses against the data you collect to validate the problem, current state, and business impact.

TIME SAVER
Cut to the Chase and Ask Five Whys

Prepare yourself with "cut to the chase" questions to make the most of limited time with leaders, subject matter experts, and stakeholders. These shortcut questions can be a great starting place for quickly getting to the heart of a business problem. By asking different stakeholders and subject matter experts the same questions, you can compare their responses and identify differences that may point to unaligned goals, overlooked perspectives, and organization gaps.

Cut-to-the-chase questions include:
- What is the most important thing that needs to change?
- What is currently driving the need for this change?
- What will happen if we don't solve this problem?
- If you could wave a magic wand, what is the *one* thing you would do to solve this problem?
- How will you know if this problem is solved?

The five whys method, developed from the Toyota production system, is a quick way to guide stakeholders through the process of identifying a needs assessment problem. The process is straightforward: Ask *why* five times, or repeatedly until the question can no longer be answered. This process will eventually lead to the identification of the key business problem that can be addressed through a needs assessment. You can start with a trigger question to get started like *"Why is this a problem?"*

Identifying Stakeholders

▶ **Why is this important for your strategy plan?** Stakeholders are the people who need to solve the key problem, are responsible for solving the problem, or have a vested interest in the problem (and therefore have a vested interest in the needs assessment).

► **When can you skip it?** Never. If no one has a stake in the key problem, then there is no reason to conduct a needs assessment. You need support, input, insight, and aligned expectations with the right stakeholders.

► **What's the MVP?** It will include a list of key stakeholders. Ideally, one of these stakeholders will be a project sponsor—a leader who can help guide the scope and ensure the completion of the needs assessment.

Stakeholders are people within an organization who are interested in the needs assessment, will be affected by the results of the needs assessment, are responsible for the problem being solved, or may benefit from solutions. In other words, stakeholders have a vested interest in the needs assessment. The larger the problem, the more stakeholders you're likely to have.

When in doubt about stakeholders, start by asking, "Who is responsible for this process, department, system, policy, or result?" Corporate shareholders, for example, are invested in a business's financial success; needs assessment stakeholders are invested in (and often responsible for) solving a business need. You'll learn more about working with stakeholders in chapter 6.

Different stakeholders have different levels of investment in a needs assessment. We like to start by listing all the project stakeholders and categorizing them as a sponsor, key stakeholder, advisor, collaborator, or partner:

- **Sponsor.** Needs assessment projects usually have a sponsor—a primary stakeholder who leads or is responsible for the business function's role in the needs assessment. Often, the sponsor is the person who requested the needs assessment, but they may also be assigned by a more senior leader. The sponsor usually shares responsibility with the needs assessment practitioner for completing the project and provides final approval. Sponsors may have the authority to implement recommendations.

- **Champion.** A champion is a leader with the insight, influence, authority, and interest required to guide the goals of your needs assessment, secure resources, and support recommended solutions. Champions can provide support at a higher leadership level than what you may be able to do on your own. If your needs assessment project doesn't have a clear champion, ask yourself who will care most about the outcome. Who is the driver of the business need at stake? If that leader buys into the needs assessment, and you're able to communicate the value of the work to them, you will be able to enlist their support when you're facing challenges or it's time to share the results of the needs assessment with other leaders and stakeholders.

- **Key stakeholders.** For a needs assessment, key stakeholders include additional leaders who are responsible for or affected by aspects of the problem and subject matter experts who can contribute to understanding the problem and potential solutions.
- **Advisors.** Advisors are people inside and sometimes outside your organization who can help you by offering counsel on the problem, the needs assessment strategy, or potential solutions. Advisors will have skills and knowledge to provide technical guidance. Needs assessment advisors may be members of the business line you are supporting, training professionals, or leadership mentors.
- **Collaborators.** Collaborators are people who can assist you in doing the work of a needs assessment, such as collecting and analyzing data. Look for possible collaborators on your team, in other training areas, or in specialized roles such as data analysts or human resources business partners.
- **Partners.** Partners are people in your organization who have insight that will help you complete your project. Partners don't usually take an active role in the needs assessment, but they can help steer you in the right direction when you're not sure where to look for the information you need.

Once you've identified your stakeholders, work with them to determine the scope, expectations, and resources available for the needs assessment as you clarify the key questions that need to be addressed and the data that you'll need to answer those questions. Before you can clearly determine the needs assessment project scope and expectations, you must determine your research questions. It's time to grab your detective hat!

Identifying the Methodology: Start With Research Questions

▶ **Why is this important for your strategy plan?** Your research questions will determine the strategies you need to collect and analyze data and set the scope for the needs assessment.

▶ **When can you skip it?** Never. Conducting a needs assessment without specific research questions is like going grocery shopping without a list. You might gather the wrong things or skip the things you need most.

▶ **What's the MVP?** It will include a clear question, or several questions, about the key problem that you can solve by collecting and analyzing data.

Once you've identified the problem, current state, goal state, and business impact, you can develop research questions to guide your data collection and data analysis processes. You can start by writing a working draft of research questions, but be sure to review them with your key stakeholders before you begin collecting data. Your stakeholders may be able to clarify, correct, or enhance your research questions. Align with stakeholders on the research questions to ensure your data collection process is as effective as possible.

TIME SAVER
Making Research Questions Relevant

Here are a few notes to help jumpstart your process:

- Good research questions can't be answered with a simple yes or no—instead, they provide depth and breadth for the needs assessment topic.
- Focus on the information stakeholders need to make informed decisions—don't include "nice to know" questions that aren't directly related to the problem you're trying to assess.
- To evaluate the relevance of a potential research question, ask your stakeholders, "What could you do if you had the answer to this question?"
- If you're new to writing research questions, feel stuck, or don't have enough information about the business problem, start by asking your stakeholders the top three things they'd like to know about the problem you are investigating.

If your shoestring is incredibly short, frayed at the edges, or barely hanging on, start with the two most basic research questions:

- What is causing this problem?
- What needs to change to solve this problem?

Your research questions set the scope for your needs assessment. Often, you may develop a primary research question with a few supporting subquestions. This allows for large investigations to be broken down into smaller segments. Asking clear questions will help you identify data sources and ensure that you have the right information to complete the needs assessment.

Your research questions kickstart your needs assessment methodology—to answer them, you must determine what data you need to collect and analyze. You can add, modify, or remove research questions as needed when you begin collecting data and learn more about the key problem you are trying to solve. You'll learn more about data collection and analysis in chapters 2 and 3.

Identifying the Project Scope

▶ **Why is this important for your strategy plan?** The project scope defines expectations for requirements, results, deadlines, budgets, and resources. Without clear expectations, you may quickly experience scope creep.

▶ **When can you skip it?** Small needs assessments or those addressing problems with minor-to-medium business impact may not require a detailed project scope. If you're conducting a needs assessment for a single team or a single process, you can stay on track through informal alignment with stakeholders on goals and expectations.

▶ **What's the MVP?** The MVP will include an agreement with stakeholders on what the needs assessment will and won't include, how and when it will be completed, and what resources are available.

As you plan and conduct a needs assessment, you'll wear many hats—including a detective hat, consultant hat, analyst hat, and project manager hat. Sometimes, managing the project can be just as challenging as collecting and analyzing the data. One of the most important steps for managing your time, resources, and stakeholders' expectations is to clearly determine the needs assessment project scope as early as possible.

To understand project scope, it's helpful to identify the high-level milestones. The major milestones for a needs assessment are universal, but the timeline is usually determined by the project's scope and available resources, including support staff, data sources, data collection and analysis tools, access to participants if needed, and budget. The milestones in Figure 1-2 can be used to track significant points in the project.

Figure 1-2. Needs Assessment Project Scope: Milestones

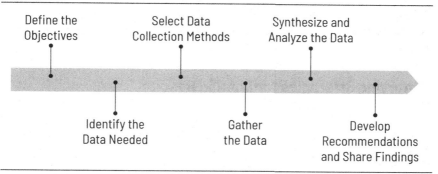

You don't need a formalized project management system to conduct a needs assessment, but you do want to align with your team, leaders, and stakeholders on the project expectations, deadline, and budget. Defining the project scope is the best way to avoid *scope creep*—delays, increased costs, and inefficiencies caused by adding requirements, expectations, or additional problems to a needs assessment project once it's started. In short, determine what's in scope for the needs assessment—what problem will you research, and what findings, conclusions, and recommendations are required for the project to deliver expected results?

Scope creep is a needs assessment's mortal enemy—nothing can kill your project faster. Early in her career, Kelly was assigned a needs assessment project to determine why faculty members were reluctant to use a university's learning management system (LMS). That project quickly derailed into a series of wish lists and demands so large that the only solution seemed to be adopting a new LMS, which would have cost more than six figures and taken months to implement. Luckily, the project had a strong sponsor who was able to refocus the scope and advise Kelly to ask different questions. Kelly went back to each faculty member and asked, "How is using the LMS different from your usual classroom teaching, and what concerns does this cause?" That approach shifted the focus from the LMS's features and got to the heart of the instructors' real concerns—they weren't using the LMS because they believed their syllabi, course content, and instructional materials would become the intellectual property of the university, could be seen and judged by their peers, or be "borrowed" and used by other instructors. Kelly was then able to provide that insight to the academic leaders who in turn developed a faculty intellectual property policy, addressed instructors' concerns, and required access and security settings in the LMS. Faculty usage doubled within a semester and grew steadily after that.

Identifying Strategies for Sharing Results and Recommendations

- ▶ **Why is this important for your strategy plan?** A needs assessment ends with key findings about the problem, and usually, recommendations for solving the problem. You need to know what stakeholders expect to see as the result of conducting a needs assessment—what are the key deliverables?
- ▶ **When can you skip it?** Needs assessment projects that are small, informal, or internal (projects done by your team for your team), or those addressing problems with minor-to-medium business impact, may not require a full results report. However, you will need to share results with key stakeholders.
- ▶ **What's the MVP?** It will include alignment with your stakeholders on their expectations for the delivery of the needs assessment results (and recommendations, if applicable), including what will be shared, how results will be shared, and who results will be shared with. An MVP can be as simple as sending them an email with your key findings and recommendations.

There isn't one right way to share results and recommendations, but it's important to plan a strategy for doing so. Sharing the results of a needs assessment gives you the opportunity to make your organization aware of problems, relevant explanations, causes, implications, and solutions. A common share strategy is delivering a results report or presentation, often via multiple versions for specific audiences. In our experience, the executive summary of the results report is the most valuable medium for sharing results. (See chapter 4 for more details and an example.) Work with your stakeholders to develop a communication plan so you can meet expectations for effectively sharing the results of your needs assessment.

When building your needs assessment strategy, ensure you understand all the audiences for the results and recommendations so you can identify the best strategies for keeping them informed and engaged. Remember that different audiences have different needs and different sensitivities related to the needs assessment problem, business impact, current state, goal state, and recommended solutions. Consider the various points in time when it will be helpful to inform audiences of project milestone statuses. We recommend discussing communication expectations with your stakeholders early on so that you'll know the best ways to share the results of the needs assessment for your specific audience.

Identifying Constraints: Limitations and Delimitations

- ▶ **Why is this important for your strategy plan?** Constraints provide boundaries for your needs assessment project, and clearly defined boundaries will help you determine what's in and out of scope and what options for data collection and analysis are feasible.
- ▶ **When can you skip it?** Small projects, or those addressing a problem with minor-to-medium business impact, may not require you to detail or document constraints, but it's always helpful to define them for yourself, even if just informally for your own understanding of the project.
- ▶ **What's the MVP?** It will include the project deadline or timeframe expectations and list of available data sources (who you can include in interviews, surveys, or observations and what documents you can access). Also, outline what is realistic with the data collection strategy you select (which you'll learn more about in chapter 2).

As you plan your needs assessment strategy, you'll need to identify the project constraints—limitations and delimitations. *Limitations* are things you cannot control, such as budget, timeline (if the deadline is set by someone else), location of employees, lack of resources, and project scope determined by leadership. *Delimitations* are limitations you choose to impose on a needs assessment to prevent scope creep, manage expectations, and meet deadlines. For example, if your budget is a limitation, and you don't have enough resources to conduct multiple focus groups, you may have to choose electronic questionnaires as a data collection delimitation.

Clearly defining limitations and delimitations also helps prevent scope creep. Remember the customer service scenario? They were facing many problems in addition to employee retention. You can try to collect data related to other problems during the needs assessment, but focusing on the key problem will help you focus the needs assessment on the primary purpose. *(Remember: One problem at a time!)*

Research projects always seem to draw attention from others. In Jody's experience, she has noticed that research and data sparks interest and curiosity in many people—which can be a great thing. People will ask, "Did you consider [*fill in the blank*]?" or "Did you investigate this specific aspect of the situation?" During a past project, Jody remembers that she shared preliminary data about a website's usability with a stakeholder. The usability findings were interesting, providing insight about user patterns and most frequently visited sections. This specific stakeholder quickly jumped in with questions like, "Did you ask managers what they thought?" and "Are you sure you gave them enough time to respond?" The stakeholder's excitement and questions about the data gave the impression that they were requesting additional feedback or data points. However, Jody was able to share the project limitations and delimitations with the stakeholder to describe the scope of work—what she decided to include, not include, and why. Being prepared with this information was an effective way to address the stakeholder's concerns and define the scope of work throughout the project.

As you design the needs assessment, discuss the limitations and delimitations associated with your stakeholders to reach consensus, and then document them within the project scope. Use the prompts in Table 1-2 to identify constraints.

Table 1-2. Prompts to Uncover Limitations and Delimitations

Limitations	Delimitations
• What is the specific project scope, and why? • What methods are available to collect data? • What resources and attributes of the working environment support your plan? • What barriers are in place?	• What information are you *not* going to gather? • What is an adjacent topic that's *not* within the scope? • Why are you *not* collecting the information?

We recommend revisiting constraints throughout a need assessment project—often, you'll identify additional limitations and delimitations as the work progresses.

Identifying Success Metrics for Recommendations

▶ **Why is this important for your strategy plan?** If stakeholders expect the needs assessment results to include recommendations for ways to solve the problem, you need to know how to evaluate potential solutions. In other words, if you're providing recommendations, how will you know if those recommendations will solve the problem?

▶ **When can you skip it?** If your role is to assess the problem but not make recommendations for solving it, you can skip this step. If the needs assessment project is small, or the goal is to solve a problem with minor-to-medium business impact, you may be able to revisit recommendations after key findings are shared with stakeholders and not necessarily need to include solutions in your results. Be sure to align with stakeholders on their expectations for recommendations.

▶ **What's the MVP?** The MVP for each needs assessment will vary based on stakeholders' expectations and project goals. Best practice is to include a scale of options for recommendations:

- Solutions that are inexpensive and can be implemented quickly to provide some improvement for the problem
- Solutions that require a small investment or more time but can solve more of the problem
- More expensive or longer term solutions that may completely solve the problem

Remember that conducting a needs assessment works best if you work backward. Before you start brainstorming recommendations for solutions to solve a problem, you want to identify the metrics that you'll use to evaluate the effectiveness of any potential solutions. In collaboration with your stakeholders, decide how you will measure the results of solutions before implementing them. Those metrics may include KPIs, OKRs, and ROI:

- **Key performance indicators (KPIs).** Current state measures and benchmarks—KPIs measure what *is* as of today.
- **Objectives and key results (OKRs).** Goals and milestones—OKRs are metrics for the goal state and measure progress.
- **Return on investment (ROI).** Cost of the solution versus the return on results—ROI measures value.

You'll learn more about building recommendations in chapter 4, but for now, keep the goal results in mind as you work with stakeholders to plan the needs assessment strategy. Once the problem, current state, and goal state are clearly defined, it will be much easier to determine success measures.

Identifying Value Measures for the Needs Assessment

▶ **Why is this important for your strategy plan?** Demonstrating the value of a needs assessment justifies the time, effort, and cost (if applicable) of the project. This is especially important if the needs assessment requires time from many employees or a budget, or if stakeholders require specific results that affect major business areas or initiatives.

▶ **When can you skip it?** Small-scale projects, those that only require a few total hours of employees' time, or those that could be completed quickly and easily may not require justification.

▶ **What's the MVP?** You should be able to explain why the needs assessment was worth completing. The MVP might be a statement such as "The needs assessment results help us identify [*specific training needs*] that will help us close the skills gap in support of our strategic plan."

Needs assessments are filled with value-packed insights, but identifying the valuable measurements can be a tough job. Calculating the real value of a needs assessment can have two parts: the value of recommended solutions (if implemented) and the value of the needs assessment. By showing the value of the needs assessment, you will gain buy-in, increase leaders' and stakeholders' understanding of the value of needs assessments, and increase your team's role as a trusted business partner.

However, many needs assessment projects, while incredibly valuable to an organization, don't include the financial metrics required to calculate ROI. If you can't calculate ROI, work backward to identify the potential value measures of your needs assessment. Envision the end of the project and consider how the needs assessment helped the company identify gaps and solutions, as well as the time, effort, and money that may be saved as a result.

Part of working backward is thinking ahead to the result, and that means strategizing how you might show the value of the needs assessment work before it's even begun. See chapter 8 for strategies and questions to help you brainstorm ways to measure the value of your needs assessment project.

DEEPER DIVE
Needs Assessment Strategy and Best Practices

Want to learn more about needs assessment theory, approaches, and best practices? These are some of our favorite resources:

- Catherine M. Sleezer, Darlene F. Russ-Eft, and Kavita Gupta, *A Practical Guide to Needs Assessment*, 3rd ed. (San Francisco: Pfeiffer, 2014).
- Hadiya Nuriddin, "Get the Whole Picture With a Performance Assessment," *TD at Work* (Alexandria, VA: ATD Press, 2018).
- Beth McGoldrick and Deborah D. Tobey, *Needs Assessment Basics*, 2nd ed. (Alexandria, VA: ATD Press, 2016).
- Kristopher Newbauer, *Aligning Instructional Design With Business Goals: Make the Case and Deliver Results* (Alexandria, VA: ATD Press, 2023).
- ATD (Association for Talent Development), *Needs Assessment: Design and Execution for Success* (Alexandria, VA: ATD Press, 2018).

A Shoestring Summary

As you develop your needs assessment strategy, ensure that you have gathered all the elements of your planning worksheet and reviewed them with your stakeholders. Like a detective organizing a case file, this foundational planning will help you gather the necessary information to accurately determine needs and requirements for planning effective solutions. Before you begin collecting data, be sure you've identified the following elements:

- The key problem—current state, future state, known gaps, and business impact

- Stakeholders
- Methodology—research questions, data collection, and data analysis
- Scope, expectations, and resources available for the needs assessment
- Constraints—limitations and delimitations
- Success metrics for evaluating recommendations and solutions
- ROI measures for the needs assessment
- The plan for sharing needs assessment results and recommendations

And as a reminder, the best place to start is with identifying the problem. The intake discussion (when you first meet with a sponsor about a needs assessment project) is important, and not having answers to your intake questions can cost you serious time and effort down the road. Some of the most important intake questions include:

1. When did this problem start?
2. What is causing this problem?
3. What needs to change to solve this problem?
4. What is currently driving the need for this change?
5. What has already been tried to solve it?
6. What will happen if we don't solve this problem?
7. How will you know if this problem is solved?

2
Building the Case: Data Collection

When a detective is assigned a new case, their gears start turning immediately into search mode. If they catch the scent of a clue, they won't stop digging until they've uncovered the truth. They may track down witnesses, run background checks, search financial records, talk to neighbors and colleagues, conduct interviews, scan fingerprints, stake out suspects for observation, or send evidence to the crime lab for analysis. As a needs assessment practitioner, you won't run a CSI-style lab, but you will ask a lot of questions and examine a lot of data to uncover actionable insights for the problem you're investigating.

During the case building phase of your needs assessment project, you'll continue wearing your detective hat while building a case to understand and address the problem (Figure 2-1). You'll gather information from a variety of sources, analyze the data you collect, and use your findings to develop recommendations for solutions that meet the business need. This chapter and the next will guide you through the process of answering your needs assessment research questions.

Figure 2-1. Needs Assessment Methodology: Build the Case

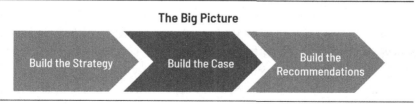

You may be tempted to jump right into collecting information, especially if you're operating on a shoestring and pressed for time. After all, you likely have

a dozen other tasks to manage, and your stakeholder is requesting answers. Simply writing a survey and sending out an email to solicit responses may seem like the path of least resistance and a reasonable decision. However, without a data collection strategy, you may run into problems, such as:

- The survey didn't ask the right questions or missed key questions that should have been asked.
- People who should have been included were overlooked.
- Efforts were duplicated if data had already been collected or created by someone else at your organization.

Jumping into data collection without a plan may end up costing you time and leave you without important information. Before you take a shortcut, pause and consider the big picture of your needs assessment landscape. This chapter will give you a wide overview of data collection strategies, and from there, you can identify which paths are worth your time and which ones you can skip over while still reaching your goal.

Data Collection and Data Analysis: Two Sides of the Same Coin

Data collection is the process of gathering the information needed to answer your research questions. *Data analysis* is the process of interpreting the data you collect. As you plan your data collection strategy, focus on what you need to know, and why you need to know it. When you analyze data, focus on what is significant and *why*.

Once you determine what you need to know, and why you need to know it, you can design a plan for collecting data—find data that already exists at your organization, decide who you can interview or survey, and determine what you can observe.

A needs assessment is a flexible, often nonlinear process, which makes it possible to do even if you're time constrained—you don't have to set aside a week of other work to perform a needs assessment or ask others to do the same. You can plan your needs assessment approach and then iteratively take on the work in smaller sections. You may begin analyzing one dataset while also starting to collect another. For example, you may send out a survey and review results while also scheduling and conducting interviews.

Every piece of data that you collect and analyze will help you build insight to address the needs assessment problem, but your time and resources will be limited. Start strong by identifying the most relevant sources available for collecting the most valuable data as quickly as possible.

Data Sources

Imagine if a detective interviews only one suspect and immediately thinks they've solved the case. That interview may be a critical clue, but unless it's a signed, recorded confession, is it enough to make an arrest and convince a jury? Now imagine that the detective also has crime scene video footage, DNA reports, and statements from multiple witnesses, all analyzed and verified by experts. The combination of multiple data sources and validated analysis builds a much stronger case—for both mysteries and needs assessments.

After you write your research questions, the next step is identifying data sources that can provide answers to those questions. Ask yourself, "Who else might know more about this? What data, reports, or records might exist? Where can I learn more?" Usually, the more data sources you have, the better, but realistically, you should avoid getting stuck searching for too many for too long. Aim to collect internal information (from within your organization) directly from the source or as close to the problem as possible. In some cases, this source is a physical location (such as observations at the sales counter or interviews with frontline employees) while in others it may be a moment in time (such as reports from last quarter).

As you consider the information you'll need to address your research questions, the following prompts can help you identify potential data sources:

- Whose work is most likely affected by the need you're assessing?
- Which departments or teams would be most likely to handle requests, issues, or communications related to this problem?
- Who in your organization would be most likely to write or collect reports about this topic?
- Where is information about the topic currently stored?
- Who in your organization may be aware of available data repositories?

Best practice is to collect data from multiple sources so that you can compare and validate your findings. Ideally, a needs assessment includes three data sources (such as a survey, a series of interviews, and a document analysis).

Having three sources allows you to triangulate data—compare three data points for consistency—but operating on a shoestring sometimes means that you won't have the time or resources to complete multiple rounds of data collection. There's good news, though! You can design a solid needs assessment with only one data collection source if you plan carefully and get creative.

TOOL
Data Collection Plan Template

In appendix A, you'll find a data collection plan template with some tips that you can use as you strategize the sources and methods you'll need to answer your research questions. Meanwhile, in appendix B's "Data Collection" section, we used the customer service needs assessment scenario to provide a worked example of a data collection plan.

The trick to triangulating data when you only have one source is to create at least three points of comparison. For example, if your only data collection method is interviews, ask the exact same interview questions of participants from different departments or with different levels of experience at the organization. If you only have documents to work with, ask three stakeholders to review them, and then ask them the same questions to gather their feedback in ways that can be consistently compared. (Bonus! If you ask effective questions, you can essentially conduct mini interviews with stakeholders while they review the documents and discuss their feedback with you. Be sure to take good notes.)

If you are only able to leverage one data source, you can mitigate that limitation by noting it in the project scope and results report. You can explain to stakeholders that this needs assessment project is a starting point toward addressing the problem, but further investigation may be needed to gather more feedback and bring more value to the organization. When you're operating on a shoestring, you can approach needs assessment projects in phases, peeling back layers one at a time to iteratively get to the core of the problem you're trying to solve. Start with the avenues available to you and build on those findings—you might kick things off with a survey, for example, and then share those survey results with stakeholders to get support for conducting follow-up focus groups or observations.

How Much Data Do You Need?

Whether you're operating on a shoestring or have enough funding to buy the entire shoe department, you must answer an inexplicable question: How much data do you need? Unlike a Google search to find a specific answer, a needs assessment is a research project, and research doesn't have a clear end point. When is research work *done*? Running out of time or not being able to find the data sources needed to address your research questions may bring your project to a halt, but that's not the same thing as knowing when you've collected enough data to continue on to analysis. So how will you know when you have enough data for your needs assessment, and how can you plan a strategy to help ensure you're able to reach that point?

Your goal is to reach data *saturation*—the point of diminishing returns when continuing to collect more data is no longer worth the effort because the data points stop returning new information. In formal research studies, saturation is determined when the study is deemed replicable, and this concept can be helpful for your needs assessment. If someone else duplicates your data collection, would they likely hear the same feedback and reach the same conclusions? You know you've reached saturation when you aren't learning anything new or different from incoming data and don't need additional responses or examples to confidently predict responses.

It's important to plan your data collection methods carefully so that you can reach saturation. If you are surveying 100 people, you should not send them 100 different surveys—you should use only one so that you can compare results for each question. If you ask the same interview questions with all participants, you can detect patterns and recognize the point when answers become repetitive. But if each interview and focus group includes different questions, or you don't follow the same protocol for multiple observations, you won't have consistent points for comparison and it may be impossible to determine saturation.

Triangulation—comparing data to valid information from three or more credible sources—is one of the best ways to reach saturation and ensure data is accurate and trustworthy. By collecting multiple data sources and comparing data points across at least three sources, you can be more confident about the data you're using to solve the needs assessment problems. The more consistency you find in each dataset and across multiple datasets (seeing the same feedback in survey responses, interviews, and documents, for example), the more likely you are to reach data saturation.

There are no hard and fast rules for determining how much data you need, and professional researchers disagree on many standards. But you don't have to be a professional researcher to conduct an effective needs assessment. Design your strategy plan so that you can triangulate data and aim for saturation—those are two of the best ways to ensure that you collect enough of the right data to complete your needs assessment with results you can confidently use to help your organization. In the next section, we've included notes and best practices for reaching data saturation with different data collection methods.

TIME SAVER

Concurrent Data Collection and Analysis

Whenever possible, don't wait until you've finished collecting all the data before you start your analysis; instead, collect and analyze data concurrently. If you analyze as you go, you will recognize the data saturation point faster.

For example, if you plan to interview 30 employees, analyze each interview as soon as possible and begin comparing answers after the first two. Continue to analyze and compare responses after each interview. If you're hearing the same responses to the same questions after the first dozen interviews, you may have reached a saturation point. Instead of completing all 30 interviews, you may be able to stop at 12 and still have a solid dataset.

If you're interviewing different audiences, though, be careful not to assume you've reached saturation too soon. For example, if you scheduled multiple interviews with managers and frontline employees, don't assume saturation if the managers' answers are all similar—the frontline employees may have very different viewpoints. However, if you're careful, stopping at the point of saturation is a great way to save time without cutting corners.

Data Collection Methods

When operating on a shoestring, you must select the method that is best suited to collecting the information you need. For example, if your goal is to identify what processes employees are actually using, you don't want to rely on analyzing standard operating procedure (SOP) documentation. Instead, you will want to ask employees directly or observe them on the job.

The following sections include an overview of the five most common data collection methods—documents and work products, surveys, interviews, focus groups, and observations (Figure 2-2).

Figure 2-2. Five Most Common Data Collection Methods

| Documents and Work Products | Surveys | Interviews | Focus Groups | Observations |

As you gain more experience with needs assessments, you'll develop favorite methods for data collection. Documents and other existing data are usually our go-to source. Analyzing documents allows us to gain a contextual understanding of the business problem, see what research has already been done, get a sense of organizational or process history, find potential subject matter experts (SMEs), and identify conflicting, outdated, or missing information. In addition, collecting and analyzing documents helps us design more targeted questions for interviews, focus groups, and surveys, as well as pinpoint things to watch for during observations.

Sometimes, the project scope determines your methods; for example, if you need to collect 1,000 responses, the most realistic option is probably a survey. As you conduct needs assessments, you'll learn which methods work best for different audiences and problems, and which ones best compliment your strengths and preferences.

To save you time and effort and help you get started regardless of your experience conducting needs assessments, we've provided a shoestring friendly overview of the best uses, cautions, considerations, and realistic best practices for each data collection method.

Documents and Work Products

Documents and other forms of existing data can be a great resource for quickly accessing information, saving time, and avoiding duplicating work. Regardless of the topic of your needs assessment, it's likely that *some* type of relevant documents exist within your organization. This is the most effective way to gauge the data landscape and determine what information you may already have and what information you need to collect next. You don't want to waste participants' time by asking them questions that are already answered in existing documents and work products. Whether you're operating on a shoestring or have enormous resources at your disposal, starting your data collection with existing documents is always a good idea.

Existing documents and data may include sales target reports, customer satisfaction data, employee pulse surveys, quarterly performance reports, data from employee recruiters and exit interviews, departmental reports and presentations, KPI reports, quality assurance reports, and safety reports. Completed work products—like product release data, policy and process documents, employee handbooks, and training materials—are also forms of data you can collect.

Table 2-1 offers a few things to keep in mind if you're considering data collection via existing documents and work products. (And you absolutely should!)

Table 2-1. Best Practices for Documents and Work Products

👍 **Best Uses**
- Gaining understanding of the background of the needs assessment topic
- Gathering multiple data points and determining which are relevant for your project
- As a starting point for developing questions for surveys, interviews, and focus groups or items to include in observation protocols
- Learning more about operating procedures and past performance
- Investigating a certain point in time or how things have changed over time
- Validating the problem, current state, and business impact
- Identifying potential stakeholders and SMEs
- Finding internal research or work that's already been conducted on the business problem
- Triangulating data and identifying saturation points

⚠ **Use With Caution**
- Not all existing documents and work products will be useful to the current needs assessment.
- Documents may be outdated, incomplete, or limited in content.

Table 2-1. Best Practices for Documents and Work Products (Cont.)

- Data will need to be reviewed with stakeholders or SMEs for accuracy and relevance.
- Ask your sponsor and key stakeholders for help when you encounter challenges. They may be able to help remove barriers so that you can stay focused on the project. In this case, brainstorm alternatives, such as asking an HR analyst to summarize the file and remove all employee identification data.

 Time Considerations

- Be sure to plan the time needed to gather and review the documents. They must be identified, requested, located, and sent to you before you can analyze them.
- Determine where and who you can get information from. If you are new or have limited knowledge, this might take a lot longer, and you may need help.
- Once you receive the documents, allow time for a data review so you can become familiar with the content, check for accuracy and relevancy, and identify any follow-up questions you need to ask. The time needed to review and analyze each document will vary depending on the document's length and complexity. For a very rough minimum estimate, plan to spend one to three hours on each document—but be prepared for this work to require significantly more time.
- Schedule time to meet the staff members who created the documents and work products so you can ask them clarifying questions.
- Allocate time for a stakeholder review of documents, keeping in mind demanding schedules and workloads.

 Resource Considerations

- You may need stakeholders' support to access existing data.
- You may need access to the staff members who created the documents and work products.
- You'll need a process and platform for collecting and storing documents, as well as sharing them with team members who are working with you on the needs assessment.

 Budget Considerations

- While you'll need time and internal resources to collect and review existing documents, there isn't a budget cost for internal documents.
- If you need to purchase external documents, such as industry research reports, you may need a budget or approval to make that purchase.

 Saturation Point

- It depends on the scope of your project, the consistency of information you find among the documents, and the purpose of each document.
- You can stop collecting documents when you're confident that you've found accurate information that answers your questions or provides enough background to help you move forward.

Surveys

A survey is a form that individuals complete to answer specific research questions. They're a great way to learn about a large population by sampling members of the group or quickly gathering information from specific participants. A well-designed survey is easy for participants to complete and can provide both qualitative and quantitative data to address the needs assessment research questions. (For simplicity, we're using *surveys* as a stand-in for both closed-ended surveys and open-ended questionnaires.)

Surveys can be the fastest and most cost-effective method for collecting data from your needs assessment audience, so they are an accessible option for practitioners operating on a shoestring. But there are two significant challenges: Good surveys aren't easy to design, and many people experience survey fatigue, both at work and outside work. Because survey tools are easy, inexpensive (or free), and capable of reaching a wide audience in seconds, they can get overused. Don't fall for the temptation to "just send a quick survey." The best surveys are quick and easy for respondents but require significant time and effort to create.

A Few Must-Know Notes About Surveys

When using a survey as a collection tool you need to be aware of a few common formulas. These formulas will be helpful when you are collecting data as well as when you are sharing the results with stakeholders. You need to know three numbers: the total number of people you *invited* to take the survey (target), the number of people who opened and *started* the survey (response), and the number of people who *finished* the survey (completion).

- **Target.** How many people will you ask to complete the survey? If you're hoping to survey a team or department, how many people are in the group, and how many do you need to complete the survey to reach your research goals?
- **Response rate.** How many of the people who received the survey opened and started it, but did not submit answers for every question? To calculate the response rate, take the number of people who opened and started the survey and divide that number by the total number of people you sent the survey to (then multiply by 100 for the percent).

A low response rate may signal that participants did not know how to answer the questions, did not want to answer the questions, or had a poor experience with the survey design.

- **Completion rate.** How many people who started the survey submitted answers for every question? To calculate the completion rate, divide the number of *complete* surveys by the number of survey respondents (then multiply by 100 for the percent). Note the difference between invitees and *respondents*—not everyone who receives the survey will open it, and not everyone who starts it will complete it. You need to know how many in your target group submitted incomplete surveys (response rate) and how many answered all the questions (completion rate). When you analyze survey results, you will need to note how many responses you got in total *and* how many responses you got for each question.

If, according to survey math, your response and completion rates are high, but you only heard from fewer than half of the participants you tried to reach, the survey data can still be useful, especially if the survey isn't your only data collection method. You can compare the survey results against documents and work products, interview responses, and observation notes. You can also review the survey results with stakeholders to determine if you have enough information to move forward, or if you need to consider a different approach.

ON THE CHEAP
Free Sample Size Calculator

The survey notes we've provided are the tiniest tip of the iceberg. Survey analysis also includes statistical calculations for sample size, confidence rates, and margins of error. SurveyMonkey offers a free sample size calculator, which you can access at surveymonkey.com/mp/sample-size-calculator.

Table 2-2 offers a few things to keep in mind if you're considering data collection via surveys.

Table 2-2. Best Practices for Surveys

👍 Best Uses

- Collecting data that is easy for participants to provide in a short time period across multiple geographic areas
- Learning more about a large group by surveying a small sample
- Describing participants' characteristics, opinions, attitudes, beliefs, preferences, behaviors, and previous experiences
- Conducting a survey prior to conducting interviews, focus groups, and observations to help you write more targeted interview questions and more specific observation protocols.
- Using survey data to triangulate data from subsequent interviews and focus groups.

⚠️ Use With Caution

- Beware of survey fatigue. Most people receive more surveys than they ever want to complete.
- Survey requests are easy to ignore.
- Surveys often have functionality problems.
- Not all participants will respond to survey requests, lowering your response rate. If surveys are required, participants may be resentful or unwilling to share their honest perspectives, so data may be unreliable.
- Poor survey design can also cause low completion rates.
- Surveys are self-reported data—you can't control the accuracy of participants' responses.
- Closed-ended questions limit the depth and detail of information you'll be able to collect.
- Responses could be affected by recent events; survey participants usually respond based on most recent memories versus holistic views.

🕐 Time Considerations

- Surveys can gather a large amount of quantitative data in very little time and be analyzed quickly using statistical software.
- If you use printed copies of surveys to collect responses, enter all responses into a survey analysis tool.
- Analysis of qualitative data can be time consuming. If your survey includes open-ended questions, be sure to plan for how you will analyze those responses and allow time to do so. (See the "Data Analysis Strategies" section in chapter 3.)

👥 Resource Considerations

- Consider colleagues who may be available to help you who have access to specialized software and experience processing data.
- Consider using a software or survey tool that can assist with the data analysis process. Look for tools that have built in analysis or artificial intelligence (AI) features.

Table 2-2. Best Practices for Surveys (Cont.)

- Get leadership approval before collecting data using external survey tools to ensure you're complying with your organization's IT and data privacy policies and network requirements.

 Budget Considerations

- Use a survey delivery and reporting tool—such as SurveyMonkey, Google Forms, or Qualtrics—many of which are available for free.
- Save money by making your own survey using tools that are standard-issue within your organization, such as Microsoft Forms.
- Be sure that you can download data in Excel or as a .csv file—a summary PDF of your results will not give you the detailed data you need for analysis. Sometimes, free survey tools don't the capability to export the results in the formats you need.

 Saturation Point

- Strive to get completed surveys from the right people who can give you the information you need to make decisions.
- Be realistic with survey expectations. Start by identifying how many people are in your target audience and set a goal for how many responses you need to meet your research needs.
- Use the following estimates to gauge the success of your survey:
  - **Response rate below 10%:** Very low. You may need to redesign the survey or opt for a different data collection method.
  - **Response rate around 25%:** Acceptable. You may have enough data to continue, but review carefully to verify that enough of your target audience is represented in the results.
  - **Response rate above 50%:** Excellent. Pat yourself on the back and carry on with your analysis!

Interviews

Interviews are one-to-one conversations in which individuals are asked open-ended questions. Used strategically, interviews are powerful tools for gathering *rich* data (detailed responses in participants' own words), especially when you need to understand complex issues or learn from organizational leaders, but they are time consuming to conduct and even more time consuming to analyze.

Interviews can be formal or casual, structured or semi-structured. A *structured interview* follows a specific protocol (the interviewer asks each participant the same set of questions in the same order). A *semi-structured interview* also includes a questioning protocol but allows flexibility for adding or customizing questions as needed during the interview. Interviews can be in-depth discussions if participants trust the interviewer, but confidentiality concerns can hinder responses, so be sure to explain all privacy expectations. Depending on your project goals, you can ask interview questions in the moment to get spontaneous answers or send the questions to participants in advance so they can reflect and prepare for the interview. You will not be able to conduct endless interviews or redo interviews that don't go as well as you'd hoped, so it's critical to determine which participants can best serve the goals of the needs assessment, and make the best use of the time you have with them during interviews.

Table 2-3 offers a few things to keep in mind if you're considering data collection via interviews.

Table 2-3. Best Practices for Interviews

👍 **Best Uses**
- Clearly defined audiences questioning specific individuals
- Getting pre- or post-survey clarity
- Asking about broad or complex needs assessment topics
- Personalizing your strategy for data collection
- Conducting interviews in person, virtually via a digital meeting app like Zoom or Google Meet, or over the phone

⚠️ **Use With Caution**
- Be strategic about whose perspectives you most need to hear—you can't interview everyone.
- Remember that interviews result in deep knowledge from a narrow well—you can learn a lot, but you can't extrapolate those findings to generalize about a larger population.
- You must be able to build rapport quickly, keep the conversation flowing, and listen attentively (while managing your time with the participant).
- Keep your reactions and opinions to yourself. Objectivity is incredibly important.
- You will need a strategy (and a backup strategy) for taking notes during interviews.
- If more than one person will be conducting interviews, it's important to follow the same protocol for questions and to share notes (and recordings, if available) with all interviewers as soon as possible after each interview.
- Be honest with participants about how their responses will be used, and whether their responses will be anonymous. If anonymity is important, you will need to compile and summarize responses so that individual participants can't be identified when you share the results of the needs assessment. Never, ever share interview responses inappropriately.

Table 2-3. Best Practices for Interviews (Cont.)

 Time Considerations

- Ahead of the interviews, allow time to develop your protocol, coordinate scheduling with participants to reserve meeting rooms if needed, and prepare.
- Schedule each individual interview for 30 to 60 minutes. Give yourself at least 15 minutes to capture last minute thoughts and impressions after each interview.
- After the interviews, allow time to transcribe each one and interpret and compare large sets of qualitative data.
- For each interview, plan one to two hours for the first round of analysis (basic review and initial themes) and then two to five hours for deeper analysis (comparison, connections, and holistic themes).
- List your questions by priority so that you can be sure to collect the information you need most if time does not allow for all questions to be answered.
- Include a pre-interview survey to quickly capture demographic data or other information from participants.

 Resource Considerations

- Create an interviewer guide with a script for interviewers to follow (such as a welcome message, the purpose of the interview, and an icebreaker question) and the order of the interview questions.
- With participants' permission, record interviews using a software program that can provide a transcript.
- Have a backup note-taking strategy in place—never rely on recording devices to capture interview data.
- Provide information for participants' supervisors (if needed) to ensure they can participate.
- Ask a team member to participate in a mock interview so you can ensure each interview question is clear and make changes to the protocol if needed.
- Be sure to send a follow-up thank-you note to participants after each interview.

 Budget Considerations

- The interview process can cost more in terms of time and resource investment, but the results are generally more reliable. If feedback from specific people is important to your research, interviews are a great buy!

 Saturation Point

- Conduct enough interviews to gain the perspectives of individuals who represent the defined audiences in your research.
- Target 10 to 15 participants for each interview dataset.

Focus Groups

A focus group is a collaborative interview (usually 60 to 90 minutes long) with a small group of people (usually six to 12) who can address your research questions. When operating on a shoestring, focus groups might seem like a lot of work (planning and facilitating) that produce even more work (debriefing and data analysis). But a focus group can be a great way to conduct multiple interviews at once, gain collective insight from a group, and learn more than you might from an interview if participants build on each other's responses. Like interviews, focus groups can be a great starting place for building a needs assessment survey, clarifying survey responses, or designing more in-depth interview questions. This method works best when you want to ask broad, open-ended questions for group responses.

Focus group planning includes participant selection and recruitment, event logistics, facilitation processes, and a data analysis strategy. They can be conducted in person or online—regardless of the location, remember that you want to facilitate a welcoming environment that is conducive to conversation. When conducting a focus group virtually, whiteboards and chats allow individuals to provide additional information and expand on interview questions. Focus groups are fantastic tools for capturing a lot of information from a group of participants during one meeting.

Table 2-4 offers a few things to keep in mind if you're considering data collection via focus groups.

Table 2-4. Best Practices for Focus Groups

👍 Best Uses
- Working with clearly defined audiences who can address your research questions
- Conducting a small focus group as a pilot test before spending time planning larger focus group, multiple focus groups, or a major survey project
- Prior to designing individual interview protocols

⚠ Use With Caution
- Plan for how you will capture data while facilitating the event. You may need someone to serve as a note taker, even if the focus group is recorded—don't take the risk of a technology glitch costing you all the data if the recording fails.
- Encourage conversations while managing group dynamics (some participants may try to dominate the conversation, for example) and time so you can hear from participants in depth and still address all your questions. Focus group discussions can get heated and stressful, so be prepared.

Table 2–4. Best Practices for Focus Groups (Cont.)

- Be honest with participants about how their responses will be used, and whether their responses will be anonymous. If anonymity is important, you will need to compile and summarize responses so that individual participants can't be identified when you share the results of the needs assessment. Never, ever share focus group responses inappropriately.

 Time Considerations

- Find a time when you can gather enough people together (in person or virtually). Each focus group's collaborative interview usually takes 60 to 90 minutes. You will need the support of stakeholders and managers to use employees' time for focus groups.
- To maximize time with focus groups, send participants some type of prework or reflection questions so they are prepared to contribute.
- In virtual meetings, ensure participants can hear and be heard before starting. Plan for extra time to troubleshoot audio and video inputs, or assign a staff member to be the technical troubleshooter.
- Give yourself at least 15 minutes to capture last minute thoughts and impressions at the end of each focus group session.
- For each focus group, plan two to three hours for the first round of analysis (basic review and initial themes) and then two to five hours for deeper analysis (comparison, connections, and holistic themes).

 Resource Considerations

- Prepare facilitator materials that include an introduction script to set expectations, the focus group interview questions listed in order of importance, and a closing script to thank participants.
- With participant permission, record the focus group to free up the facilitator from note taking. Also, select a recording program that can provide a transcript.
- Give each participant a pen and paper, or a place to take digital notes, and invite them to record any comments that they don't want to share with the group. Collect their notes at the end of the focus group—this will help you hear from everyone.
- If one is available, ask a cofacilitator or coordinator to monitor group dynamics and attend to any logistical concerns that may arise. For virtual focus groups, partner with a producer who can facilitate chat and whiteboard tools, support participants with technical issues, and serve as a backup note taker.

 Budget Considerations

- If you're meeting in person, book a conference room or meeting space.
- If possible, budget for providing refreshments or lunch during the focus group. If you have small swag items or other giveaways available, a token of appreciation for participants is always a good idea.
- When people are dispersed across office locations, or people work from home, conduct the focus group using the virtual meeting platform your organization provides.

Table 2-4. Best Practices for Focus Groups (Cont.)

 Saturation Point

- Your project timeline will heavily influence the quantity and scheduling of the focus groups. You must balance the pressures of meeting project timelines with the time needed to conduct enough focus groups to collect the data required to answer your research questions.
- Focus groups will reveal themes and connections that are just under the surface of participants' comments. You can stop conducting focus groups when these themes and connections are no longer surfacing. If possible, best practice is to conduct at least three focus groups for each needs assessment topic.

Observations

Observations are a structured process of watching work in action. You can gather valuable data about the workplace through observations, including the physical environment, processes, performance, interpersonal interactions, and employee communications. Before conducting observations, it's imperative to gain the necessary approvals, communicate with supervisors and employees before scheduling an observation, and ensure that you are observing during a time that will not cause disruption. Consider how you will introduce yourself to employees on-site and ways to explain why they are being observed. It's important to communicate the purpose of the observations so that employees don't think they are being evaluated, judged, or criticized. Work with stakeholders and managers to develop the best approach for each audience.

The most important thing to plan for conducting observations is a strategy for capturing field notes—which are observations of what you see and hear. If possible, and with participants' and supervisors' permission, take photos or videos during observations. If you're conducting multiple observations, create and use an observation field notes checklist so you can ensure you're capturing the same data from each location or session. Be sure to label your field notes with the date, time, and location of each observation, and if possible, include the names and job titles of the employees you observe. Capture as much dialogue as you can—it's also helpful to note employees' comments, questions, and interactions.

Table 2-5 offers a few things to keep in mind if you're considering data collection via observations.

Table 2-5. Best Practices for Observations

👍 Best Uses

- Collecting behavior, process, and usability data
- Collecting data concerning the physical environment
- Gathering data from employees with limited availability (employees are not required to stop their regular job responsibilities during observations)
- Capturing information about employee skill levels and skill gaps, performance, behaviors, and interactions with the workplace environment

⚠ Use With Caution

- Employees may change their normal behaviors when they know they are being observed. It's important to prepare employees, and their managers, before an observation so they understand why it's happening, what it means for them, and what they can expect.
- Observer bias and confirmation bias can skew how you see and interpret a situation. It's difficult to capture all the data that you will observe. Observers will need to be trained in capturing objective, detailed notes using an observation checklist and protocol.

⏱ Time Considerations

- Observations of people doing their job can occur at any time.
- Plan for time to review and analyze field notes, photos, and videos, and compare your findings against other data you collected for the needs assessment.
- Add additional notes immediately after each observation while it is still fresh in your mind.

👥 Resource Considerations

- If possible, ask managers to provide information from their observations so you can compare their impressions to yours.
- Use observations to prepare for more in-depth interviews, focus groups, and follow-up surveys. You can also use documents that you've collected to develop your observation checklist and field notes protocol.

💲 Budget Considerations

- If travel is required, secure approval or budget to complete observations on-site.
- If possible, budget a small expense to purchase lunch, treats, or small swag items for the employees you are observing. They are a nice thank you at the end of an observation.
- Consider observation methods that are always in place, such as video cameras or screen share software. If it's possible to complete an observation remotely, you can save on travel expenses.

Table 2-5. Best Practices for Observations (Cont.)

Saturation Point

- Consider your research goal and target population to determine the number of observations needed. For example, if you are investigating the needs of a manufacturing plant that uses multiple shifts, you should set up observations to include a sample for each shift.
- The free-flowing nature of observations will offer insight into employee performance, the workplace environment, and other unexpected data sources. Take advantage of all the sources and continue your observations as long as you are receiving data that informs the research question.
- Once the observations are no longer providing new information, you can conclude your efforts.

Tips for Writing Survey, Interview, and Focus Group Questions

It's important to align each question you ask on a survey; during a focus group, interview, or observation; and while reviewing documents to the research questions guiding your needs assessment. Your research questions can be considered *project facing*—questions that guide your needs assessment—while data collection questions (questions you ask participants or while analyzing existing documents), can be considered *participant facing*. A marketing department isn't likely to ask customers why their sales are down; instead, they'll ask customers about frustrations, feature requests, or things they value. Participant-facing questions should be user friendly and aligned with project-facing research questions so the data they collect will help you solve the needs assessment problem.

Participant-facing questions are designed to gather information from your intended audiences, and they must be written carefully to be effective. We coach many practitioners on writing effective questions—this is an aspect of a needs assessment that can be especially challenging. It's incredibly frustrating to put effort into launching a survey or facilitating a focus group that ends with unclear, incomplete, or unusable feedback from participants. Data collection design takes time and experience to learn, but the following best practices cover the most common mistakes and will help you write good questions for interviews, focus groups, and surveys:

- **Use clear, simple language.** Avoid using buzzwords, acronyms, and business jargon.
- **Ensure the question is free of bias and judgment.** As a detective, don't lead the witness. Stay neutral. You're collecting data, not selling something.
- **Avoid asking two questions at once**—also known as a compound question. For example, "Was the time and location of this training convenient?" is asking about the timing of the event *and* the location of the event. Ask only one question at a time.
- **Avoid using double-negative questions.** We've probably all experienced these questions as voters. For example, "Do you not oppose allowing the board to pass Resolution 200?" may appear on a ballot. The word *not* is usually a clue that you're asking a double-negative question. Consider the clarity of "Which of the following is *not* important to you?" compared with "Which of the following is *least* important to you?"

The best way to ensure you have designed good questions is to test them. Try them out on your team members and pilot test your data collection instruments for readability, ease of use, functionality, and data collection. The feedback you receive may inform the wording, questioning process, and survey design. In addition, structure survey questions in priority order, starting with the most important questions. Include space on the survey for participants to add comments or expand on their answers.

Mitigate user errors through careful survey design. Thoughtful survey design includes clear instructions, the minimum number of questions required to gather necessary information, user-friendly question wording, and intentional question-type selection. You won't be able to clarify or explain survey questions, so it's essential that they are structured to be as user friendly and clear as possible.

Make a plan for your survey distribution to ensure you are reaching your target audiences. Use communication as a marketing tool to promote the survey's value and the request for participation. You must use multiple communications to promote your survey.

Which Data Collection Method Is Best?

We are often asked which data collection method is the *best* one. The answer is . . . it depends. Remember that when you conduct a needs assessment, you're wearing a detective hat—where you look for clues depends on what you are investigating. Always start with your research question: What do you need to learn? Next, consider where you need to go to get the information you are seeking, and then select the data collection methods that will get you there.

When Jody has the time and budget to do it, her favorite method is to gather some existing documents and then conduct virtual focus groups. Virtual focus groups are flexible and can cover a lot of ground, literally. When working with a geographically distributed workforce, you can use virtual focus groups to gain employees' perspectives regardless of their physical location. Participants can join from their workstation, cubical, or home, and the familiar setting can help make them more comfortable. Virtual meeting apps may also support features that help with data collection, such as whiteboards and chats. It is best to keep the number of participants small; Jody never invites more than 10 to make it manageable in a virtual setting. Despite her preferences, each project is unique, and Jody likes to reserve the right to pick the best data collection mix according to the need.

Kelly usually prefers interviews over focus groups. Her favorite data collection strategy is to gather and analyze documents and then conduct interviews—usually, she aims for 12. Interviews work well in person or through a virtual meeting app, can be done while drinking a cup of coffee, and often allow for more individual flexibility and anonymity than focus groups. One-to-one interviews also let Kelly focus more on personalized conversations than group facilitation, and usually result in more thorough answers from participants. But for different types of needs assessments, Kelly's methods shift based on the project, and there are times when a focus group, observation, or survey is a more viable option for data collection.

Remember that needs assessments are flexible, not linear, and a lot of work can be done iteratively. You can schedule a focus group or series of interviews before or while you write the interview questions. You can start identifying participants for a survey before or as you're designing it, or you can start working on an observation checklist while you review existing documents.

Your project scope may also dictate your data collection methods. Do you need access to employees to gather data and insights? Use a simple decision tree to choose data collection methods based on the number of employees you have access to (Figure 2-3). If you're trying to select a method and are unsure of where to start, consider whether you'll be able to access employees and, if so, how many you may be able to reach.

Figure 2-3. Decision Tree for Choosing a Data Collection Method

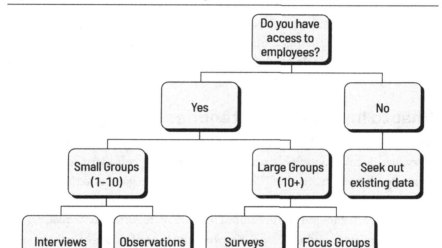

Once you have determined your collection methods, check out chapter 6 for strategies on identifying and working with needs assessment participants and getting the support you need to allow employees to participate.

DEEPER DIVE
Data Collection Methods

This chapter gave you a high-level overview of the most common data collection methods, and you might want to learn more! Here are some of our most recommended resources for conducting surveys, interviews, focus groups, and observations:

- Megan Cole, "Surveys from Start to Finish," *TD at Work* (Alexandria, VA: ATD Press, 2016).
- Sheila B. Robinson and Kimberly Firth Leonard, *Designing Quality Survey Questions* (Thousand Oaks, CA: SAGE Publications, 2019).
- Herbert Rubin and Irene Rubin, *Qualitative Interviewing: The Art of Hearing Data*, 3rd ed. (Thousand Oaks, CA: SAGE Publications, 2012).
- Neal Chalofsky, "How to Conduct Focus Groups," *Infoline* (Alexandria, VA: ATD Press, 2001).
- Sharon Boller and Laura Fletcher, "Sample Observation Guide," appendix in *Design Thinking for Training and Development: Creating Learning Journeys That Get Results* (Alexandria, VA: ATD Press, 2020).

What to Investigate: Categories of Insight

Now that you know the primary methods for collecting data (documents, interviews, focus groups, observations, and surveys), consider the categories of data you'll need in terms of the insight you want to gain. Whether the data you need to collect exists within or outside your organization, the insight you need to gain can generally be organized into four categories: *contextual*, *organizational*, *operational*, and *individual*. Knowing the type of information you need will help you locate it faster and help focus your data collection efforts on the most valuable sources.

The following sections provide an overview of the four broad insight categories, along with suggestions of what you might build, borrow, or buy to collect meaningful data within each category. You can use this information to design your data collection plan based on the scope of the problem you're investigating and the types of insight you need to gain.

Contextual Discovery

Contextual discovery will help you gain insight into the background and current circumstances of your organization's industry by helping you understand what has happened in the past, what is happening today, and what may happen in the future. Contextual data may include sources within your organization as well as external data sources, such as industry trends, laws, legislation, supply chain shortages, labor shortages, changing employee and customer demographics and expectations, geographical considerations, increased costs, and technologies shaping the industry.

For example, if you conduct a needs assessment focused on hospital employee burnout in 2023, you will need to consider the many impacts of the COVID-19 pandemic. To determine contextual data relevant to your needs assessment, ask yourself what you understand and what you need to learn about the external, historical, and current forces that have shaped and are shaping the organization you're working to help.

While historical context and predictions based on current trends and business outlooks can be essential in gaining contextual insight about your organization, be careful about spending too much time looking backward or forward—it's easy to get lost and collect too much data. Prevent getting stuck by defining up-front what you need to understand from the past and how far back in time you need to go, as well as identifying the future-based data that is most relevant to the problem you're addressing in the needs assessment.

Sources you can build, borrow, or buy to collect contextual data include:

- **Build**
  - Curate internal sources of contextual information (such as company, department, and team history), accomplishments, community service involvement, awards won or given, and professional contributions (including boards, conferences, and advisory groups).
  - Curate a list of external sources that may provide contextual information, such as relevant professional associations, industry research groups, blogs, podcasts, magazines, and newsletters. (Ask stakeholders and company leaders for references—what data sources do they rely on?)
  - Conduct interviews, focus groups, observations, or surveys.
- **Borrow**
  - Strategic plans, business goals, and OKRs
  - Company and department presentations and reports
  - Reports and press releases published by the organization
  - Employee demographics
  - Employee satisfaction and retention data and exit interview data

- Employee reviews on websites like Glassdoor and Indeed
- Employee and customer reviews and social media posts related to the organization
- Training course and program results and employee feedback
- Intranet articles and internal communications (Slack or forums)
- Competitor data, such as "Best Place to Work" and "Best in Class" award recipients

- **Buy**
  - If possible, invest time and resources to attend company, department, and industry meetings (such as conferences).
  - Published industry reports
  - Case studies
  - Industry benchmark reports
  - Research and whitepapers published by ATD and other industry experts
  - Consulting services or reports from firms such as LinkedIn, Gartner, McKinsey, or PwC

Organizational Discovery

Organizational discovery will help you gain insight into your company, even if you already know it well. The more you learn about your organization's mission, purpose, values, structure, past and current performance, challenges and opportunities, and goals, the more effectively you can analyze the data you collect. At this point in the process, you've identified the problem, as well as its current state, goal state, and business impact. What do you need to know about internal and external factors affecting the organization? Technology adoptions, department reorganizations, supply chain shortages, and recent or upcoming mergers and acquisitions are a few examples of major organizational impacts. This insight will help you align your needs assessment and recommendations with the company's strategic goals.

Sources you can build, borrow, or buy to collect organizational data include:

- **Build**
  - Employee and customer journey maps
  - Timelines to describe important areas of company growth and change

- ° SWOT (strengths, weaknesses, opportunities, and threats) analysis and similar risk or opportunities assessments
- ° Interviews, focus groups, observations, and surveys to understand different perspectives and capture the current state and anticipated future goals
- **Borrow**
  - ° Company documents, such as long-term business strategy plans, annual goals (OKRs), town hall presentations, job family structures and job descriptions, compensation or incentive bonus structures, monthly reports and dashboards, and company-wide annual survey data
  - ° Resources from other teams to assist with data analysis
- **Buy**
  - ° Invest time by participating in department and industry meetings.
  - ° Attend industry conferences and tradeshows.

Operational Discovery

Operational discovery will help you gain insight into how things are currently done at your organization and why. The more you understand about daily practices, processes, policies, resources, performance, goals, and current challenges, the faster you'll be able to identify the data needed to understand the business needs of the problem you're assessing. Many workplace processes and policies are documented, but remember that the reality of what happens on the job may vary from the documentation. Observations, interviews, and focus groups may provide better insight than relying on policy and procedure documents alone.

Sources you can build, borrow, or buy to collect operational data include:

- **Build**
  - ° Flowcharts to document current practices and processes
  - ° Skills and knowledge inventories and assessments
  - ° Employee and customer journey maps
  - ° Performance and process observations
  - ° Interviews, focus groups, observations, surveys
- **Borrow**
  - ° Internal knowledge management resources (such as employee intranet articles, forum discussions, or Slack channels)

- Standard operating procedure (SOP) documents
- Quick reference guides and job aids
- Employee resource groups (ERGs) or guilds
- Existing training data (such as course reports and surveys)
- **Buy**
  - Ask for time to interview company leaders and SMEs.
  - Connect with external operational specialists (such as LEAN, Six Sigma, product owners, or project managers) to gain insight.

Individual Discovery

Individual discovery will help you gain insight into company culture by understanding more about the people who work and do business there and the perceptions they have of the organization. Individual data describes a person's lived experiences and will help you uncover their wants, needs, interests, skills, attitudes, motivations, and challenges. To complete this investigation, you will need access to people who are a part of the desired audience groups for the needs assessment, including employees, managers, leaders, clients, and customers.

Sources you can build, borrow, or buy to collect individual data include:

- **Build**
  - A visual summary of employee and customer satisfaction
  - A visual summary of employee and customer perceptions of the organization
  - Employee and customer personas
  - Employee journey maps ("hire to retire" experience) and customer journey maps
  - Skills and knowledge inventories and assessments
  - Performance and process observations
  - Interviews, focus groups, observations, and surveys
- **Borrow**
  - Employee demographic data
  - Employee satisfaction survey results, retention data, performance data, and exit interview data
  - Employee, department, and company awards received or given
  - Relevant company, department, and employee community service efforts

- ° Employee reviews on websites like Glassdoor and Indeed
- ° Employee LinkedIn and social media posts related to the organization
- ° Customer satisfaction data, reviews on e-commerce and social media sites, and social media posts related to the organization
- ° Training and development course or program results and feedback
- ° Intranet content and internal communications (Slack and forums)
- ° Feedback from ERGs (including leaders and participants)
- ° Competitive employer data, such as "Best Place to Work" and "Best in Class" award recipients

- **Buy**
  - ° Invest by participating in company, department, and industry meetings (such as conferences) to gain insight.
  - ° Purchase external reports on relevant employee demographics, workplace trends, and workforce development research—some are available for free!
  - ° Use assessments (such as 360-degree reports) to provide leaders with more insight into their effectiveness.
  - ° Consider hiring an external consultant to conduct interviews, focus groups, surveys, and observations if objectivity, privacy, or anonymity are concerns.

Thinking about the data you might need to collect from each category—contextual, organizational, operational, and individual—can kickstart your efforts with increased focus. Once you've determined the data to collect and the methods you'll use to collect it, the next step is planning how to analyze the data you collect. In the next chapter, we will walk you through data analysis methods and processes. Data analysis is hard work, so we've included tips to help you work as quickly and efficiently as possible.

TOOL
Insights Exercise

In appendix B, we use the customer service needs assessment scenario to show one way to use the four categories of insights to guide your data collection plan.

If Opportunity Presents

Sometimes, during a needs assessment, you discover opportunities to collect more data than you expected. For example, you might have planned to interview a department manager and were invited to tour the department's location when you arrived for the interview—presenting an opportunity to conduct an informal observation and capture some field notes. We call this "opportunity data," and these spontaneous opportunities for gaining insight can be incredibly valuable.

Opportunity data can also expand your scope, analysis demands, and project timeline. However, opening a new door of opportunity data can also lead you off course from your strategy plan. Every needs assessment needs constraints—limitations and delimitations that provide parameters and stop points. You could spend years researching a problem and still find new opportunities for data collection.

So how can you make the most of opportunity data while staying focused on your finish line? We suggest leveraging it as an insight gain instead of an additional data collection method. Do that quick observation and take notes, but instead of including them in your data analysis and findings, use those notes to give more insight during data analysis or while writing conclusions. If the opportunity data warrants a change to your data collection plan, do what's best in service of solving the problem you're investigating. Just be sure to update your dataset summary document and analysis plan so you can make any needed adjustments to your project timeline or task schedule.

A Shoestring Summary

Building the case of your needs assessment requires thorough investigation and data collection. To uncover all the essential evidence, be sure to:

- Keep an open mind and continuously ask questions to gain insight across the four domains of discovery: contextual, organizational, operational, and individual.
- Gather quantitative and qualitative data from multiple sources—triangulate to validate!
- Align survey questions, interview questions, observation checklists, and document reviews to the research questions guiding the needs assessment.
- Pilot test your data collection instruments.

3
Building the Case: Data Analysis

A box of evidence isn't useful until it's been studied. All the information that detectives collect—witness statements, background checks, financial records, interviews, observations, fingerprints, and DNA—must be analyzed. Detectives must determine what all the evidence means before they can close the case. They follow strict rules and best practices to analyze evidence based on the type of data, protocols, and requirements for maintaining the chain of evidence, preventing loss and contamination, and ensuring usability. Your needs assessment data won't require evidence bags or legal paper trails, but you will want to analyze it correctly and ensure that your analysis is accurate, relevant, and usable. Keep your detective hat on as you examine all the data you've collected.

Analysis is the process of building insight from all the data you've gathered. Like the larger needs assessment process, data analysis is both an art and a science. It's a systematic process of investigation and interpretation. The result is a holistic story of business needs with actionable proposals to meet those needs. In short, it's how you make sense of the data you have collected. After analyzing the data, you will synthesize your research to complete the needs assessment by organizing your findings (answers to the research questions), reaching conclusions (the significance of those findings), and building recommendations (viable solutions). See chapter 4 for strategies for organizing your findings, reaching conclusions, building recommendations, and sharing the results of your needs assessment.

While they're usually paired in descriptions of needs assessments and other research projects, data collection and data analysis are two very different processes that require different skills. Some practitioners are highly skilled at collecting data but struggle to analyze it. Other practitioners could happily spend all day analyzing data but struggle when conducting interviews and focus groups. You might excel at analyzing numerical data in Excel but feel overwhelmed when facing a large qualitative dataset of interview transcripts. When you're operating on a shoestring, you'll probably have to stretch your skills a bit and challenge yourself to dive into new research challenges—but ask for help when you need it! Sometimes, one conversation with a colleague can help you get unstuck.

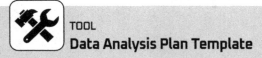

TOOL
Data Analysis Plan Template

In appendix A, you'll find a data analysis plan template with some tips that you can use as you strategize ways to analyze and apply all the data you've collected. Meanwhile, the "Data Analysis" section in appendix B provides a worked example of a data analysis plan.

Jody's first needs assessment was overwhelming. So many steps and moving parts, and then the analysis—analysis, ugh! Despite the anxiety, she pressed on and now she finds the process enjoyable and very rewarding. She started by acknowledging the things that caused her to worry—the tasks that she was under-skilled in, specifically, managing the time needed for deep concentration during her busy workday. Jody set up "study halls"—long blocks on her calendar when she could organize, interpret, compare, and make meaning from the data she collected. She scheduled them in the morning on her less busy days because mornings are her most productive times and she'd have the mental energy to do the work. Early on, those blocks were half-days. Now they are usually shorter, but she still tries to block off at least two hours at a time, weekly for the duration of the analysis.

Another tactic that Jody still uses is talking about her work with a trusted colleague. Sometimes, when she gets stuck in her own head during data analysis, she finds that talking about it in a free-form way allows the data to take on a new life. Talking yourself through data analysis can help you think about your needs assessment as a story—the characters, the conflict, and the resolution. If you have a colleague to bounce ideas off of, the questions they ask may also help you think about your data differently or more deeply.

Kelly loves qualitative data collection and analysis—designing questions, conducting interviews, facilitating focus groups, and diving deep into the rich data they bring. The logistics of data collection are more challenging for her—scheduling, finding, and reserving space; managing calendar conflicts; and ensuring all technology is set up and working ahead of time. When she was a team of one, she worked hard to keep those details organized because she knew that the logistical work would be challenging. She stuck poster-sized sticky notes to her office wall to visually keep track of the moving parts of each needs assessment project, and she set frequent calendar reminders to help her stay ahead of the details. Today, Kelly's strengths still align with qualitative research methodology (and she still uses wall posters and whiteboards during analysis). She can usually rely on logistics assistance from a coordinator, but now her work often requires collecting and analyzing large quantitative datasets. She has to enlist the support of people who are skilled in quantitative analysis to ensure that data is analyzed correctly by those with more expertise in that area. It can be a vulnerability challenge to acknowledge your own limitations in this way—and she's actively building her quantitative data analytics skills—but knowing when to ask for help is critical for the success of any needs assessment project.

 DEEPER DIVE
Analytics for Talent Development Professionals

Do you want to increase your skills with data analytics? Check out Megan Torrance's book from ATD Press, written specifically for talent development professionals and focused on learning and performance data analytics:

- Megan Torrance, *Data & Analytics for Instructional Designers* (Alexandria, VA: ATD Press, 2023).

We can't give you a template for estimating the time and effort needed to analyze data or a formula you can follow for each phase (although, we wish we could!), but we did include some general estimates in the "Data Collection Methods" section of chapter 2 to help you get started. The time and effort required for analysis depends on the size and complexity of your datasets, as well as your skill level and the resources you have available. Analysis paralysis is real and it's easy to get overwhelmed or stuck.

Here are a few shoestring-friendly strategies based on our experience to help you with the difficult work of data analysis:

- **Dedicate time blocks for analysis for the duration of the project.** Set aside regular time blocks on your calendar—at least a couple hours each—and guard them fiercely. Turn off email and instant messenger; maybe even silence your phone. Data analysis is complicated, so reducing distractions can help give you both the calendar space and the headspace you need to complete the work.
- **Talk it out.** As Jody mentioned earlier, talking out your analysis can be incredibly helpful. You need a colleague who will listen, ask good questions, and let you bounce ideas around. Make sure to keep confidential details confidential, but discuss what you see in the data, what it might mean, and what you might be missing.
- **Get messy.** Grab a whiteboard, cover a table with butcher paper, pull out the markers and sticky notes, and scribble away—analysis is messy. You can type your findings and make them neat and tidy later. During analysis, you're asking your brain to process a lot of information, see connections within that information, recognize themes and patterns, and draw inferences that won't be explicitly spelled out for you. Get up and move, put things on walls, and write all over your notes—whatever helps you make sense of your data.
- **Make it a story.** Flex your creativity by framing your needs assessment as a story. Your characters (the stakeholders and participants) are facing a conflict (to solve the business problem) and to do that, they must perform some action (solution to the needs assessment problem and story resolution). Make a chart of characters, conflicts, and potential resolutions as a brainstorming analysis exercise.
- **Take breaks.** Have you ever opened 20 tabs in your browser and watched your computer freeze from the task overload? Your brain is similar—if you open too many idea tabs or look at too much data at once, you might feel like your cognitive processor is frozen. Take a break from the data and let your subconscious take over for a while. We all know that feeling of getting a great idea in the shower or while driving—sometimes, your brain does its best work when the rest of you is on autopilot. Give the data time to percolate in your mind. Go

for a quick walk, dance it out for a few minutes, or maybe even sleep on it and come back to the analysis tomorrow.

- **Stay hydrated.** (Analysis is hard work.)
- **Ask for help.** Even if you're operating on a shoestring, you don't have to work in isolation. There are lots of strategies in this book for enlisting the support of people who can help with your needs assessment, but that only works if you're willing to ask. Especially during analysis, having another set of eyes and another perspective can be invaluable. Just be sure to return the favor when it's someone else's turn to conduct a needs assessment!

Make the Data Make Sense:
The Data Analysis Process

Data analysis is a multifaceted process made up of multiple stages of organizing and studying multiple *datasets*. Each collection method results in a dataset—related groups of data that are organized together to address a research question. If you conducted interviews, collected documents, and sent out a survey, you'll have three datasets, each with subdatasets. (Each interview is part of the interview dataset, each document is part of the document dataset, and each survey response is part of the survey dataset.)

The stages of data collection and analysis often overlap, but the general process of analysis includes four parts: organizing, interpreting, comparing, and making meaning (Figure 3-1).

Figure 3-1. The Data Analysis Process

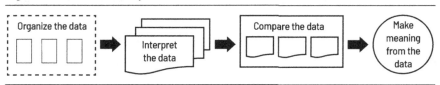

Organize the Data

The first step of analysis is to organize all the data you collected so that you can examine each dataset in isolation, understand the amount of data you have to analyze, review for quality assurance, identify any errors, determine how much of the data is usable for your final analysis, and decide how you can use it during and after the analysis. If you collect additional opportunity data after your official data collection phase is complete, go back and add that information to your dataset summary.

As you begin collecting data, we suggest creating a dataset summary document to help you stay organized. It's important to organize datasets so you can compare findings from each collection method (for example, how do survey results compare with interview responses?), within subsets (for example, how do the field notes from Observation 1 compare to Observation 2?), and across datasets (for example, if "working remotely" becomes a theme as you analyze data, you'll want to compare survey responses, interview notes, and documents that contain data related to working remotely).

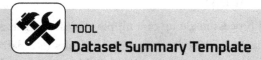

TOOL
Dataset Summary Template

In appendix A, you'll find a dataset summary template you can use for your own project, along with a few tips to help you make the most of this tool. Meanwhile, the "Dataset Summary" section in appendix B provides a worked example of the dataset summary template we created for the customer service needs assessment scenario.

Huge, complex needs assessments usually include data governance plans to set standards for consistency in file naming conventions, document tagging, and file storage and access. For the purposes of this book and conducting a needs assessment on a shoestring, we won't get into the weeds of data standards; just consider the basics for keeping your data organized in ways that are useful to you and your team.

Interpret the Data

Once you've organized your data, the next step is to examine each dataset separately. This examination process is when you interpret the data to determine what it's telling you. Your goal is to uncover what the data says about the problem you're investigating. At this point, you're only looking for the interpretation—a summary of answers that can be organized into findings. (How did respondents answer the survey questions? What did interview participants say? What did you observe? What did you learn in answer to the research questions you posed?)

Complete the interpretation analysis process for each dataset you collected (such as surveys, focus groups, interviews, and collected reports). Analyze each one separately to discover the key takeaways from each. For example, if you sent out a survey, completed interviews, and conducted a set of observations, you would analyze the data from each to arrive at three interpretation summaries (one from the survey results, one from the interviews, and one from the observations). Treat each dataset as its own set of findings so you can clearly articulate their results. What did you learn from each set? How would you summarize the key takeaways from each one? After you evaluate the datasets, you'll be ready to deepen your analysis by comparing them.

Compare the Data

After interpreting each dataset, the next step is to compare their findings to identify consistent themes and outliers and determine the holistic findings based on your combined interpretations. If the findings of each dataset are wildly different, you may have a data quality problem that you'll need to address before moving forward with your analysis. If comparisons across all datasets yield similar results and themes, you can be more confident that your findings are reliable (consistency across datasets means that if you collected additional data, those findings would also be consistent with your current data) and valid (meaning that the findings accurately address the questions you sought to answer).

Comparing your data will help you identify any gaps so you can collect additional data, if needed, or verify data that needs to be validated. For example, if an interview participant in the customer service needs assessment scenario shared that the employee turnover rate was below 10 percent 10 years ago, and the real turnover problems started when salaries were cut in 2013, you would need to find additional data sources to verify that information before including it in your findings or using it to build recommendations.

In a needs assessment, having multiple pieces of data that point to the same themes and conclusions is most effective. *Triangulation*—verifying information from three or more credible sources—increases the likelihood that you have gathered reliable data and gives you a way to validate what you've seen and heard from participants. Needs assessment recommendations require multiple inputs of data to be translated into something that concisely informs the situation and offers high-quality and feasible solutions. Triangulation is particularly important when you borrow data because you are not in control of how that data was gathered or analyzed. Never use information that you have not verified in your needs assessment.

TIME SAVER
Triangulate on a Shoestring

You can triangulate data several ways, but these two strategies can be used in nearly every needs assessment:

- Collect multiple sources of data using a mixture of qualitative and quantitative sources so that you can compare both types of data for the same research questions.
- Ask at least two other knowledgeable people to review the data, and then compare their findings with yours.

Comparing data will also help you deepen your understanding of your findings. Interview responses can add nuance to survey responses. Survey responses can highlight the importance of something you noted during an observation. Focus group data can expand on insight gained from analyzing collected documents. Whenever possible, have another person (or two) compare the findings of each dataset with you; comparing your interpretation against others' is an excellent practice for needs assessments. This requires you to review and analyze data multiple times and ideally, from multiple perspectives. It is worth the time investment—deeper data dives always yield more meaningful results.

Make Meaning From the Data

When you organize data, you gain a holistic understanding of your needs assessment datasets. When you interpret the data, you learn how each dataset can answer the research questions. When you compare the datasets, you identify which findings and themes are consistent across all datasets. At this point, you can answer the questions you sought to address. The next step is determining what those answers mean.

Making meaning is more subjective than the other steps of data analysis, and it is often the most difficult step. The meaning you make from needs assessment data will vary depending on the business problem you're trying to solve, the needs you've identified, the goals and values of your organization, your stakeholders' priorities, and even your own biases.

TIME SAVER
What Does This Mean to You?

Making meaning from data analysis results is a subjective process that can be challenging to do alone, especially if you're not an expert in the needs assessment topic. It can be helpful to ask others for their reaction to your findings and then compare those perspectives. An if-then framework can be a fast, easy-to-use method for determining the real meaning of your findings from the viewpoint of the people most invested in the needs assessment. Here are a few examples:

- The survey results showed _____. What does that mean to you?
- The documented performance reports indicated _____.
  What does that mean to you?
- During observations, we saw _____. What does that mean to you?
- Focus group participants agreed on _____.
  What does that mean to you?

You can even ask your stakeholders these questions early in the project before analyzing the data to help identify clues to watch for during analysis. For example:

- If the survey results show _____, what would that mean to you?
- If the documented SOP and the work product varies, what would that mean to you?
- If we observe that employees aren't _____, what would that mean to you?
- If the focus groups agree on _____, what would that mean to you?

Let's revisit the customer service needs assessment scenario. Suppose that the data analysis results showed that most employees attributed the department's high turnover rate to a negative department culture, uncaring managers, and low morale. The data analysis also revealed that most front-line employees' salaries were higher than the industry average, that managers' workloads were much higher than their employees' perceptions of their workloads, and that frontline employees' productivity rates were not meeting the expected KPIs. A business efficiency analyst may determine that frontline employees were overpaid and that salary corrections and performance-based reviews were required. A manager may determine that an additional management position was needed to help with the demanding workload. A quality assurance expert may determine that more automated processes were needed to measure and improve performance.

People tend to make meaning based on their primary perspective at work: An HR professional will make meaning through a human capital lens; a salesperson will make meaning through a competitive lens; a CEO will make meaning from a profitability lens. As you approach the challenge of making meaning from your data analysis, remember the four categories of insight we discussed in chapter 2: contextual, organizational, operational, and individual. Ask yourself what your results mean within each category. The What? So What? Now What? model is incredibly helpful for this work. You will learn more about this model and how to apply it to your needs assessment project in chapter 4.

Data Analysis Strategies

There are many excellent books about data analysis, but our goal is to help you analyze data on a shoestring, so we're only including a few go-to strategies here. To learn more, check out the "Deeper Dive" resources listed at the end of this section.

Data is either quantitative or qualitative, and the way you analyze it depends on the type:

- **Quantitative data** is countable, measurable, and expressed as numerical values. Analysis results in counts, percentages, statistical frequencies (mean, medium, mode, and standard deviations), charts, and graphs.

- **Qualitative data** is descriptive, subjective, and expressed in words. Analysis results in rich descriptions, themes, categories, labels, narratives, word clouds, and excerpts.

Quantitative analysis strategies include measuring and counting values, calculations, and statistical analysis. There are many quantitative analysis tools available today, including spreadsheets like Excel and Google Sheets, statistical analysis software like SPSS and SAS, and data visualization software like Tableau and PowerBI. Some survey systems include analysis tools, such as SurveyMonkey and Qualtrics. Depending on what tools you have at your disposal for quantitative (and qualitative) analysis, you'll need to factor in whether buying the tool fits into your budget; see chapter 8 for more guidance on resource management decisions.

Qualitative analysis strategies include frequency counts (for example, key words and phrases) and coding. Most of these are manual processes, but new text analytics software is available and offers advanced support tools, including NVIVO, MonkeyLearn, ATLAS.ti, MeaningCloud, and CodeIT.

Table 3-1 presents a quick summary of analysis strategies for qualitative and quantitative data.

Table 3-1. Analysis Strategies for Qualitative and Quantitative Data

	Start with...	Do this...	End with...
Qualitative data	Extensive notes or transcriptions	Group common ideas together by coding the data. Make note of the frequency of key words and phrases. Group related codes into themes. Seek to understand the story the data is telling.	Rich description organized into thematic insights to address complex why questions
Quantitative data	Numeric data from documents, survey results, or performance reports	Calculate counts, averages, mean, medians, modes, standard deviations, and other numerical values. Seek to infer significance and meaning from numbers.	Quantified answers that address research questions (how many, how much, or how often?)

If you're new to data analysis, the process of coding can be perplexing, but it's a necessary skill for working with qualitative data, such as open-ended survey questions, interviews, and focus group transcripts. *Coding* is the process of synthesizing long-form data by labeling sections with keywords, and then organizing and consolidating those keywords into themes.

There are two basic coding methods: deductive and inductive. *Deductive coding* means labeling data using a list of predetermined codes based on your research questions—you start with a list of ideas, keywords, or important phrases—and label data with these codes as you find them in your datasets. *Inductive coding* means examining data in search of emerging codes—ideas, key words, or phrases that appear multiple times in your dataset—and labeling them as they arise. Both deductive and inductive coding are valuable, and each method leads to groups of codes that can be categorized into themes.

We suggest coding your data at least twice—once to identify deductive codes and once to identify inductive codes. Review your needs assessment strategy worksheet and create a word bank for deductive coding. The second round will help you identify more detail and emerging patterns for things like frequency, cause and effect, habits, behaviors, and differences. Table 3-2 gives a brief example.

Table 3-2. Interview Coding Example

Interview Transcript	First Round of Coding	Second Round of Coding
"I have worked for the organization for three years. I was hired by the billing department and moved to this role about 18 months ago. This team has a different culture than the other division I worked for. The work is harder in this job, and there's more of it. Also, I'm not sure which goals count in our quality reviews. My co-workers aren't sure, either."	• 0–3 years tenure • Culture • Performance	• Internal transfer • 18 months in the role • Culture differences among departments • Ambiguous goal metrics • Difficult workload

If you're coding as a team, be sure to establish initial codes before beginning the analysis and update each other regularly on emerging codes and themes.

Each person should use the same processes to code the data, and you should continuously review your codes together.

Including excerpts from interviews, focus groups, and open-ended survey questions to illustrate your key findings provides rich descriptions that help stakeholders gain a deeper understanding of important findings. You can summarize or paraphrase them to protect confidentiality, but be careful to never exaggerate or use participants' words out of context.

DEEPER DIVE
Analyzing Data

Want to learn more? Check out these great books!

- Annette Lareau, *Listening to People: A Practical Guide to Interviewing, Participant Observation, Data Analysis, and Writing It All Up* (Chicago: University of Chicago Press, 2021).
- Tiffany Bergin, *An Introduction to Data Analysis: Quantitative, Qualitative and Mixed Methods* (Thousand Oaks, CA: SAGE Publications, 2018).

In summary, analysis is the process of turning data (a collection of figures, facts, text, or numbers) into information (data grouped together meaningfully in context). Analysis makes data usable and meaningful.

A Shoestring Summary

Once you've investigated the problem and collected data, you're ready for the analysis. To uncover all the essential evidence, be sure to:

- Analyze your datasets by organizing, interpreting, comparing, and making meaning.
- Whenever possible, borrow talent to assist you with data analysis—multiple perspectives are invaluable.
- Continue to ask questions as you move from analysis to synthesis and work to organize your findings, reach conclusions, and build recommendations.

4
Building the Recommendations

When a detective solves a mystery, the work doesn't end when they figure out "whodunit." They know the answer, but the case isn't closed. Detectives must convince others of their findings—a judge with the authority to issue warrants, a prosecutor who will determine the legal merits of the case, and jury members who must examine the evidence. There's a lot riding on the credibility of the detective's conclusions and their ability to communicate the results of their investigation.

Your needs assessment won't end with a dramatic courtroom conclusion (at least we hope not!), but after the hard work of building the strategy and the case through data collection and analysis, there may be a lot riding on your conclusions. Even if the stakes are low, you should suggest solid solutions that will help your team solve the business need. Your goal at this point is to leverage all you've learned through data analysis to build actionable recommendations and then share the results of your needs assessment with stakeholders (Figure 4-1).

Figure 4-1. Needs Assessment Methodology: Build the Recommendations

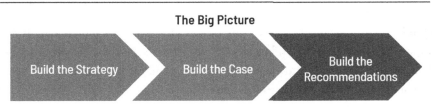

The Big Picture

Build the Strategy → Build the Case → Build the Recommendations

During data analysis, you'll examine all the data you collected in detail and compare findings across datasets. The next step is to synthesize your research by zooming out and considering the big picture, putting patterns together, and weaving the results together. You will have a lot of information to synthesize, summarize, and share—but you may not have much time to do so. You need to identify solutions quickly and ensure those solutions are feasible. Then, you should bring your analysis and recommendations together into a concise results report that provides stakeholders with the insight they need to make strategic decisions about the problem you've assessed. This chapter will walk you through considerations and strategies to complete your needs assessment project on a shoestring and effectively communicate your results.

Work Backward: Needs Assessment Results

Why do we keep telling you to work backward? For needs assessment projects, you start with the end goal and then design strategies to reach that goal. You can also work backward by thinking about the long-term big picture and how your needs assessment project connects to your organization's strategic goals and initiatives. Needs assessments can become valuable work products. Remember our advice to start your data collection with existing documents? Well, after your needs assessment is finished, the results report and associated files become documents that might support research for future efforts—for yourself and others. Needs assessment results can also be used as tools for strategic planning and continuous improvement.

When she starts working on a new initiative or major project, Kelly's first step is to review any needs assessments or studies about the topic that have been completed within the last three years, even if those needs assessments were for small projects or limited to training programs. Knowing who was included (stakeholders and participants), reading the project notes, and reviewing the results report and any information on solutions that were implemented tells her what work the organization has already done related to the current initiative. This strategy helps her start new projects faster and more effectively and share valuable insights with the initiative team.

Before your needs assessment project can bring value to your organization, you must finish the work. After building your needs assessment strategy and collecting and analyzing data, it's time to:

- **Organize your findings**—identify answers to your research questions.
- **Reach conclusions**—determine the significance of the findings.
- **Build recommendations**—suggest viable solutions (based on your findings and conclusions) to solve the problem.

This process can be overwhelming, difficult, and time consuming, so we suggest working backward with the end results of your specific needs assessment project in mind. Your goal is to turn the data you analyzed into meaningful conclusions that you can then use to recommend viable solutions. You want to be able to walk stakeholders through a logical results summary to describe the most relevant findings, illustrate the importance of those findings in terms of business impact, and explain the ways in which your recommendations for solutions align with business strategy. (Read more about presenting a logical summary in the "Weave a Golden Thread" section at the end of this chapter.)

If you're feeling stuck (or wondering *how* you're supposed to identify these things), keep reading! Next, we'll discuss the What? So What? Now What? model and how you can use it to develop findings, conclusions, and recommendations.

What? So What? Now What?

The What? So What? Now What? model is a versatile, easy-to-use tool for critical reflection and data-driven decision making (Borton 1970; Driscoll 2007). Answering the three questions seems simple, but this model will help clarify your understanding, challenge your assumptions, ensure you're focused on the right things, and consolidate your ideas. It has three parts that align perfectly with the three parts of needs assessment results:

- **What?** These are the *findings* of the needs assessment (the answers to your research questions). The question "What?" describes the problem that needs to be solved and the most relevant data points that provide evidence of that problem. You want to quantify the business impact of the problem as much as possible.
- **So what?** These are the *conclusions* of the needs assessment (the significance of your findings). Answering the question "So what?" will help you articulate the implications of the problem within the context of the business impact—why business leaders should care

about this problem and why they should address it. You identified the business impact during your needs assessment strategy planning, and after analysis you should have the data to verify and quantify it. Each conclusion you draw should be directly connected to findings based on the data you collected and analyzed. Sometimes, your conclusions will provide more insight about the key problem but not identify the main cause of the problem. In those cases, you can conduct a root cause analysis, and then add the root cause to your conclusions and determine which solutions will best address it.

- **Now what?** These are the *recommendations* (suggested solutions to address the key problem). Once you verify the problem, and can demonstrate why it's important to solve (and whenever possible, determine what's causing it), you can brainstorm with stakeholders and leverage your professional expertise to identify possible solutions. The question "Now what?" is shorthand for "What should we do to solve this problem?" It's important to maintain objectivity when building recommendations. Solutions may be chosen by business leaders, and those decisions may ultimately be out of your control. Your job is to provide options so that stakeholders can make the best possible decisions based on the data you collect and analyze and the recommendations you provide.

You can use the What? So What? Now What? model as you work your way through needs assessment findings, conclusions, and recommendations. We suggest using it as a:

- Way to start processing your findings, conclusions, and recommendations
- Strategy for staying on target as you work through the details of each
- Tool for brainstorming and aligning with stakeholders on solutions

Use this model again when it's time to recommend the best of those solutions and write your results report. It is incredibly versatile—you'll probably find additional uses for it beyond your needs assessment projects. (In fact, it is so helpful that Kelly keeps a sticky note with the questions "What?" "So what?" and "Now what?" inside her planner to help her remember that most projects can be approached this way).

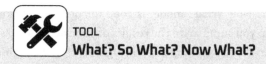

TOOL
What? So What? Now What?

You can use the What? So What? Now What? model to consolidate your data analysis, work through the needs assessment results with stakeholders, brainstorm solutions, and summarize your findings, conclusions, and recommendations. A blank version and a tool for visualizing the results appears in appendix A.

What? *Needs Assessment Findings*	So What? *Needs Assessment Conclusions*	Now What? *Needs Assessment Recommendations*

• What is the real business problem?
• How do we know this is the real problem?
• What data support the identification of the key business problem as we've defined it?
• Why does this problem occur? What caused the problem, or what factors contribute to the problem continuing?
• Who is involved or affected by this problem?
• Where does this problem occur? What other areas does it affect?
• When does this problem happen (or how long has it been happening)? When did it first occur?
	• What is the relevance and business impact of this problem?
	  ∘ Performance
	  ∘ Profit
	  ∘ Resources
	  ∘ Budget
	  ∘ Measurement or data
	  ∘ Process
	  ∘ Environmental
	• What will happen if this problem is not addressed?
	  ∘ Safety risk
	  ∘ Security risk
	  ∘ Compliance risk
	  ∘ Financial risk
	  ∘ Operational risk
	  ∘ Performance risk
	  ∘ Opportunity risk
	  ∘ Reputation risk
		• What is needed to solve the problem? [*For each potential solution, include constraints, necessary resources, costs, timeline estimates, and steps required for implementation.*]
		• What are the pros, cons, and potential results of each solution?
		• How will you know when the problem is solved?
		• Consider success measures for each solution, and use the information you gathered about the current state and the goal state to identify potential impacts and evaluation metrics.

Source: Adapted from Borton (1970) and Driscoll (2007).

While the What? So What? Now What? model is good for processing, you might need a visual tool to help you summarize the results of your needs assessment. Consider the example structure we've provided in Figure 4-2, and imagine how you may fill in the blanks as you identify findings, conclusions, and recommendations and ensure that they align. Start by listing each key finding in the first row, and then add your conclusion about each finding in the middle row. If you need to determine the root causes of your conclusions, you can add them to the conclusions row after they are identified. Once you've determined recommendations, add them to the last row, and review them to see if the logic moving from each finding to each recommendation is clear. The great thing about using this layout is that your recommendations will be aligned with your conclusions, which will be validated by your findings.

Figure 4-2. Example Needs Assessment Results

Findings
The most relevant
results of data analysis

- The current employee turnover rate is 43%.
- The current workforce gap is 15%.
- In the last 30 days, 39 employees (82%) have considered resigning.

Conclusions
The significance
of key findings

- Employee retention is a significant business problem with a high risk of escalation.

Recommendations
Potential solutions
to solve the problem

- Monitor resignations and terminations for the next three months, and collect exit data for each separation.
- Design and implement employee engagement strategies to encourage retention.
- Revise or reassign responsibilities to provide department managers with time to support frontline employees.
- Provide coaching for department managers.

Strategies for Synthesizing Research

Now that you have a starting point for synthesizing your research, the next sections will give you more detail and strategies for organizing findings, reaching conclusions, identifying root causes, brainstorming solutions, making recommendations, and sharing the results of your needs assessment.

Organizing Findings

The process of organizing your findings may seem daunting. You have just completed a ton of work analyzing hundreds or even thousands of data points, and now you must decide how to consolidate those findings to illustrate the impact of the problem you're trying to solve. Organizing your findings is a process in which you step back to answer the question, "What did the data say?" (Remember, organizing findings answers the question "What?" in your data analysis.) Your goal is to consolidate the key findings from your data analysis into a clear, concise, unbiased summary. We recommend these strategies for organizing your findings:

- Consider multiple data points from each data collection source and include the most relevant and validated findings, especially those that triangulate across sources.
- Include the good and the bad findings, but don't exaggerate or dramatize. Hyperbole isn't helpful and makes your analysis less credible. Let the data speak for itself.
- Be careful not to focus only on the findings that matter most to you personally, support a particular stakeholder's agenda, align most with your department's goals, or are otherwise biased. Maintain objectivity and clearly list the most important facts you've uncovered.
- Group your key findings into categories of topics or themes or in order of priority or complexity. Categorizing your most relevant findings will help you draw conclusions based on the summary and significance of the findings, and then you can work to design solutions that address each conclusion.
- While you can't include every data point in a needs assessment report, be sure to save all your data so you can reference it as needed.

Effectively summarizing your findings will make it clear to stakeholders that the problem is real and help them see the business impact. Once you've identified your key findings and organized them into categories, the next step is to determine the significance of those findings by answering the question "So what?"

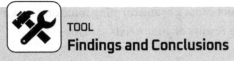

TOOL
Findings and Conclusions

The "Findings and Conclusions" section in appendix B includes an example of organizing findings from the customer service employee retention needs assessment scenario.

Reaching Conclusions

What's the difference between findings and conclusions? *Findings* are a collection of facts you uncovered during data analysis, and *conclusions* are explanations of how those facts illustrate business impact. Findings show that the problem you researched does, in fact, exist. Conclusions explain how that problem affects the business.

There's a big difference between reaching conclusions and making assumptions. If you hear thunder and then see people walk into your office building carrying umbrellas, you can logically assume that it's raining. But in needs assessments, you should avoid assumptions and, instead, draw conclusions based on your findings—you must go to an office window to see that it is indeed raining. It's important not to expand your conclusions beyond what the findings show.

Conclusions answer the question "So what?" to explain why stakeholders should invest the time, effort, and resources required to address the problem. Findings are facts; conclusions are implications. Conclusions are more subjective than findings. You can count, measure, and validate findings. To reach conclusions, you must examine your findings in the context of the problem and determine their relevance to your organization. Your goal is to illustrate the significance of your findings. We recommend the following strategies for reaching conclusions:

- Revisit the notes you took during data analysis when you made meaning from your data. Can you draw multiple conclusions from each set of findings? Compare different interpretations and examine how they align with your findings. Ask your project sponsor, champion, or trusted colleague for their interpretations or for feedback on your conclusions.

- Remember that correlation does not prove causation, and at this stage, you're not yet determining the cause of the problem. For now, stay focused on determining the importance of your findings.
- Review your conclusions with stakeholders *before* sharing them more widely or using them to build recommendations to ensure they are clear, relevant, meaningful, and actionable. If stakeholders disagree with your conclusions, address those concerns before moving forward with identifying root causes and solutions. Time spent revising conclusions is not wasted—it's better to correct course now.

You can group all your key findings into one synthesized conclusion or develop a conclusion for each category. Sometimes, your conclusions will describe the symptoms or impact of a problem, but you may need to do some additional analysis before you can determine what's *causing* the problem. If the cause of the problem isn't completely clear after data analysis, a root cause analysis will help you fill in the missing pieces. And don't worry—root cause analysis may sound like a time-consuming process, but it doesn't have to be. Keep reading for some shoestring strategies to get to the root of the problem you're assessing.

Root Cause Analysis

Stakeholders and clients often jump to solutions before analyzing the root cause of their current problem, but it's important to identify what's causing a problem before suggesting corrective actions. Every problem has a root cause (or root causes)—the central factors that need to be resolved. As you analyze data, look for clues to identify the problem's root cause—this is a good time to use the five whys strategy discussed in chapter 1. If your data analysis reveals complex problems, or multiple symptoms of a problem but not a specific cause, conducting a root cause analysis can help you get closer to identifying the right solutions.

There are many root cause analysis tools, processes, and best practices, but if you need to determine root causes while working on a shoestring, we recommend a simple exercise: Classify the problem into a problem category. Almost all organizational problems can be assigned a root cause category, and once you know the type of problem you're facing, you can focus on solutions best suited for it.

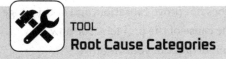

TOOL
Root Cause Categories

We've included a root cause category template in appendix A. You can use it to categorize the root cause of problems and their potential solutions so you can ensure your recommendations align with the type of problem you're trying to solve.

Let's discuss the most common root cause categories.

Knowledge Problems

Knowledge problems are caused by information gaps. Usually, the information exists in some form but may not be available or accessible to everyone who needs it. Knowledge may be bottlenecked in the heads of only a few people or may have been lost when key experts left the company. Resources may be outdated or difficult to find, user manuals may not be user friendly, or managers may not be providing the time and support required for employees to access, understand, and apply all the information they need.

Solutions for knowledge problems may include training, support documentation (job aids and reference guides), knowledge bases, intranet articles, communication campaigns, and change management initiatives.

Skill and Behavior Problems

Skill problems are caused by performance gaps due to a lack of ability or know-how. People may not have the skills needed to perform a job or task, or they may not be practicing the behaviors required to perform the job or task. *Behavior problems* are caused by a performance gap due to a lack of motivation. If the answer to the question, "Do they know *how* to do this?" is yes, then you're likely facing a behavior problem. This doesn't immediately mean that employees are refusing to follow a process or perform a task, and it doesn't usually mean that you're dealing with incompetency or opposition. Often, behavior problems are caused by a lack of time, support, or resources or a misunderstanding about the *why* behind the process or task.

Solutions for skill and behavior problems may include training, practice opportunities, simulations, coaching, job shadowing, workforce development, upskilling initiatives, communication strategies to ensure employees understand the why of required processes, procedure manuals, policies, change management strategies, and team building activities.

Resource Problems

Resource problems occur when knowledge, skills, and behaviors exist, but there is not enough time, people power, materials, hardware, or other resources available to complete the job, process, or task.

Solutions for resource problems may include capital investments, technology solutions, digital transformations, budget reallocations, hiring additional staff, workforce development, upskilling initiatives, outsourcing, and performance improvement strategies such as Lean Six Sigma and 5S (sort, set, shine, standardize, and sustain).

Process Problems

Process problems appear when performance outcomes are inconsistent from person to person due to the absence of standardized steps. Evidence of these problems may show up in quality control findings or an audit could uncover inconsistency in operational procedures. Process problems can also include a lack of knowing *how* to do something.

Solutions for process problems may include training, support documentation, knowledge bases, held desks, policies, communication campaigns, quality assurance strategies, compliance programs, change management initiatives, technology solutions, digital transformation, and performance improvement strategies such as Lean Six Sigma and 5S.

Leadership and Culture Problems

Leadership and culture problems can be attributed to a collection of issues such as tolerance of poor performance, lack of acknowledgment of good performance, not developing staff, or not communicating organizational performance expectations.

Solutions for leadership and culture problems may include leadership development programs, mentoring programs, assessments (such as 360-degree reviews and employee pulse surveys), organizational communications, change management initiatives, employee development and appreciation activities, and team building activities.

Additional Considerations

Organizational problems usually have several contributing factors. Under-standing the root cause—or identifying the general root cause category—will help you identify and prioritize solutions. But remember, they don't appear by magic (although the list of examples provided here may give you a place to start).

Brainstorming Solutions

Once you have a clear sense of your conclusions, and have identified any root causes, it's time to start considering ways to solve the problem. We like to start this process with structured brainstorming sessions to get creative ideas churning and to think about the problem from different angles.

Identifying solutions requires both creative and critical thinking, which can be difficult to set aside time for when you're in a rush. However, even if you think the solution is obvious, it's worth considering alternatives. There are many ways to solve problems, and the more creative, objective, and flexible you can be while brainstorming, the more solutions you'll be able to consider.

What follows are a few of our favorite strategies for brainstorming solu-tions. Add your own techniques to this list and try some of ours to see which ones are most helpful for your needs assessment projects.

Mind Mapping

When Jody is brainstorming solutions, she likes to consider as many ideas as possible because often the best solution is a combination of several ideas. She likes to use the mind mapping brainstorming technique, which aims to gener-ate many ideas rather than one single idea and can be used independently or with groups. The first few ideas usually come easily, but then ideation becomes more difficult. When she hits that point, she uses prompt questions, such as "What can be removed?" and "How can we take advantage of what is working well?"

Jody likes to capture ideas visually and then draw lines to connect concepts together, as shown in Figure 4-3.

Figure 4-3. Using Mind Mapping to Brainstorm Solutions

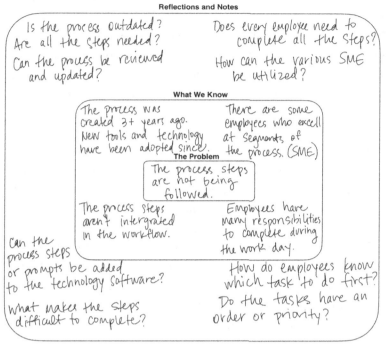

Reflections and Notes

Is the process outdated?
Are all the steps needed?
Can the process be reviewed
and updated?

Does every employee need to
complete all the steps?
How can the various SME
be utilized?

What We Know

The process was
created 3+ years ago.
New tools and technology
have been adopted since.

There are some
employees who excell
at segments of
the process. (SME)

The Problem

The process steps
are not being
followed.

The process steps
aren't intergrated
in the workflow.

Employees have
many responsibilities
to complete during
the work day.

Can the
process steps
or prompts be added
to the technology software?

How do employees know
which task to do first?

What makes the steps
difficult to complete?

Do the tasks have an
order or priority?

The 80/20 Rule

The 80/20 rule, also known as the Pareto principle, explains that about 80 percent of results are caused by 20 percent of actions. Identifying the 20 percent of causes that drive 80 percent of results is key to determining priorities. To use the 80/20 rule for brainstorming needs assessment solutions, follow these steps:

1. Organize your key findings into business impact categories.
2. Assign a value to each key finding based on its impact and then rank them in numerical order. Calculate the top 20 percent.
3. Focus on ideas for solutions to address the top 20 percent.

Minimal Viable Solutions

Swap your detective and project manager hats for an engineer's hat during this brainstorming process. When solving software problems or creating new products, many developers start by identifying and implementing an MVP—minimum viable product—to gain early buy-in and collect enough data to determine next steps.

Practice the exercise of identifying *minimum* and *maximum* solutions to solve the problem you're facing. Rank potential solutions by cost, feasibility, complexity, and time requirements and categorize them into "minimum, low cost, and immediate," "better, moderate cost, and soon," and "maximum, higher cost, and long-term" options.

Synthesize the Findings

You can spark ideas for creative solutions by synthesizing your needs assessment to frame the findings in multiple ways and examine multiple solutions. Rank your findings in each of the following ways:

- Priority order from most to least severe
- Chronological order from the oldest data point to the most recent
- In order of cause of effect—in what order should they be solved?
- In order of complexity from clear to ambiguous

After each step, ask, "What should be done first to address this problem?" and then compare answers for your lists. What do the solutions have in common? Which solutions apply to the most findings?

Futures Wheel

The Futures Wheel model is a visual brainstorming tool developed by futurist Jerome C. Glenn (2009) to identify the potential future consequences—benefits and risks—of a proposed change. To create a futures wheel, follow these steps:

1. Write the proposed change (needs assessment solution) in the middle of a page (or screen). This is the central idea.
2. Brainstorm a list of immediate consequences for the proposed change, and then add each one as a circle connected to the central idea. These circles are first-order consequences. To create the list of first-order consequences, ask, "What would happen if . . ." and identify all possible outcomes you can think of—positive and negative, direct and indirect. It's also helpful to color code each layer of connected circles so you can identify first-order consequences from second- and third-order consequences as you continue to brainstorm.

3. For each first-order consequence, brainstorm a list of potential second-order consequences that could result from each first-level result. Repeat this process if needed to identify third- and fourth-order consequences—but going to the second level will most likely be all you need to do.

4. After diagramming the consequences that could result from the proposed solution, analyze the results. What does the big-picture visual of ideas tell you?

5. For positive possible outcomes, brainstorm how you can leverage them to their best advantage. What other problems might this solution help solve? For each negative possible outcome, brainstorm how you might mitigate the consequence. Is the risk worth the benefit of the proposed solution?

Case Studies Benchmarking

If you're not sure where to start with brainstorming solutions, or want to prime a group with example solutions to consider before a brainstorming session, it may be helpful to begin by searching for case studies that explain how other organizations have solved problems like the one you're facing. You may want to look at organizations that are similar in size and structure to yours, or slightly larger or smaller, or those that are similarly profitable, less profitable, and more profitable to create benchmarks for comparison. You can find case studies through *Harvard Business Review*, business journals, ATD, and other professional associations.

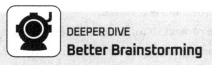

DEEPER DIVE
Better Brainstorming

Want to learn about more techniques for strategic brainstorming and creative thinking? These are our go-to books for inspiring ingenuity.

- B. Kim Barnes, *Building Better Ideas: How Constructive Debate Inspires Courage, Collaboration, and Breakthrough Solutions* (Oakland, CA: Berrett-Koehler Publishers, 2019).
- Michael Michalko, Thinkertoys: *A Handbook of Creative Thinking Techniques*, 2nd ed. (New York: Ten Speed Press, 2006).

- Chris Griffiths, *The Creative Thinking Handbook: Your Step-by-Step Guide to Problem Solving in Business* (New York: Kogan Page, 2019).
- Wendy K. Smith and Marianne W. Lewis, *Both/And Thinking: Embracing Creative Tensions to Solve Your Toughest Problems* (Boston: Harvard Business Review Press, 2022).
- Donella H. Meadows, *Thinking in Systems: A Primer* (White River Junction, VT: Chelsea Green Publishing, 2008).

Making Informed Recommendations

Depending on your role in the organization and the nature of your project, you may not be able to implement solutions following a needs assessment, but you may be responsible for making recommendations based on your findings. Providing multiple viable solutions—especially when they're ranked by priority, potential impact, feasibility, cost, or timelines—adds value to the needs assessment results for your stakeholders and the entire organization. Once you've identified several possible solutions, it's time to decide which ones to recommend as options for solving the problem. Stakeholders can then make decisions based on the problem's impact, business priorities, and available resources.

Sometimes, the most practical recommendation is the least popular option. You may face the dilemma of presenting tough choices or making recommendations that, while ultimately beneficial for the organization, may be met with resistance, reluctance, or initial resentment. In those situations, especially, you need to be able to explain the purpose, goal, and reality of the assessment's limitations to gain buy-in and move forward.

Kelly once worked on a large-scale project to implement a new company-wide performance review system, including doing a needs assessment to determine the best way to train 3,000 employees on the new system. The stakes were high—the company had a deadline for performance reviews that was tied to annual bonuses and could not be extended, and there were only a few weeks between that deadline and the rollout of the new system. With an understaffed training department, no budget for outsourcing additional help, and a scalable solution needed immediately, the needs assessment team recommended virtual training sessions leveraging a train-the-trainer approach. To overcome the lack of resources, the team borrowed a dozen facilitators from functional training groups, organization development, and HR teams to help deliver the mandatory virtual training sessions over a two-week period.

Here's how this solution became a somewhat unpopular option. Each *borrowed* facilitator had to deliver the hour-long training session 10 times. They had to pause other projects for three weeks—a week for train-the-trainer sessions and preparation and two weeks of training delivery. Repeating the same virtual session 10 times in a row became tedious. Employees weren't enthusiastic about mandatory training on short notice. HR staff had to enforce the training requirement, keep track of attendance, and follow up with stragglers. And a few makeup training sessions were required at the last minute. But in the end, the solution worked—employees received the training they needed to use the new system before the deadline, and performance reviews were submitted on time. In this case, the need justified the means, and the tedious solution proved to be highly effective.

While weighing the pros and cons of potential solutions, focus on the bottom line, and start by determining possible evaluation metrics before deciding which solutions to recommend. How will you know if your recommendations are successful if implemented? Work backward to determine how potential solutions can drive performance (KPIs), support business goals (OKRs), have a positive impact on the business's bottom line (ROI), or deliver other value measures to the organization.

We briefly discussed these metrics in chapter 1, but let's dive deeper into each one:

- **Key performance indicators (KPIs)** are measured on an ongoing basis and can alert organizations to problems that need to be solved. KPIs measure the current state and provide data for benchmarking. When you start a needs assessment project, current KPIs will help you determine the problem, current state, and future state, and you may identify additional KPIs that need to be tracked in the future. In our customer service scenario, employee retention was being tracked by the organization as a KPI; those measurements helped determine the purpose of the needs assessment.
- **Objectives and key results (OKRs)** capture the most important goals (usually three to five objectives) that should be reached along

with the key results (measures of how objectives are being met) and milestones (when and how key results should be measured). OKRs keep everyone aligned on goals and allow you to track your progress. Because reaching a major objective may take a long time, key results and milestones allow you to evaluate progress toward major objectives. OKRs are goals and measurements of change that show how goals are being reached. In our customer service scenario, the OKR is to improve a KPI: Reduce the employee turnover rate by at least 16 percent.

- **Return on investment (ROI)** answers the questions "Was this worth doing?" and "What was the result of our investment?" It's a measure of the costs and resulting business impact. Without predetermined success metrics, it can be difficult to show how investment in time, resources, and expenditures affect the bottom line. Examples of ROI success measures are often metrics of increases or decreases, such as reduced costs, increased customer and employee satisfaction, increased productivity, and increased retention.

Challenge yourself to push beyond the surface-level metrics. Consider how the solutions can have a greater impact and make connections to show the value that potential recommendations can have on business outcomes. Align with your stakeholders on these metrics as early as possible so you have a clear sense of the investments that they're willing to make to implement recommended solutions.

Before deciding which ones to recommend, we suggest discussing potential solutions with key stakeholders and subject matter experts to ensure that your recommendations are realistic, targeted, achievable, and as efficient as possible. As a word of caution, you should always maintain professional objectivity. While most stakeholders have good intentions, their passionate perspectives may end up influencing you and, in worst case scenarios, needs assessments can become vehicles for others to advance their own agendas. It is important that you remain neutral and evaluate solutions based on feasibility and organizational goals. Collaborate with and learn from your stakeholders, but rely most on data.

For a novice practitioner, leading a needs assessment can be stressful. When you throw a challenging or biased stakeholder into the mix, it becomes very difficult. Unfortunately, you are going to encounter difficult stakeholders; that's the reality of needs assessment work. Here are a few strategies you can use to build recommendations for difficult stakeholders:

- Share the needs assessment data analysis results with all the stakeholders before you begin to discuss or brainstorm solutions. Give everyone time to review the data analysis results so they can process the information, ask you questions if needed, and manage any negative reactions before you start discussing solutions.
- Keep conversations focused on the business problem and viable solutions using facts instead of feelings. You have the data analysis results, so let them steer the discussions and use them to keep everyone on track.
- Do not reference specific people as the *problem* or the *solution*; frame them in terms of job roles instead of specific individuals. Do not assign blame or credit to specific people.
- If the stakeholder's desired (or demanded) solution requires more authority, resources, or time than you have, determine what they are willing to do to ensure the solution can be implemented successfully. Approach this conversation carefully so that you do not sound confrontational, defensive, or inept. Stick to the facts of your limitations, and ask how they envision working around those limitations. Frame the conversation as a brainstorm. Use "I" statements, not "you" statements. Explain the risks of their suggested solution in if-then terms. ("If X happens, then are you willing to do Y?")

For an example of handling difficult stakeholders at this stage, let's return to the performance review system project that Kelly worked on. In this case, the sponsoring stakeholder demanded that the training sessions be conducted virtually. In 2023 (or beyond) this probably sounds like a reasonable request, but this situation occurred well before the COVID-19 pandemic; at the time, the company had not conducted any virtual training programs. Employees did not work remotely. Video meetings were usually held in conference rooms, not on individual laptops. Not only did the facilitators need to learn the new performance management system in a very short time, they also needed to learn how to use the virtual meeting platform, strategies for virtual facilitation, and techniques for troubleshooting technical problems. The resource demand was huge. The stakeholder had their own reasons for pushing online training, and while some of those reasons made perfect sense for the problem, Kelly was concerned because the stakeholder was unwilling to consider any alternative options. She brought forth her concerns as a list of facts—employees and facilitators were inexperienced with virtual training, the virtual meeting platform had not yet been tested at this scale, and technical problems during training could increase stress and resistance in what was already a major system change for employees. She asked the stakeholder, who was in charge of the payroll system, to agree to extend the performance review deadline if, despite the team's best attempts to deliver all the training virtually, employees were not able to use the new system correctly. The stakeholder agreed—in writing. Because they were willing to accept responsibility for massive payroll work if the solution failed, Kelly agreed that the solution was acceptable.

Recommendation Categories and Considerations

Presenting your recommendations in order of implementation difficulty and anticipated resistance can help you identify which would be easiest to try first and which are worth more time, effort, and expense. One strategy for organizing recommendations is to categorize them as internal solutions, external solutions, or executive leadership solutions:

- **Internal solutions** are ways to solve a problem by making changes or leveraging resources within an organization—most internal solutions will be things you build or borrow, such as creating a new process or job aids to help employees use a new system.
- **External solutions** are usually things you buy, such as hiring a consultant, paying for external training, or purchasing a new software platform.
- **Executive leadership solutions** require buy-in from the CEO or executive leaders who can authorize company-wide solutions. Those solutions may be things an organization can build, borrow, or buy, but they can't be implemented without executive approval. For example, if your needs assessment finds that 90 percent of employees are dissatisfied with the current benefits package, an executive leadership solution will be required.

You will probably design many internal solutions, and some may require borrowing resources from one area of your organization to help another area solve a problem. For example, if your needs assessment is focused on internal sales reps, and you determine they need more knowledge about customers, an internal solution might be asking the marketing team to provide customer personas and journey maps and share excerpts from customer focus groups and surveys.

Sounds like a win-win! You can address the problem effectively without a budget. Right? Maybe, but before recommending a *borrowed* solution, you should understand that borrowing internal solutions requires the people providing the solution to *borrow* the burden of the problem the solution is designed to solve. Never assign burden without first discussing bandwidth—the resources you're *borrowing* will not appreciate being "voluntold" instead of being asked if they are able and willing to cooperate. Borrowing internal resources to solve one problem could create another problem if you don't consider the borrowed burden. If you do recommend borrowed internal support as a solution, set clear expectations, parameters for the request, and a cut-off date. Limitations must be in place so no one's time is *borrowed* to the point that their own performance suffers.

Recommendation Blueprint

When making recommendations to solve a business problem based on your needs assessment, your goal is to tell an effective story that links the current state of the problem to the goal state through solutions that address the gap. Recommendations have five key components: Define the problem, the approach, success, the timeline, and the resource requests. Use Figure 4-4 on the next page as a model to build a recommendation blueprint for your project.

You can also use the build-borrow-buy framework to organize recommendations:

- **Which solutions can be built in-house?** What resources will you need?
- **Which solutions can be borrowed?** Is there a similar solution that is being used by another area of the organization that you can leverage or use as a template?
- **Which solutions must be bought?** What is the potential ROI of that expense? Be sure to share any cost savings that you've identified.

Figure 4-4. Key Components of a Recommendation

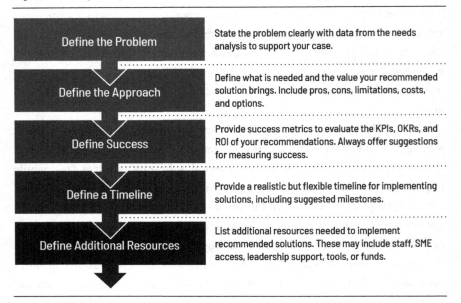

Define the Problem	State the problem clearly with data from the needs analysis to support your case.
Define the Approach	Define what is needed and the value your recommended solution brings. Include pros, cons, limitations, costs, and options.
Define Success	Provide success metrics to evaluate the KPIs, OKRs, and ROI of your recommendations. Always offer suggestions for measuring success.
Define a Timeline	Provide a realistic but flexible timeline for implementing solutions, including suggested milestones.
Define Additional Resources	List additional resources needed to implement recommended solutions. These may include staff, SME access, leadership support, tools, or funds.

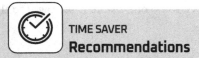

TIME SAVER

Recommendations

In the "Recommendations" section of appendix B, we use the customer service needs assessment scenario to demonstrate how you can apply the three recommendation categories with the build-borrow-buy framework to formulate the recommendations you might consider presenting to stakeholders.

In addition to the recommendation blueprint and build-borrow-buy framework, we suggest the following strategies for sharing the results of a needs assessment:

- Highlight any connections where the recommended solutions could help other areas of the organization or address other problems—build once; use often.
- If you evaluated case studies of how similar organizations solved similar problems, provide those comparable points of reference.

- Conduct a pilot test to generate the data needed to evaluate the effectiveness of solutions before fully investing in them. If a pilot test is possible, propose when and how you will perform it and what resources you will need.
- Discuss the cost of not taking any action. This outcome of needs assessments is often overlooked—your recommendation may be to take no action. Regardless, it's always worth discussing the potential outcomes of taking no action. Calmly highlight these risks and support them with data from your analysis (such as projected lost revenue or employee retention).

  TIME SAVER · ON THE CHEAP
Crawl-Walk-Run

Crawl-walk-run is a well-known concept in the business lexicon, and it is a great way to position your recommendations in a pilot-iterate-scale model. The crawl-walk-run process helps you identify the most important outcomes at various stages while the decision to progress and scale occurs, along with data to support it. We have also seen it work to get things moving quickly.

The crawl-walk-run approach may be right for your project if:

- A pilot test is needed to determine whether recommendations can effectively meet the organization's needs.
- The recommendation is experimental and bugs need to be worked out before it is scaled to a larger group.
- Gaining buy-in and stakeholder approval is needed at multiple time intervals. For example, stakeholders are not willing to fund the entire project but are willing to fund a project with a smaller budget.

Sharing Results

Now that your data collection and analysis are complete, and you've brainstormed solutions and selected recommendations, your needs assessment project is nearly complete. It's time to summarize and share the results! Sharing results is a critical step in the process. This is your opportunity to make the organization aware of the problems that exist and to provide recommendations on how to solve them.

As you review your assessment results and recommendations, consider returning to the stakeholders and asking for their feedback on the draft results report as you write it. By sharing some initial samples of your work, you can get feedback that you can implement iteratively. Sharing your results along the way will also ensure you and your stakeholders are not faced with last minute surprises when they review the final report. While requesting feedback can undoubtedly cause short-term pauses as you wait for replies, think of this as a potential long-term time saver.

We recommend that you create a needs assessment results report and a brief presentation summarizing it. Depending on the nature of the project, you may also need to create a version of the report and presentation for participants that contains less detail than the stakeholder's version. And you may want to create a one-page summary or a single slide, which serves as the most consolidated presentation of the problem, impact, current and goal state, key findings, and recommendations. Remember that different audiences will have different expectations, requirements, and sensitivities to the data included in your report—consider each one carefully when preparing materials.

Jody's primary lesson learned from writing needs assessment results reports is to set up the document at the beginning of the project and fill in the details as she goes. Using this write-as-you-go method will lessen the burden of writing your report if you are under pressure to complete the work and scrambling to remember or gather all the details. When using this approach, remember that you are not creating a polished and perfect version.

Write the executive summary last—it will be much easier once the rest of the report is complete. Early in the project, focus your write-as-you-go efforts on the background, investigation, and key findings sections. Using this approach, Jody has been able to reduce the amount of time she spends writing reports. A small-scope needs assessment results report can be as brief as 10 to 15 pages or can be presented in slides, omitting the report completely.

What to Include: Need to Know vs. Nice to Know

Deciding what information and how much detail you should include in a needs assessment report or presentation can be challenging, especially when consolidating results into an executive summary. You worked hard to learn a lot, and it's natural to want to share all this knowledge.

One strategy is to write a version of the results report that includes all the information you've gathered—this *full detail* report can be helpful for later reference too because it includes all your findings, notes, and potential solutions. Then, label or color code each sentence or data point in the full report as "need to know" or "nice to know."

Need-to-know content includes key information and data points stakeholders need to understand the impact of the problem and the rationale behind the recommended solutions. *Nice-to-know content* includes reference information and full results details—it's important to save this information for decision discussions, ROI measures, and future evaluation of solutions. You can use nice-to-know content as talking points or speaker notes for presentations, but removing it from slides or summary pages will help you keep your reports as visual as possible and ensure they're concise and easy to read.

TIME SAVER
Elevator Pitch

One way to differentiate need-to-know from nice-to-know content is to use an imaginary timer as if you were limited to explaining your needs assessment results as an elevator pitch. If you only have five minutes with decision makers or only one page to explain the needs assessment and make your recommendations, what information would you include and why?

You can create outlines based on five minutes, 10 minutes, or 20 minutes; one or two pages; three or four slides; and so on. This exercise will help you summarize your main points and effectively present the most important facts.

Needs Assessment Results Report

The results report contains an overview of each element of the needs assessment from start to finish—background, methods, key findings, and recommendations. The strategy worksheet you've been using is a helpful resource for this process.

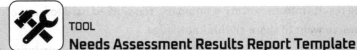

TOOL

Needs Assessment Results Report Template

Appendix A includes an outline you can use when creating your needs assessment results report. It covers space for your executive summary, introduction to the report, background on the problem, methods for collecting data, key findings, recommendations, references, and an appendix. Meanwhile, in the "Results Report" section of appendix B, we use the customer service needs assessment scenario to provide a worked example of a results report executive summary.

Here is an outline you can use when creating your needs assessment results report:

- **Executive summary.** The executive summary is a synopsis of the needs assessment that includes a short summary of each section of the report. Cut to the chase, include only the most critical details, and use data visuals when possible. The executive summary is best placed at the beginning of the report, but we recommend writing it last. This approach will help you capture the most important details from each section of the report in a concise, easy-to-read format.
- **Introduction.** The introduction provides an overview of the problem, its impact on the business, the current state, goal state, and gaps. This section should explain why the problem was worth investigating and what's at risk if no action is taken to address it. Sometimes this section is labeled "purpose" instead of "introduction."
- **Background.** The background section provides a brief summary of the insight you've gained (contextual, organizational, operational, and individual). Highlight the information that is most relevant to the rest of your report or needed to understand your findings and recommendations. Sometimes this section is labeled "overview" instead of "background."
- **Methods.** The methods section is a detailed summary about the needs assessment investigation—what research questions guided the work, what data did you collect, and how did you analyze the data? Sometimes this section is labeled "investigation," "assessment," or "research" instead of "methods."

- **Key findings.** The key findings section is a summary of the results of your data analysis. It can be helpful to include both quantitative and qualitative data here—an interview quote that further explains a survey question calculation, for example. Include a limited list of the most relevant findings that support each conclusion. Additional findings such as full survey results can be included in an appendix if needed. Note: When you conduct needs assessment work, you organize findings and then reach conclusions based on those findings. For the purpose of the needs assessment results report, findings and conclusions are usually combined into one key findings section.

- **Recommendations.** The recommendations section lists the action steps of your report and is where you describe the solutions you recommend to address the problem. For each recommendation, describe the conclusion it addresses, and include the rationale (Why is this a potentially viable solution?), pros, cons, limitations, costs, timeline estimates, required resources, and suggestions for measuring the results if implemented. You can present recommendations in order of priority, feasibility, impact, implementation time, or cost. If you're recommending a crawl-walk-run approach, you can present those recommendations as solution phases.

- **References.** If you cite publications or other copyrighted materials in your report, include a list of citations in a references section at the end of the needs assessment results report.

- **Appendix.** The appendix can include additional information such as the list of stakeholders, copies of relevant reports or benchmarking data, background information, and solution details (potential vendors and pricing options). If you want to include a summary of the needs assessment's ROI, it can be placed before or within the appendix.

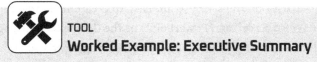

TOOL
Worked Example: Executive Summary

In the "Results Report" section in appendix B, you'll find a sample executive summary for the customer service scenario.

Results Summary Presentation

Remember that the time you have with any audience for sharing the results of your needs assessment comes at a premium—time and attention are sacred resources. A summary presentation of the needs assessment results report is often more useful for sharing results than the actual report. Take the time to create a visual presentation that's tailored to meet the needs of your audiences. Table 4-1 provides a presentation content outline you can adapt for your own reports.

Table 4-1. Outline for Results Summary Presentation

Introduction Slide	Customize the introduction based on your audience. Consider the content from your stakeholders' point of view—WIIFM (What's in It for Me?).	
Content Slides	• Business problem • Investigation approach	• Findings • Recommendations
Closing Slide	Customize your conclusion by specifying the call to action on behalf of the audience you are presenting to.	

Like your report, your presentation can include an appendix with slides that provide additional details or information—separating this content into an appendix will allow you to share the most important results quickly and then dive in deeper as time permits to facilitate Q&A or more in-depth discussions.

Visuals

Sometimes, a picture really is worth a thousand words—or at least a lot of data points. Visuals can add value to needs assessment reports and presentations by giving you options for displaying and drawing attention to key findings or other important aspects of your results. Consider using tables, pie charts, and figures to display your data findings—these are easy to create in simple tools like Microsoft Office (Word, Excel, and PowerPoint) or the Google Suite (Google Docs, Sheets, and Slides). You don't have to be a graphic designer to use visuals effectively. Just follow a few best practices:

- Label each table and figure.
- Use color and bolded fonts when formatting headings in table columns and rows.

- Ensure that each visual is self-explanatory, and provide footnotes as needed to expand on or clarify the information. Link any footnotes to information in the appendix or references.
- Keep all visuals professional and streamlined. Don't use clipart, flashy colors, or animations.
- Ensure that all text is legible. Don't use fonts that are too small or difficult to read.
- If you have photos from observations or other data collection methods, include the one or two that most clearly illustrate the situation you observed. However, don't forget to preserve the participant's privacy.

Visuals are powerful because they grab attention and can convey data quickly and effectively. However, don't overload your audience with too many visuals or too much information all at once. Our short-term memories have a limit on how much information they can process simultaneously. When using visuals to deliver information, borrow from some of the best practices offered by John Sweller's cognitive load theory. Build your data story by adding visual information gradually rather than dumping it all at once. Consider dividing information into chunks that can be more easily processed—our brains can process five to nine chunks of information at a time (Sweller 1994).

Visuals can be a great tool to complement your report and presentation. And while it may seem counterintuitive, remember that text is also a form of visual information. Our brains process white space, blocks of text, headings, and other spacing in documents visually as well as textually, so cognitive load best practices work well even if your visual options are limited only to word processing tools.

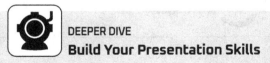

DEEPER DIVE
Build Your Presentation Skills

There are many great resources to help you develop your presentation skills, from storytelling to graphic design. Check out these tried-and-true options:
- Cole Nussbaumer Knaflic, *Storytelling the Data: A Data Visualization Guide for Business Professionals* (Hoboken, NJ: John Wiley and Sons, 2015).

- Nancy Duarte, *Resonate: Present Visual Stories That Transform Audiences* (Hoboken, NJ: John Wiley and Sons, 2010).
- ATD (Association for Talent Development), *10 Steps to Successful Presentations*, 2nd ed. (Alexandria, VA: ATD Press, 2019).
- MJ Hall, "Make Your Data Dance," *TD*, March 1, 2018. td.org/magazines /td-magazine/make-your-data-dance.
- Mike Parkinson, *A Trainer's Guide to PowerPoint: Best Practices for Master Presenters* (Alexandria, VA: ATD Press, 2018).

Weave a Golden Thread

Remember the exercise at the beginning of this chapter (in Figure 4-2) when you outlined your findings, conclusions, and recommendations in aligned rows? Now that you've done all the work of completing a needs assessment, wrap everything up in a neat, logical bow as you create the final report by weaving a (metaphorical) golden thread of connections through your results.

Figure 4-5. Connecting It All Together

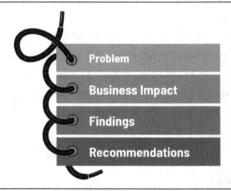

Make it as easy as possible for your audience to see the logic connecting the problem, business impact, key findings, and recommendations. The reasoning behind your recommendations should be crystal clear and solve the problem being addressed—if your key findings are solid enough to stand on their own and your recommendations are clearly aligned, your audience can focus on the implications, instead of the rationale, of your results.

It may seem counterintuitive, but if you can summarize your needs assessment results so succinctly that a few sentences (and maybe a visual aid or two) can convey the whole story, you've succeeded in synthesizing a complex problem into simple components with compelling recommendations based on accurate data. If all those things are aligned with stakeholders' expectations and specific business goals, then you've hit rock star status! Creating clarity from complexity is a needs assessment practitioner's superpower.

A Shoestring Summary

Now that you know how to build a needs assessment project from start to finish, and you've learned about dozens of strategies and resources to help you along the way, take a few minutes to reflect on what you've learned so far.

What are your top five takeaways?

1. _____

   _____

2. _____

   _____

3. _____

   _____

4. _____

   _____

5. _____

   _____

Which "Deeper Dive" suggestions do you most want to learn more about?

1. _____

_____

2. _____

_____

3. _____

_____

Which three strategies will you use for your next needs assessment project?

1. _____

_____

2. _____

_____

3. _____

_____

PART 2
BORROW

In part 1 of this book, you learned how to build a needs assessment. Part 2 will help you execute that work using the internal and external resources you can access on a shoestring.

Borrowing your way through a needs assessment is a savvy way to get the work done. The chapters in this section offer guidance on how to borrow smartly to repurpose existing resources, information, and content, as well as strategies for identifying and leveraging collaborative opportunities.

In this part of the book, you'll learn how to identify and use:
- Relevant internal and external data
- Existing expertise within and outside your organization

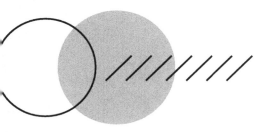

5
Borrowing Existing Data

Detectives work hard under pressure to solve cases correctly, quickly, and efficiently, and they need to discover data that antagonists are working equally hard to keep hidden. Hopefully, your needs assessment work won't be antagonistic, but you'll likely face challenges when it comes to identifying, accessing, and using data that already exists within your organization or is available externally. During a needs assessment, consider borrowing any data that may assist you. And like a savvy detective, you should uncover, verify, and use any information that helps you close the case without leading you down the wrong trail.

Get creative and consider all the relevant data that may exist and ways you can gather, validate, and reuse that information. Think of the data sources as falling into two buckets: internal and external.

- *Existing internal data sources* include information created within your organization such as training assessments, employee retention data, customer demographics, revenue statements, annual reports, press releases, competitive analyses, findings from previous surveys and focus groups, quality assurance observations and checklists, process and policy documents, budget narratives, employee handbooks, product brochures, marketing materials, and the organizations' social media channels.
- *Existing external data sources* include information created by experts, researchers, or competitors outside your organization, such as benchmarking data, industry reports, case studies, and quarterly earnings statements.

Not all "borrowable" data is valuable or accessible, so it's important to have a strategy in place to make the best use of your time, effort, and resources.

Borrowing Data Strategically: Repurpose on Purpose

When you are operating on a shoestring you may not be allotted the time or access required to generate all your own data. Instead, borrowing data is a strategy to identify, access, verify, and use credible information that can help you accurately answer the research questions of your needs assessment within the available timeline, budget, and project scope. Being a savvy data borrower will help you reduce workload, avoid redundancy, build credibility, and save time. Strategically borrowing existing data will also expand your organizational and industry knowledge, develop your analytical skills, and help you make more informed recommendations. Figure 5-1 presents our recommended strategy for being a savvy data borrower.

Figure 5-1. Data-Borrowing Strategy: Eight Steps to Success

1. Determine information standards.
2. Identify credible data sources.
3. Identify access options.
4. Save and cite each source.
5. Evaluate, validate, and triangulate.
6. Format for usability.
7. Use with acknowledgment.
8. Appreciate and reciprocate.

Like shopping for a high-quality preowned item, you want to have a strategy for identifying options, determining requirements, ensuring quality, and getting the most value. Costs and challenges involved with accessing existing internal data include awareness and relationships, political capital or leadership support, time, delays, and hidden labor costs. Costs and challenges with accessing existing external data include the expense of purchasing reports or content from publishers, the process of gaining permission to reuse data if needed, time required for contacting sources and data to be delivered to you, and time needed to evaluate, validate, and format data. There's not a magical, easy way to gather existing data, but there are strategies to help you determine what you should build yourself (review chapters 1, 2, and 3), what makes the most sense to purchase (coming up in part 3), and what's worth borrowing.

In the following sections, we will share best practices for borrowing existing data for needs assessments.

Step 1. Determine Information Standards

After determining what data you need to collect, but before investing the time to collect the data, identify standards for information usability. Remember the professors who required you to use library databases instead of Wikipedia for research papers? That requirement was created to ensure you used peer-reviewed sources. You don't have to follow academic research standards for needs assessments, but you do need to establish criteria for determining which borrowable sources are worthy of inclusion.

Criteria to consider include:

- **Currency.** How old is too old for a source to be considered credible? What date ranges are acceptable for your needs assessment data? It may be helpful to set an expiration date for current data sources.
- **Authority.** Who are the trusted experts in the field? Do you and your stakeholders consider the organizations, researchers, thought leaders, or industry report authors credible and trustworthy? Is the information bias free? Be careful when considering information offered as part of a sales pitch—not all vendor whitepapers are valid data points.
- **Accuracy.** How can you verify the data you're borrowing? Does the data triangulate with other information you've gathered?
- **Relevance.** Is the data aligned with your needs assessment research questions? If you're evaluating benchmarking data or case studies, are the examples relatable to the problem you're trying to solve?

- **Quality.** How confident are you in the data you're borrowing? What quality measures are you evaluating against? What research methods were used to create the data source?

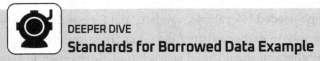

DEEPER DIVE
Standards for Borrowed Data Example

Here's an example of standards that we examine when considering whether to borrow data. Before deciding to use ATD's 2022 research report, *Succession Planning: Preparing Organizations for the Future*, for a leadership development needs assessment project, we looked for details about the research methodology. The whitepaper included all the information we needed to gauge currency, authority, accuracy, relevance, and quality, including an overview of the research survey, reference footnotes, author details, statistical significance calculations, and key findings. For example, the survey overview identified:

- **Target survey population.** The target population for this research was talent development professionals across different organizations and industries. Participants from 243 organizations completed the survey.
- **Survey instrument.** The survey was composed of 22 questions, including those related to the demographics of the respondents.
- **Procedure.** ATD Research distributed a link to an online survey to the target population in March 2022. The survey closed in April 2022.

Step 2. Identify Credible Data Sources

Borrowing data will not help your needs assessment efforts if the sources aren't considered credible by your stakeholders, even if the information is accurate and meets all other criteria you've established. Thus, it's important to know which internal and external data sources are trusted and valued.

Start at the top—locate the reports and data sources your senior leaders use to make business decisions and to monitor the company's financial health. Scorecards and dashboards are examples of common organizational data outputs. Select the metrics that align with your work and follow the data trail by locating the data used to feed those reports. By following the data trails, you will likely uncover qualitative and quantitative sources. If the data feeds into the most visible reports, it is likely a credible data source. Take note of the people who are involved in creating those data reports as you build your list of go-to experts and thought leaders.

TIME SAVER
Stakeholders' Go-To Data Sources

To quickly identify information sources that will help you collect credible information, ask leaders and stakeholders the following questions:

- How do you stay informed about the industry, current news, and future trends?
- What thought leaders, media sources, blogs, podcasts, reports, conferences, and professional groups or associations do you follow most often?
- If you needed to understand the history of a current practice or process at this company, who would you ask and why?
- Who is the person (or people) at the company who can explain our strategies and goals in the simplest ways so that everyone can understand?
- If you could bring in any expert to consult with us or address the company about this problem, who would it be and why?
- What does the data validation process look like? Are regular spot checks conducted with contacts within the business?

In addition to your stakeholders' go-to data sources, identify your organizations' trusted business partners and inquire about borrowing data from them. For example, if your marketing department or business analytics team partners with an external research or consultancy group, are there reports from these groups that you can access? If your organization is a member of a professional or trade association, you may find valuable data sources there as well.

It's important to have your own list of go-to authorities for quality information to help you evaluate potential data sources, create your own benchmarks, and leverage the expertise of other talent development professionals. Organizations such as ATD, the Society for Human Resource Management (SHRM), LinkedIn, Glassdoor, and Indeed produce a variety of high-quality research reports, benchmarks, case studies, and best practices that can be borrowed for your needs assessment projects. Staying current with industry experts through trusted organizations will save you time in the long term and provide you with resources for needs assessment strategies and solutions, as well as other work, including strategic planning, budgeting, hiring, determining best practices, and conducting research.

Step 3. Identify Access Options

Once you've identified a credible data source to borrow, you'll need to identify access options and time and budget considerations.

For existing internal data, you'll need to answer these questions:

- Who currently has the data, and how can you access it?
- Do you need permission or support from executive leaders?
- Do you need time to gain access to specific systems?
- What is the deliverable timeline, considering the workload of the content owner?

For existing external data, you'll need to answer these questions:

- Who should you contact to request or purchase the data?
- Who holds any copyrights if the information was published externally?
- What is the timeline for gaining access? How long will it take for the content owner to provide the data to you?
- Is there a cost for borrowing or purchasing the data? If the full report is too expensive, can you purchase a whitepaper or an executive summary at a lower cost or access it for free?

Once you have all the access details, you can decide if borrowing the data is feasible within your project scope and deadline.

Step 4. Save Your Sources

Always keep a complete reference copy of each borrowed data file you use in your needs assessment. Also, keep the publication information for each file—author, creator or publisher, and publication date—so you can properly cite each source and find it again if needed. Note the cost associated with any purchased data and contact information for anyone who helped you access borrowed data—that information may also be useful in the future.

This references list strategy is helpful for staying current with annual reports, building your trusted information authority list and personal professional library, and budgeting for future needs assessment projects.

Step 5. Evaluate, Validate, and Triangulate

Once you've gathered the borrowed information, you'll need to review it carefully. Not all the data will be useful, so evaluate to determine whether each piece is relevant for inclusion in your needs assessment. This requires careful balancing—you should include data that's germane even if it doesn't say what you'd like it to say. Remember that you're investigating as an unbiased researcher, so don't cherry pick data that supports your recommendations while ignoring other valid data that does not align with your own opinions.

Verify any borrowed data before using it in your needs assessment. A best practice is to triangulate any borrowed data against at least two other validated information sources (for a review on triangulation, refer to chapter 3). You'll find additional strategies for evaluating and validating borrowed data in the "Borrower Beware" section later in this chapter.

Step 6. Format for Usability

Not all borrowed data files will be delivered in formats that you can immediately or easily use, and the process of extracting text and formatting data can take far more time than you expect. This sounds simple, but it's a lesson that we have both learned the hard way. For example, printed copies of reports may need to be scanned and digitized. Locked files may require passcodes to read or copy content. Older PDF files may not have copy options without Adobe Acrobat or similar PDF editing software. Spreadsheets may need to be reviewed to ensure that unusable or confidential data isn't included; tables may also need to be resorted or restructured. Plan for time to extract, format, or move data into usable forms that are compatible with the software systems and file editing programs you're using.

Step 7. Use With Acknowledgment

Always cite any direct quotations, visuals, or datasets you use in your needs assessment report and presentations. You don't need an academically formatted bibliography, but including footnotes in your report with citations in a references list is an important practice to follow to give credit appropriately, maintain your professional credibility, avoid plagiarism, and trace information for future reference.

Step 8. Appreciate and Reciprocate

Borrowing data is inevitably a necessary strategy for completing a needs assessment, especially if you are a team of one. Relationships are key to current and future information access, so be sure to acknowledge and thank those who help you identify and borrow data sources. Regardless of the data's usefulness, always be a graceful receiver. Here are a few strategies to keep in mind as you work with a data donor:

- **Be hard on facts and soft on people.** You must be critical of every dataset to ensure it is valid and accurately informs your needs assessment. However, when using someone else's work, it's important not to be critical of the *people* who are sharing data with you. Especially when evaluating borrowed internal data, keep your criticisms to yourself. If borrowed data isn't usable, thank the sender for supporting your efforts. If pressed about why you didn't include borrowed data in your needs assessment, you can explain that the information helped you gain context or background knowledge.
- **To convince potential stakeholders to share data with you, consider their perspectives.** Often you will face a situation in which you have no positional power but must instead influence others to willingly share the data with you. It is best to lead with persuasion from a position of mutual respect and make a clear case of why the data is needed and how their work will support the organization's goal.
- **Treat each contact as a valuable source.** You are likely to develop working relationships with both internal and external data owners, and you may be asked to return the favor in their future efforts. Who else in your organization might find your needs assessment results useful? Offer to share.

Jody met with an internal team that owned data she needed. From their conversation, she discovered they were looking to upgrade their current data collection software tool but couldn't get budget approval. Jody was able to use the data and offer feedback and enhancement ideas that they then used in a business case for upgrading their software. The combined need and collaboration tipped the scales for a company-wide data improvement investment.

Now that you know the essential steps of a data-borrowing strategy, let's take a closer look at borrowing benchmarking and internal data.

Borrowing Benchmark Data

Benchmarking is a measure of comparison of performance with an established standard. Benchmark data is used to gauge how your organization is performing compared with competitors and similar organizations and to discover areas for improvement. It is commonly collected to better examine current practices and determine performance metrics (KPIs).

Kelly relies on benchmarking data for strategic planning. For example, you can use talent management benchmarking to support budget requests. By researching industry benchmarks, she learned that on average, companies allocate 1 to 5 percent of their total salary costs to the employee training and development cost center. Knowing that her annual total budget request falls within that percentage based on the company's projected growth helps her build an objective, compelling business case.

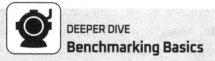

DEEPER DIVE
Benchmarking Basics

Want to learn more about benchmarking and see examples in action? Check out these resources:

- Lisa Gary, "Focusing on Alignment and Integration: Practicing What We Preach," ATD Webinar, June 24, 2021, webcasts.td.org/webinar/4289.
- ATD (Association for Talent Development), *Succession Planning: Preparing Organizations for the Future* (Alexandria, VA: ATD Press, 2022).
- Paul Elliott and Al Folsom, *Exemplary Performance: Driving Business Results by Benchmarking Your Star Performers* (Alexandria, VA: ATD Press, 2013).

Internal Benchmarking

Internal benchmarking compares groups, departments, and teams within an organization with a common set of performance standards. This data can help you understand how different groups within an organization operate, communicate, train their staff, and measure success. The process of internal benchmarking aims to identify similar operational areas so that their performance can be compared objectively. Consider gathering these internal benchmarking datasets for needs assessments:

- Descriptive information about the comparable group—size and characteristics of the team—and organizational structure
- KPIs used for annual performance reviews and for determining department success, awarding bonuses, or allocating budgets
- Current KPI measures compared to the previous quarter, previous year, or previous three-to-five years to identify trends
- Hiring and employee retention data
- Training-specific information such as onboarding standards, training program overview, annual budgets, and percent makeup of vendor-sourced and internally authored training content

While internal benchmarking data can be valuable, be aware that it takes time to discover. If you are moving swiftly, be selective by focusing on the internal areas that are most relevant to your needs assessment problem and the KPIs that inform the business problem and its impact on the organization. Also be aware that in cases of declining performance trends, data owners and leaders may be hesitant to share potentially damaging data or sensitive statistics. Your approach as a nonjudgmental, supportive professional and your ability to build positive relationships are critical to your success with borrowing internal benchmarking data and other internal data as well.

External Benchmarking

External benchmarking refers to measurements that organizations can use to compare themselves and their performance to other organizations. External benchmarking data may provide evidence to show whether the current state is meeting industry or national expectations. When considering external benchmarking data, you will likely gather information to identify *normative* and *comparative* needs (Burton and Merrill 1991). *Normative needs* are determined by comparing an organization's current state to global, national, or industry standards. *Comparative needs* are similar but home in on a specific group or team of employees and how they compare to another group of similar size, skill, and job function. Here are a few things to keep in mind as you consider borrowing external benchmarking data:

- Be aware of your organization's attributes such as industry type, company size, annual revenue, and annual training budget.
- Understand which organizations are similar to yours and which are considered competitors.
- Determine which, if any, industry benchmarking reports your organization participates in. Often, if your company contributes benchmarking data, you can access the complete research report for free or at a deeply discounted rate.

TIME SAVER
Talent Development Benchmarking Reports

Many professional organizations offer benchmarking as a service or publish benchmarking reports that are included for free with membership or available for purchase on demand. ATD's annual *State of the Industry* report provides information on training budgets, expenses, and expenditure trends from year to year and includes a breakdown of data by industry, which makes information related to competitors quickly identifiable. This report is incredibly helpful for benchmarking your annual training budget and provides data that can help you advocate for training-based solutions that emerge during needs assessments. The Learning Guild and *Training* magazine also offer a variety of benchmarking reports on many topics like training data and measurement. This information may be extrapolated and used in your needs assessment projects.

Borrowing Internal Data: Shop in Your Own Pantry

What existing internal data may be helpful for your needs assessment? It's unlikely that you'll be able to conduct a quick Google search for answers, but casting a wide, creative net of information requests can yield valuable results.

Once, as a new training manager, Kelly needed to conduct a large needs assessment that included interviews, focus groups, and questionnaires with 400 employees. She had 90 days to collect and analyze all the data, and as a new employee, she also needed to quickly learn as much as possible about the company. As a team of one, her resources were limited. Knowing that borrowing data is often the fastest path to organizational discovery, Kelly reached out to the customer support center and asked if there were recordings of customer calls available for review. In this case, recordings weren't available, but she was invited to sit with a staff member and listen to incoming customer calls. The few hours she spent listening to customer calls led to some great conversations with employees, who also shared customer emails and several documents that gave her an incredible starting point for drafting interview questions for the needs assessment. She now recommends that customer call examples be included in employee onboarding for almost every organization she works with, regardless of employee role.

For a different project, Kelly needed to conduct a needs assessment for a training program for general managers. There were more than 100 managers located all over the country, and they had incredibly busy schedules. Conducting individual interviews wasn't possible within the project deadline, so Kelly reached out to several department directors and asked if anyone had interviewed general managers for any project over the last couple years. She learned that the marketing department had conducted interviews with about 30 managers to create a persona for the HR recruitment team, and the raw interview notes and unedited transcripts were available. The interview questions were different from what she'd typically ask during a needs assessment, but the responses included great insights—participants shared why they'd wanted to work for the company, their favorite parts of their jobs, and details about jobs they'd held before becoming general managers. Reading these interviews was time well spent.

As you can see from these examples, you can find all sorts of borrowable data if you ask enough people for help. Learning who to ask for different types of information is worth the time you'll invest.

To know what internal data is available, you will need to establish a professional network within your organization, and it's best to start this effort long before you need specific datasets for a needs assessment project. In fact, we recommended beginning this process on your very first day on the job. If you don't yet have an extended internal network, don't worry! We use three simple, dependable approaches that can help you locate data within your company: the organizational charts, internal systems, and curiosity chats.

Organizational Charts

A great place to begin any internal data search is with your company's org chart. Start by identifying departments or teams in the organization that are responsible for training, process documentation, and analytics. These team members may have information about previous internal needs assessments, company reports, and performance metrics. As you make connections, ask people who have been part of previous data collection efforts about their experiences, go-to resources, and effective strategies. The company org chart can also help you identify potential SMEs across business domains—building relationships before you need them will fast-track your efforts when it's time to identify internal data sources for future needs assessment projects.

Internal Systems

If you can't find the contacts you need through an org chart, mapping your organization's internal systems is a great way to identify internal experts and potential data sources. Research what software systems and communication platforms power your company, and identify who manages those systems and platforms. Then create your own systems chart and invest time getting to know the people behind the technologies. Consider internal tools like Microsoft Teams, Slack, the LMS, payroll systems, employee intranet sites, company newsletters, customer management systems (CMSs), website content, and social media channels. Internal system data can provide insight into employee networks and help you understand how and where work occurs.

Curiosity Chats

When conducting a needs assessment, you are not required to have all the answers. In fact, your primary job is to ask questions. Curiosity is an invaluable asset, and you can actively practice curiosity like any other skill by informally interviewing people who work within your company. As you build your internal network, invite individuals to short, casual chats. This strategy works in the office and when working remotely. Structured curiosity chats can also help you build interviewing skills.

Ask people about the work they're currently responsible for, their past work experiences, why they came to work for the organization, and their favorite part of their job. Ask them how they stay current, what information resources they value, and whom they contact when they need to locate data. Before ending the meeting, ask them whom else in the company they'd recommend you introduce yourself to. Keep the questions light, the tone friendly, and the meeting short. Most people will appreciate your genuine interest in their work. Send a quick thank-you note afterward. A few minutes spent in a one-on-one meeting can go a long way in helping you create or strengthen relationships, demonstrate your approachability and relatability, and gain the trust of those you need help from. Never underestimate the power of authentic conversation.

The Art of the Ask

When it's time to borrow specific data for a needs assessment, practice the art of the ask. By this point in the project, you'll have identified the data sources and the people who can help you access them. Use the needs assessment strategy worksheet to collect contact information and track the progress of each request, and then craft a personalized ask for each data donor to ensure that you are delivering the right message to help you reach your goal.

A well-crafted ask includes five elements: the why, who, what, when, and how. You can use the checklist on the next page in Table 5-1 to outline the elements that will help ensure your initial communication request includes all the essential details needed to help you access borrowed data. Your goal is to make it as easy as possible for people to understand the need and meet your requests. Don't forget to share the results of the needs assessment or to share other data that may be helpful later to the people you're reaching out to now.

Managing Incoming Data

Borrowing data for a needs assessment adds a layer of coordination to the overall project management. Save yourself time and effort by keeping your requests to borrow data and received files organized. A simple tracking table will help you track the status of each data request, provide stakeholder updates for borrowed data, track any associated costs, and help you maintain the information needed for citing references. The Needs Assessment Strategy Planning worksheet we described chapter 1 and included in appendix A is a helpful resource for managing incoming data—document the data you need to access on the worksheet. You may list files to borrow such as past training data, survey results, benchmarking reports, or other internal business documents.

Table 5-1. Crafting the Ask Checklist

Elements of an Ask	Example
Why: Why are you requesting data? • Briefly explain the purpose of the needs assessment and why you're requesting to borrow data.	• "I am conducting a needs assessment for the customer service department with the goal of improving the current employee retention rate. I need information related to the onboarding experience of employees over the last 3 years."
Who: Why are you contacting this person? • Briefly explain why they were identified as a data donor.	• "The customer service director suggested I contact you as the HR analyst business partner."
What: What data are you requesting? • Provide specific details about the request.	• "Can you please send me the employee retention report for the customer service department for 2018–2022, including employee names and identification numbers, hire dates, start dates, and dates of separation?"
When: Timeline • Include a specific target date for data delivery.	• "I am analyzing several data points over the next two weeks. Can you provide me with the necessary reports by [*specific date*]?"
How: Call to action • Provide instructions for data delivery. • Include any follow-up steps. • Acknowledge and thank the person.	• "Please email the report to me. I will add it to my project team's shared drive for immediate review." • "After the needs assessment is complete, I will share my findings with you." • "Thank you for your help with this project. Please reach out if you have any questions."

Borrower Beware: GIGO, Red Herrings, and Confirmation Bias

Like a good detective, you'll need to leverage specific skills when borrowing data for needs assessments: effective listening, clear communication, planning, strategic evaluation, and critical thinking. You'll have to balance the art of asking and relationship management with critical data analysis to gain access to the data you need while also making informed decisions about what borrowed data to include in your needs assessment. As you borrow data, watch out for three things that can lead you astray: GIGO (garbage in, garbage out), red herrings, and confirmation bias.

GIGO (Garbage In, Garbage Out)

Even with the most advanced analysis tools, software, and strategies, your results will be worthless if the raw data you input is incorrect, incomplete, or outdated. GIGO most often occurs when you're too pressed for time to carefully review data, or when you end up relying on datasets that you don't fully understand. Data helps us make decisions, but ultimately, it's people who make decisions. The data you rely on must be accurate, especially as more tools and platforms are built around machine learning. Be careful when borrowing data from chatbots or other AI models, as GIGO can be prevalent in these new technologies. Establish criteria for verifying data, and understand the meaning and any calculations used to generate data points. It is far better to be vulnerable when receiving borrowed data and asking for help interpreting it correctly than using it incorrectly (or using incorrect data) and end up with a failing needs assessment.

Red Herrings

In mystery stories, red herrings are false clues intended to mislead or distract a detective. In needs assessments, red herrings are details that distract from the core problem you're working to solve. During a needs assessment, you will likely be presented with many red herrings as individual stakeholders share their perspectives and goals and, unintentionally, their biases, personal agendas, and blind spots. Be careful to listen critically and remain both empathetic and objective so that you do not accidentally take on others' agendas.

Confirmation Bias

A bias is a distorted, prejudiced, or faulty conception, judgment, or way of thinking. We all have biases, whether we mean to or not. In needs assessments, confirmation bias is a challenge—it is our human tendency to seek out and pay attention to information and other people that confirm our beliefs and assumptions. Confirmation bias is a recipe for failure in needs assessments because it limits our perspective and leads to selective decision making instead of objective decision making. Incorrectly comparing datasets—"apples to oranges" thinking—is a common form of confirmation bias. If data points are not directly related, they can't be compared objectively. In addition, beware of inferring causality or relationships between data points that do not actually exist. Remember, you aren't collecting and analyzing needs assessment data to prove a hypothesis. Your goal is to clearly define a business problem and identify potential solutions.

Confirmation bias can also be a challenge in needs assessments when leaders believe they already know the root cause of a problem or the best solution for a problem, do not believe a needs assessment is warranted, or want to jump immediately into action without first conducting a needs assessment. It can be tough for anyone to challenge senior leaders' opinions. Remember the crawl-walk-run example related to pilot testing? Breaking a needs assessment into smaller parts allows you to test quick fixes while continuing to collect and analyze data to identify real root causes and more effective solutions. Solid data and calm objectivity are your best tools when trying to educate, influence, or support a leader who is, intentionally or not, operating with confirmation bias.

The best way to mitigate confirmation bias is to collect and analyze data from several sources and to evaluate it through triangulation. As talent development professionals, we should continually challenge ourselves to seek input from co-workers and experts who are willing to respectfully disagree with our opinions, and practice evaluating our own decisions.

DEEPER DIVE
Mitigating Bias

You can't fully rid yourself of biases, but you can become more aware of them, as well as your organization's leaders' biases, and learn how to mitigate them. Check out these two excellent articles to learn more:

- Janet Ahn, "To Make Better Decisions, Mitigate Bias," *TD*, March 1, 2021, td.org/magazines/td-magazine/to-make-better-decisions-mitigate-bias.
- Gus Prestera, "Get Needs Assessment Right the First Time," *CTDO*, September 14, 2018, td.org/magazines/ctdo-magazine/get-needs-assessment-right-the-first-time.

Keep, Toss, or Donate: Decluttering Borrowed Data

As you borrow, collect, and generate data to fuel a needs assessment project, you'll need to decide what data to use. The keep-toss-donate decluttering model can be a simple way to decide the fate of each data point you've gathered.

- **Keep.** Use the data in your needs assessment analysis.
- **Toss.** Exclude the data from your needs assessment. Even when tossing data, keep a copy for future reference. You never know when it may come in handy for a different project, or even as an example of how to better structure datasets.
- **Donate.** Share the data. Where might this dataset be useful? Who might benefit from this information?

TOOL

Data Keep Pile Template

Use the Data Keep Pile template in appendix A to organize your sources. Here's an example for one source.

Source	• ATD's *2022 State of the Industry* report • [*Location of saved document*]
Summary	• A national summary of training expenditures within organizations
Research method and publication date	• Survey of 174 organizations; completed in mid-2021 • Published annually
Application	• I can use this source to provide reference points to common training approaches and budget benchmarks.
Cost	• This report is included in my ATD membership.

Jody likes to keep her data sources organized in a table reminiscent of an annotated bibliography containing source citation information, a brief content summary, the research method, and a short statement about how each source applies to the needs assessment. This practice helps her determine what to keep, toss, and donate based on the merits of the data and its application to the needs assessment. You can create a simple "data keep file" document or spreadsheet (like the template included in appendix A) to save all the relevant information about your data sources in one place. If you cannot complete every row in the Data Keep Pile template for a data source, it may not be worth including in your needs assessment.

A Shoestring Summary

As you plan future needs assessment projects, strategize ways to borrow data from inside and outside your organization. Considerations to keep in mind include:

- What benchmarking data (internal and external) support your needs assessment?
- What standards are you setting for borrowed data you will include in your needs assessment?
- What strategies do you have in place for building your internal professional network?
- How will you ensure your request to borrow data is clear and effective?
- How will you track, manage, and cite borrowed data sources?
- How are you mitigating against GIGO (garbage in, garbage out), red herrings, and confirmation bias when evaluating borrowed data?
- Who might benefit from borrowing your needs assessment data?

6
Borrowing Time and Talent

Detectives partner with others to scale efforts, cover more ground, or gain access to information in other jurisdictions. They may request help from a dispatcher, sketch artist, records officer, search-and-rescue team, or even a K-9 unit. (Who said all the talent you borrow must be human? Maybe in future needs assessments, we'll borrow help from AI applications.) A smart detective partners strategically—and you should too.

Borrowing time and talent is a common practice for needs assessments. Strategically borrowing internal talent will help you grow your organizational knowledge as you work cross-functionally with other business lines, functions, departments, teams, and employees. Strategically borrowing external talent will help you develop industry knowledge and professional skills like negotiation, budgeting, and project management as you partner with consultants and other providers. Borrowing external talent usually requires a cost, so we've included strategies for hiring and working with external partners in chapter 9. In this chapter, we'll focus on borrowing internal time and talent and give you strategies for working with stakeholders, SMEs, project teams, participants, and partners. And we'll share some ideas for learning from professional peers and experts outside your organization (with no cost!).

Which Hat Will You Wear?

As you build your needs assessment team, be sure to include yourself! What roles will you play? Will you be the primary project manager responsible for ensuring completion of each task within the project scope? Will you design surveys? Conduct interviews? Do you have the required skills to analyze data?

Do you have subject matter expertise related to the business problem? Evaluate your strengths and limitations so you can best define your role in the needs assessment project. Clearly defining your role will help you identify the gaps that need to be filled by others and help you narrow down the talent that must be borrowed to successfully complete the project.

Jody recalls working on a needs assessment in which she had to borrow other employees as a resource during her first week on the job. She knew the hats she had to wear for that needs assessment project—Jody was a technical SME in the process problem being researched, and she was also the project manager. Being new to the company presented several challenges: Her company knowledge was limited. She was still figuring out the business and organizational structure. And her short tenure hadn't been long enough to develop relationships with new colleagues. Because she was serving as the SME, what she needed most were partners who could help her identify additional stakeholders and target audience participants. She searched the company directory and org chart for people who might be potential partners or have insight into the needs assessment audience. Then Jody shared her contact list with the project's sponsoring stakeholder, who reviewed it, provided feedback, and added the names of trainers that Jody had not found in her search who had direct access to the learners she needed to interview. Jody asked the stakeholder to introduce her to the trainers and make any connections that would help facilitate a working partnership. This approach—knowing what hats she would wear and what hats she needed to borrow for the project—helped her hit the ground running despite not yet knowing her way around the building.

Kelly's work has shifted from wearing multiple needs assessment hats to guiding other practitioners as they learn to take on different needs assessment roles. This shift has given her a new perspective on conducting needs assessments and introduced her to two new hats—quality assurance and continuous improvement. She now designs standards and processes for needs assessment projects and works with team members to identify quality controls and efficiency opportunities. Her team is working toward new strategies for accurately identifying needs more quickly, determining the readiness level of incoming projects, and leveraging knowledge management tools to use existing data for strategy plans.

Even with our combined decades of experience, we both continue to encounter challenges with identifying and borrowing the right internal resources to get the job done. (Sadly, we still don't have the magic answer for bringing a SME back to life when they "ghost" you on a project.) Chances are high you'll need to borrow talent to conduct a needs assessment, and no matter what hat you're wearing—unless it's the CEO's—you'll probably face these challenges too. Knowing how to borrow talent to build a needs assessment team is essential to your success.

Borrowing Internal Resources: Build a Needs Assessment Team

It's virtually impossible to conduct a needs assessment without the help of others within your organization. This is one of the many reasons we continue to highlight the importance of building relationships and continuing to develop yourself as a collaborative professional. Planning a needs assessment project requires you to build a team, formally or informally. You will need the cooperation of people in several roles to be successful. Plan to borrow time and talent in support of a needs assessment for the following roles:

- **Stakeholders** are project contributors (usually leaders) who are invested—have an active stake—in the needs assessment. To identify stakeholders, consider who will be affected by the needs assessment's results and recommended solutions. Who are the leaders of the affected departments? Which stakeholders can contribute to this project, and how much time can they make available? Ideally, stakeholders will help you access existing data, complete needs assessment project tasks, and help you identify SMEs, collaborators, and participants.
- **Champions** are executive leaders who understand the importance of the needs assessment and are willing to support your efforts and help meet your resource needs.
- **Consultants** are leaders who are willing to critique your work, challenge your perspective, help you brainstorm, help you identify potential resources and solutions, and provide guidance for the needs assessment.
- **SMEs** have expertise related to the needs assessment problem, related data, or potential solutions. These practitioners can explain current

processes, practices, ways of working, and systems. When recruiting SMEs, consider how much time they can dedicate to the project, what resources they can contribute, and how they prefer to communicate and collaborate. Remember that while stakeholders have a stake in the needs assessment and are therefore invested in its success, SMEs usually don't. You will need to present a compelling case to borrow this talent and implement a strategy to ensure you make the best possible use of the SME's limited time.

- **Collaborators** have expertise outside the specific domain expertise that SMEs provide. Their skill sets—including data analysis, research, focus group facilitation, survey design, technical writing, or presentation design—are applicable to many types of needs assessments. There are probably staff members from other departments within your organization who can be *borrowed* to support your project. We recommend building a roster of potential collaborators so you can borrow their talents when their workload allows them to share time.

- **Participants** are employees who contribute data to your needs assessment research, often through surveys, interviews, focus groups, and observations. You will need to plan a strategy to identify and access participants as well as gain the support of their managers so that they are allowed to spend time away from their assigned work to take part in the needs assessment.

- **Partners** are people at work who have insight that will help you complete your project. Partners don't usually take an active role in the needs assessment work but they can help steer you in the right direction when you're not sure where to look for the information you need. For example, partners may lend a hand when you need to identify participants, understand organizational history, or determine who owns what process decisions.

A needs assessment requires the execution and management of many moving parts, so it's important for each team member to understand the inter-dependencies—how their tasks affect the overall project's completion. As you gather stakeholders, SMEs, and supporters, consider how you will align their work with individual and collective goals and rally everyone around a shared vision of continuous improvement. Organizing the project into smaller parts so action is continuous will help you keep the team fully engaged.

Ask your project champion, stakeholders, and SMEs for recommendations from their departments and teams. Sometimes, junior employees have more time to dedicate to short-term projects and can learn a lot while helping the team with needs assessment tasks.

If your organization has an exchange program, your needs assessment project may be an opportunity for an internal workforce development program. Kelly once organized the team from an ongoing, high-priority training needs assessment project into an advisory group in which volunteers served six-month rotations. This approach helped her gain buy-in, build cross-functional relationships, and provide valuable professional development experiences for the employees who volunteered their time and expertise.

Leverage cross-functional collaboration as much as possible. Internal teams from different departments can function as external consultants because they will bring a different perspective than those closest to the business problem. Jody once worked on a project that brought in a training team from another area in the organization to plan and conduct a needs assessment. The expertise and viewpoints gained by having a mixture of an internal and external team members was beneficial to the process. The internal resources were able to locate existing data, make fast connections, and translate SME language. The outside group brought value by asking clarifying questions and providing helpful benchmarking data.

Create a sense of belonging for the entire project team by acknowledging all contributions and help everyone stay focused through regular communication. A dedicated Slack channel, shared drive, or online forum will help everyone on the team communicate with one another. If possible, bring the whole group together in a kickoff meeting at the beginning of the project, and call everyone back together after the needs assessment is complete for an after-action review to gather feedback.

Borrowing the Best: Stakeholders and SMEs

Needs assessment projects can be a great experience for team members. Through the process of conducting need assessments, we have both gained long-lasting work relationships, and hope you will too. However, we would be remiss if we didn't mention that you may gain some things you don't expect or want. When you engage with others to borrow their time, data, and expertise, you may also inadvertently borrow their personal motivations, limited perspectives, agendas, or challenging behaviors. Guiding stakeholders and SMEs through the project can be tough—there's a reason why this work is often known as "herding cats."

Stakeholder management is critical in any project but especially for a needs assessment because of the symbiotic relationship between you and your stakeholders. The stakeholders will benefit from the results that you provide, and you will need them to support the project and future recommendations. You can't always choose the stakeholders and SMEs assigned to a needs assessment project, but you can leverage strategies to bring out the best in everyone by understanding the role each stakeholder may play, setting expectations, and managing disruptions.

Understand the Stakes They Hold

Stakeholders can make or break a needs assessment. The first step in working with them is understanding why they're part of the project—how deep are their stakes? Stakeholders may be reluctant team members, especially if they were assigned to the project or if the project is addressing issues within their area of responsibility. If they've been asked (or ordered) to put their process weaknesses or other professional vulnerabilities under a needs assessment microscope, they may approach the work with resentment, anxiety, or outright combativeness. Other stakeholders may be eager to dive into the needs assessment but not understand why you "insist on slowing things down with processes" when you talk them through the steps of building a strategy or collecting and analyzing data. The more you understand about your stakeholder's perspective, the better you can work with them.

Remember from chapter 1 that stakeholders usually fall into four categories:

- **Sponsor**—the person who identified the key problem or requested the needs assessment
- **Key stakeholder**—the person who has responsibilities in areas the problem is addressing or extensive expertise on the topic, or the person affected by or contributing to the problem
- **Advisors**—stakeholders who can provide guidance and support

- **Collaborators**—people with a vested interest in the project who can also assist with the work, or people who provide oversight for certain aspects of the project, such as data analytics

Stakeholders can wear multiple hats or play multiple roles. Your project sponsor may also be the project champion, or the sponsor may be a reluctant stakeholder—just because they must conduct a needs assessment doesn't mean they want to.

Set Expectations

Set expectations immediately so stakeholders and SMEs are fully aware of the time required and the tasks they'll be asked to complete. Gaining informed cooperation at the beginning of the needs assessment project will save you time and frustration in the long run. Before including a stakeholder or SME in a project, be sure to:

- Explain the business situation currently requiring a needs assessment.
- Explain why you are conducting the needs assessment now and the risks of not doing so.
- Share the team makeup and who else you're asking to participate.
- Explain why, specifically, you are asking them to be part of the needs assessment team.
- Outline what they can expect from the project and provide a realistic timeline for completion.
- Ask for the specific support you need from them. Ask if they are willing and able to dedicate the time required. (Refer to the "Art of the Ask" section in chapter 5 for tips on how to structure your request.) If they are unable to commit to the time or work required, see if they can recommend someone to serve in their place.

You may be able to identify most of your stakeholders and SMEs at the beginning, but, in our experience, this is usually an ongoing task for the duration of the project. As the needs assessment work progresses, you may need to add or remove contributors from the project team.

Manage Disruptions

Needs assessment projects can screech to a halt when stakeholders and SMEs fail to respond to information requests or complete tasks, communicate ineffectively (or not at all), or create other roadblocks for the project team. Working with difficult stakeholders and SMEs is a reality for most talent development professionals, so have strategies like these in place for managing disruptions:

- Document, document, document. Track information requests and task assignments so you have a paper trail of stakeholder and SME contributions.
- Assume good faith effort and give the benefit of doubt if someone doesn't respond immediately. They may be swamped with other work, or they may have missed the message. Sometimes a gentle nudge is all that's needed to refocus attention.
- Ensure they understand the *why* behind your requests. Remember that urgency on your part isn't necessarily urgent for others—you must clearly communicate why the information is needed or why tasks must be completed within specified timelines.
- Understand their roadblocks. They may be waiting for approval to share data, waiting on someone else's response, or stuck on a task that they aren't sure how to complete.
- Ask how you can help mitigate any challenges they are facing.

When Jody works with a challenging stakeholder, she relies on tools and techniques that help remove emotions from the situation and refocus the conversation on the problem she is solving. One strategy she uses is the cause-consequence analysis technique, which she's modified and now calls CCA+ (Witkin and Altschuld 1995). The cause-consequence analysis technique is a process for comparing inductive and deductive reasoning, but Jody has found success using her adapted version (CCA+) as a tool for identifying conflicting perspectives during a needs assessment project. She uses it to facilitate conversations between two people (for example, herself and a stakeholder or two conflicting stakeholders) to compare their perspectives about the needs assessment problem and potential solutions with a set of consistent criteria.

CCA+ can be used as a conversation framework to examine a difficult stakeholder's perspective or to help stakeholders resolve conflicts in a productive way. When points of view differ, stop and discuss them to understand the differences so you can realign and move forward.

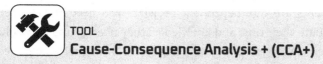

TOOL
Cause-Consequence Analysis + (CCA+)

Here is an example of Jody's CCA+ tool, which is a great technique for facilitating conversations when stakeholders or team members disagree about the key problem, findings, conclusions, or recommendations. It's also great to use when you're clarifying the key problem at the beginning of a needs assessment. There is a blank version in appendix A that you can adapt for your own projects—add or change the points for comparison as needed.

	Jody's Perspective	Stakeholder's Perspective
Highest priority needs	Frontline managers	New employees
Causes	• Stressful work environment • Unclear expectations for employees • Lack of training and support for managers	• Open vacant positions due to high turnover • Lack of training • Lack of internal succession plans
Consequences	• Low morale • Employee turnover • Low productivity	• Increased hiring of entry-level employees (hiring costs and productivity costs) • Increased employee turnover
Difficulty to correct	High	High
Critical rating	High	High
Recommendation	Leadership training for frontline managers	Onboarding and new-hire training
Measurements	Employee perceptions, surveys, HR attrition report, and training completion reports	Employee perceptions, HR attrition report, and training completion reports

Source: Adapted from Witkin and Altschuld (1995).

Needs assessments are interdependent projects. You need stakeholders and SMEs to contribute their time and knowledge; they need you to help solve performance problems. Your job is to ensure alignment throughout the project by maintaining your objectivity, staying calm, communicating clearly and often, keeping the team focused, setting and reinforcing expectations, managing roadblocks as soon as they occur, and intentionally facilitating a valuable experience for team members.

If the strategies you try don't yield results, and stakeholder challenges are putting the project at risk, escalate your concerns. Sometimes, champions can nudge stakeholders and stakeholders can nudge SMEs. If you've done all you can to communicate, support, and mitigate, the last option is to escalate the roadblock to the appropriate leader who can help. No matter how frustrated you feel, keep your escalations and feedback about stakeholders and SMEs professional and objective. You may have to work with them again, and it's important to maintain as positive a relationship as possible. See chapter 9 for more strategies on working with stakeholders.

Borrowing Perspective: Identifying Participants

Once you've established your needs assessment strategy and gathered the team, you need to define the audience (or population) from whom you will collect data—this may include individual contributors, managers, executive leaders, additional SMEs, or even entire teams or departments. Select the target audience carefully by determining who has the information you need to answer your research questions. You'll need to know where they're located, how to contact them, and what approvals are needed to allow them to participate. There's no point in wasting time hoping to get a hold of a segment of participants you know won't be available. Work with your stakeholders to identify participants and determine how you will share the results and recommendations of the needs assessment with them, if it's appropriate to do so.

You will likely be limited in time, resources, or budget (maybe all three). Constraints will require you to be smart and selective about how you engage participants—it's not usually possible to talk to every single person identified as a potential participant. You will likely need to work with a *sample* of the greater population, which should be the best representation available within the project's constraints.

The two most common population selection techniques are *convenience sampling* and *purposeful sampling*. You may also be able to use a combination of both:

- **Convenience samples** are the people most available within the target population. Convenience sampling is the fastest approach for projects that require a tight turnaround or are being managed to a specific timeline. In the customer service example scenario, we may need to gather data from the group during a specific week, and if so, we will only get information from the people that are scheduled to work that week.
- **Purposeful samples** are collections of specific groups of people who are targeted because they can provide a needed perspective. If you need to collect data from specific employees, managers, or SMEs, you will need to manage the project timeline based on their availability.

If you are not sure where to start, creating a mind map can be a useful strategy for brainstorming participant selection and considerations. The Participant Mind Map tool provides some prompts to help get your ideas flowing.

TOOL
Participant Mind Map

Use a mind map activity to plot and visualize your population group. Draw lines and circles to connect ideas related to the population selection.

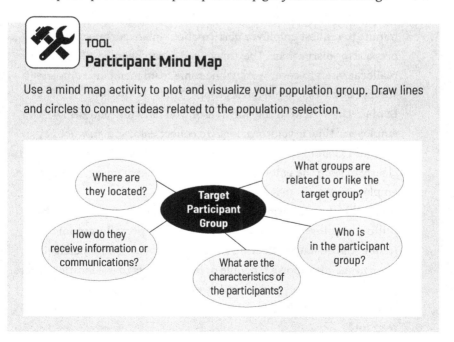

Borrowing Others' Time: Accessing Participants

As a needs assessment practitioner, asking for employee participation in surveys, focus groups, and interviews probably seems like an effective way to collect essential data. But for a manager who's overworked, understaffed, and striving to meet KPIs, a request for employees to spend time away from their necessary work may seem silly, wasteful, or disruptive. Remember, you're not the only person at your organization operating on a shoestring.

So how can you get access to the employees who are essential participants in your needs assessment? First, appreciate the weight of your request. Asking a call center manager to devote 90 minutes of their employees' time away from serving customers for a focus group is asking for a heavy lift—time away from phones can hurt the department's productivity scores for the day. Make sure the weight of the request matches the priority of the data needed so that the employee time you ask for is worth the cost for those donating that time.

Even if resources aren't spread so thin, you may face workplace bureaucracy when requesting permission to hold interviews, send surveys, or conduct observations on the job. Here are a few strategies to try when you need to convince gatekeepers to grant access to participants' time:

- **Give them as much notice as possible.** Do not wait until the last minute to request employee participation—managers need time to prepare for disruptions. They may need to reschedule shift times or reallocate staff to cover work while some team members complete surveys or participate in focus groups.
- **Explain the WIIFM.** If the only reason you have for requesting employees' time is your own need to collect data, you may not get very far in gaining cooperation. Make sure you've considered and can clearly explain the potential benefits for the department, manager, or employees. What's in it for them?
- **If possible, brainstorm ways you can help cover gaps caused by pulling employees away from their work or provide support to help with the data collection process.** Can you assist a manager in revising an afternoon's schedule or bring tablets to the location where your targeted survey participants work if they don't have access to computers? How can you make the request easier for gatekeepers to grant?

Borrowing With Positive Intent: Working With Participants

Your needs assessment strategy will include a clear, specific purpose and a defined audience of participants who will contribute data to answer research questions. Always remember that in terms of roles, priorities, and perspectives, they are people first, employees second, and needs assessment participants third. People deserve to be treated respectfully at work, so never make the mistake of approaching a *human* request as if it's a *research resource* request—your participants aren't lab rats. (This is why we always use the word *participant* instead of *subject* when describing needs assessment roles.) You aren't conducting a needs assessment *on* them; you're conducting it *with* them. And sometimes, the data you need carries a level of risk for employees who are willing to share it. It's your job to mitigate those risks and ensure participants do not have a negative experience because of your needs assessment.

Jody recalls intentionally keeping participants' names confidential as a best practice while working on a training needs assessment project. During data collection, participants shared that they were not lacking knowledge; rather, the process they'd been told to follow was not working. The participants shared this under the assumption of confidentiality. They were willing to provide candid feedback because they knew their names were not going to be attached to it. The insight about the new process's ineffectiveness was not received well by the project's stakeholders. In fact, the stakeholders had trouble believing the feedback, because they thought the process was flawless. When a stakeholder demanded to know who reported the process problems, Jody was able to protect that participant from any retaliation because she intentionally planned for participant anonymity and was prepared to address that issue. Although she did not disclose the participant's name, she was still able to maintain a positive relationship with the stakeholder by explaining that the data collection methods were anonymous.

While working with participants, you should always prioritize ethics and respect so you can actively mitigate risks while maintaining a healthy work culture and positive relationships. Keep this formula in mind:

Consideration + Action = Trust

Building trust with needs assessment participants is a multifaceted process. Consider their perspective—it can be risky for many people at work to share their honest feedback, appear critical of current practices, or question leaders. How can you help them feel heard and safe when sharing their feedback? Demonstrate consideration for participants by following these best practices:

- **Provide a clear explanation for your data requests.** Be upfront about the purpose of surveys, focus groups, interviews, and observations, and explain why they're being asked to participate.
- **Communicate proactively with participants** by anticipating their questions and concerns. Provide a summary of the needs assessment project or an FAQ document they can review before participating. Include contact information so they know whom to reach out to if needed.
- **Ask stakeholders or department leaders to communicate with participants** so employees know that their managers support their involvement in the project.
- **Plan for privacy concerns, and be transparent about privacy expectations.** Will survey results be anonymous? Will interview transcripts be attributed to individuals by name? Confidentiality is an important factor and must be handled carefully.

Follow up after needs assessments through clear actions by sharing the results and solutions with participants, as appropriate. Consider what actions participants will expect to see. Lack of follow-through erodes trust. For example, if employees get an annual survey every year, but never see communications about results or company changes based on those results, they will not trust the survey source and will be less willing to participate in the future. Plan to share next steps and anticipate how the collected data can be acted on in ways that will be meaningful to your participants.

Borrow Broadly and Inclusively: Not Just the Usual Suspects

When you face the challenge of identifying and recruiting stakeholders, SMEs, supporters, and participants for a needs assessment, you may be tempted to ask people you know well or already have a relationship with. While this may be a time-saving approach in the short term, over time this practice will skew your data with bias, narrow your results, and limit your ability to capture the full, real story of a business problem that can only be told by engaging across the entire organization.

To mitigate the risk of exclusion, ask yourself and stakeholders who you might be forgetting or overlooking. Don't assume you have thought of every-thing because there is no such thing as a perfect perspective. Search the organi-zation for silos by examining the org chart and internal systems. Also consider dependencies, relationships, or processes that may exist and affect participant selection. Ask yourself:

- Whom might I have missed?
- How does this team or department work with others?
- Are other teams or departments dependent on this group?

As much as possible, include everyone who needs to be heard. Challenge yourself to ensure you are not creating a limited view of the problem.

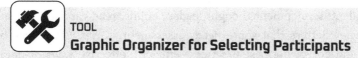

TOOL
Graphic Organizer for Selecting Participants

In appendix A, you'll find a tool to help you organize the business areas and teams connected to the needs assessment problem. This visual overview can help iden-tify potential stakeholders, SMEs, supporters, and participants for your needs assessment project.

Borrowing Expertise: Learn From Peers and Thought Leaders

Ultimately, needs assessments are learning projects, even when you're in a rush. Keep your skills sharp by investing time and energy in your own lifelong learn-ing and continuously nurturing your curiosity. In addition to the Deeper Dive resources throughout this book, we encourage you to actively practice learning from others at work, online, and within your own professional network (while continuing to expand your network).

Earlier in this chapter, we mentioned how Jody worked with a team that included internal and external training experts. This experience helped her develop professionally, deepen organizational capacity, and build interpersonal skills. Each time you engage in a needs assessment, use the project as an opportunity to build your talent development capabilities by learning from others within your organization—if you approach experiences and relationships with a learning mindset, you will gain insight from leaders, employees, participants, peers, stakeholders, and SMEs. Keep a journal where you can reflect as you document your successes and challenges and remind yourself of what you've learned.

Challenge yourself to meet and interview at least two talent development professionals outside your organization each year to learn about their needs assessment experiences. You can reach out to peers on LinkedIn, contact your local ATD chapter, or look for professors in instructional design programs at local universities. If you're able to attend professional conferences, make it a goal to meet with at least three talent development peers from other industries and connect with them on LinkedIn, and then invite them for a short, virtual coffee chat.

Follow talent development thought leaders online, read case studies, and subscribe to newsletters that share needs assessment stories. Stay sharp by seeking out and borrowing best practices—efficient, effective ways of doing things that experts have identified through research, trial and error, or historical trends. You can locate best practices through professional literature, associations, talent development awards, successful business leaders, researchers, authors, and practitioners who contribute to the advancement of the talent development field.

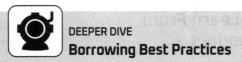

DEEPER DIVE
Borrowing Best Practices

ATD publishes an annual issue of *TD* magazine featuring BEST and Excellence in Practice Award winners who have been recognized for exceptional work in the talent development field. The issue includes examples from nearly 100 companies worldwide. To learn more, visit td.org/td-magazine/best-practices-2022 -td-magazine.

Be Borrowable: Gain Experience by Helping Others

In addition to experience on the job, you can gain professional expertise and build your needs assessment capabilities by helping others. Remember, just because you're operating a needs assessment on a shoestring, and might feel pressed for time, doesn't mean your work is happening in a vacuum; other people have their own shoestring projects they're urgently scrambling to get done. If you want people to let you borrow their time and talent, model this collaboration by letting others borrow yours.

An easy place to start is within your own organization. Remember the list you made of potential collaborators for your needs assessment work? Consider how you might be a support for someone else. You'll learn while creating cross-functional opportunities for development and collaboration. Additional opportunities to build your skills by being borrowable include:

- **If your company has an internship program, request an intern** to help you conduct a needs assessment project. Mentor the intern and provide a positive learning experience for them.
- **Mentor a graduate student or be a resource for them.** Help them design and conduct a needs assessment, or share your experiences with needs assessment projects, lessons learned, and key takeaways. Grad students often need to interview current practitioners; you can be a borrowable resource for them. Kelly participates in a few interviews with graduate students each year. Reflecting on her experience is good practice for her, and her feedback helps the students complete assignment requirements.
- **Volunteer to help a nonprofit organization conduct a needs assessment.** Nonprofits are often fueled by volunteers who donate their time and talents. The skills associated with needs assessments are highly transferable and can help organizations in many ways. Explore your local area and personal interests to locate a nonprofit that you can contact to offer your services.
- **Reach out to your local ATD chapter** and ask about opportunities to volunteer with needs assessments or support graduate students. Local chapter leaders may have contacts at nonprofits and universities. Even better, consider volunteering with your local

chapter! Their needs may not include a needs assessment project, but many of the skills you'll gain as a volunteer will transfer to needs assessment work.

- **Consider presenting at a local conference or writing a blog post or LinkedIn article** to share a needs assessment case study with your talent development peers.

Professional service is an important form of leadership, regardless of your current job title. As you learn more from each needs assessment project you complete, consider how you can share your knowledge and skills with others.

A Shoestring Summary

Conducting a needs assessment requires you to borrow the time and talent of others within your organization. You'll need to balance roles as project manager, collaborator, team lead, researcher, guide, mentor, and advocate. As you build a team and work with participants, consider how you will handle each challenge and opportunity. Here are some key takeaways:

- Set expectations early and reinforce them often. Mitigate problems as soon as they arise. Acknowledge contributors and design a valuable experience for all team members.
- Scale your needs assessment team by creating development opportunities for others.
- Show consideration to participants and follow up with actions to build trust.
- Think broadly across the organization to ensure inclusive collaboration and diversity of thought.
- Use time with stakeholders and SMEs to learn the lexicon of their business domain.
- Invest your time in learning from peers and talent development thought leaders.
- Practice service leadership to gain experience by helping others.

PART 3
BUY

Part 3 explores all the things that can be bought during a needs assessment. Don't worry, this section isn't exclusively about spending money; rather, it will cover several ideas and concepts that include resource management strategies for conducting needs assessments.

In this part of the book, you'll learn how to:

- Estimate and advocate for the time needed to conduct a needs assessment and manage time effectively
- Plan and manage a project budget and find free or cost-effective tools that you can use to conduct needs assessment
- Gain buy-in from leadership, stakeholders, partners, and participants

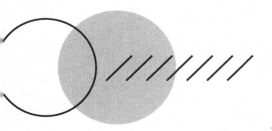

7
Budgeting for Time

Detectives always work against the clock—time management is essential so the trail of clues doesn't run cold. For a needs assessment, you won't be outsmarting a villain, solving a crime, or deciding whether to cut the blue wire or the red wire while a clock counts down to potential doom, but you will be pressed for time. Needs assessments are worth the time investment, but budgeting for time, managing timeline expectations, tracking project progress, and ensuring the work progresses at full speed while managing competing priorities, inevitable delays, and intricate tasks can be challenging. Time management is especially critical for teams of one. You will be the strategist, detective, researcher, project manager, and communicator. Use the tips in this chapter to stay on schedule while performing all those roles.

You Pick Two: Quality, Time, or Cost. Managing the Iron Triangle

If you've taken a project management course, you've probably been introduced to the iron triangle, which is also known as the "triple constraint" or the "project management triangle." This conceptual triangle represents the idea that every project has a balance of time, cost, and quality, and you can control for only two of these three factors, as shown in Figure 7-1 on the next page.

The project timeline includes many variables, but one of the most important is your methodology—the process you'll use for data collection and analysis. Balancing your methodology and deadlines is a challenging push-pull situation. If there is no wiggle room in your deadline, for example, you will need to select data collection methods that can be completed quickly, but then you may miss data that could add more valuable insight. It's important to align with your stakeholders on these decisions so that expectations are clear and project deadlines are manageable.

Figure 7-1. The Iron Triangle

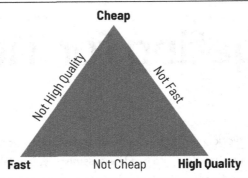

The project can be done...	But it won't be...
Fast and cheap	High quality
Fast and high quality	Cheap
Cheap and high quality	Fast

In chapter 1, we discussed the project scope. It's important to define your scope clearly with stakeholders and understand their priorities in terms of the iron triangle. What do they value most in the needs assessment project's scope—time, cost, or quality? Make sure you understand the *why* of this priority. Is the business problem costing the company money every day that it continues? If so, *time* may be the top priority. Is the business problem ambiguous, complex, and layered, and has it been ongoing for a long period of time? If so, *quality* may be the top priority for the needs assessment strategy to ensure you accurately identify the problem and the factors contributing to it.

Unless you have unlimited resources, unlimited time, and an unlimited budget, you'll have to make compromises based on your needs assessment project's strategy. Realize that when problems arise, there is always a project *penalty* that will be paid—in time delays, increased costs, or decreased quality. Align with stakeholders as early as possible on their top priority (time, cost, or quality) and apply that key value to the decisions you make when planning your strategy and managing the needs assessment project.

Consistency is critical—you can't start a project with time being the driving priority and then shift gears halfway through to prioritize quality instead.

The priority will shape the scope; the scope will shape the strategy; the strategy will shape the project execution. Stakeholders may say they want it all, and tell you to figure out how to deliver high-quality results fast and cheap. In reality, it's usually impossible to meet those demands, and it will be your job to explain that. A big part of managing a needs assessment is managing your stakeholders' expectations.

Do You Want It Done Right? Managing Stakeholders' Expectations

One of the most common challenges when conducting a needs assessment is determining the project timeline. Stakeholders who aren't familiar with needs assessments may not understand the time demands involved. Once an urgent business problem has been identified, stakeholders will want to solve it as quickly as possible. And once you indicate that a needs assessment is required to identify the best solution, they may request that you meet a deadline for the needs assessment that isn't possible.

Often, needs assessments don't happen because of a perception that they take too long. You will need strategies for saving time and ensuring that the time you have allocated for the project is well spent. Wasting your stakeholders' time is a guaranteed way to lose their support. Spend time carefully strategizing the project. What data is needed most, and how can you collect it efficiently? Remember the power of iterative work—as you break down the needs assessment tasks, you may be able to start one before finishing another, or work on multiple pieces concurrently.

One of the most challenging and frustrating things when conducting a needs assessment is managing deadlines for work that you cannot complete yourself. You're often at the mercy of stakeholders and SMEs, competing priorities, and overpacked calendars. You may not be able to manage these people—you're unlikely to be their supervisor—but you can manage expectations for the project timeline by communicating the impact of delays before they occur.

To manage expectations, we suggest outlining the project's timeline in terms of interdependencies and time ranges instead of using specific dates. List the tasks in the order in which they must be completed, and include the timelines for each task. See Table 7-1 for an example of a project timeline breakdown.

Table 7-1. Sample Project Timeline

Task	Timeline	Next Step Dependency
Identify interview participants.	3 days	Gain manager approval.
Gain manager approval for employees' time.	3 days	Schedule interviews.
Schedule interviews.	3 days	Conduct interviews.
Conduct interviews.	7 days	Perform interview data analysis.
Perform interview data analysis.	6 days	Analyze additional datasets.

Include timeline impacts for each major task. If the data collection falls a week behind, for example, then analysis will begin a week later than scheduled. Explain project milestones as if-then timelines; for example, "If documents are provided by [*date*], analysis can be completed by [*date*]." Keep the project status updated on a shared project management board or spreadsheet, and document delays. Adjust timelines if delays occur to keep everyone on the same page and to manage expectations for the final project completion date.

TIME SAVER
Add 20 Percent

Sometimes, you will have to push back on deadline expectations, but it's important to do so at the beginning of the project during the strategy planning phase, not later—after work has begun—when you suddenly realize that the deadlines will be impossible to meet. The best advice we have is to estimate time requirements as realistically as possible, and then add 20 percent. It's better to under promise and over deliver. No matter how well you plan your project, delays *will* happen. Padding the project timeline from the start by adding 20 percent to your time estimates will help you manage the unexpected things that happen during the needs assessment while still meeting deadlines.

Structuring a needs assessment project based on smart estimates of the total time required to complete the work in terms of total hours, days, or weeks is more effective than agreeing to a deadline and then facing delays that are beyond your control. If you estimate three weeks for data analysis, you can document the time spent on that task separately from project deadlines. In other words, if you complete the data analysis in three weeks, but are two weeks late on the project schedule because of delays caused by stakeholders during data collection, you'll be able to accurately show time spent on task completion versus time spent waiting for project deliverables. Clearly documenting and communicating timelines is not about assigning blame; it's about ensuring accountability, transparency, and efficiency.

Estimating the Timeline: Break It Down

Estimating timelines for needs assessment projects can be tricky due to the complexity of managing multiple interdependent moving parts. The first step in demystifying the timeline is to break down the needs assessment project into phases, milestones, and tasks. Think of it this way: If a needs assessment was a book, the phases would be parts, milestones would be chapters, and tasks would be paragraphs. The phases of a needs assessment include planning, data collection, data analysis, recommendations, and reporting.

For each phase, determine the milestones and the tasks that roll up to major steps. For example, if your data collection includes document review, interviews, and surveys, you will have three data collection milestones, which will each have multiple tasks required to complete the milestone. Try to write down everything you anticipate being necessary for each phase.

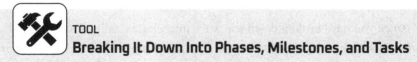

TOOL
Breaking It Down Into Phases, Milestones, and Tasks

In appendix A, there's a tool you can use to organize a needs assessment project by breaking it down into different phases, milestones, and tasks.

If you're a list maker like Kelly, freewriting a messy task list and then moving them into a simple table may help you organize the breakdown of work (Table 7-2).

Table 7-2. Kelly's Style of Breaking Down Tasks

Phase	Milestone	Tasks
Data collection	Collect documents	• Create a list of required documents. • Determine document owners. • Contact owners to request documents. • Track requests and deliveries.

If you're a visual thinker like Jody, a color-coded outline or timeline stack of tasks may be a helpful approach, like in Figure 7-2.

Figure 7-2. Jody's Style of Breaking Down Tasks

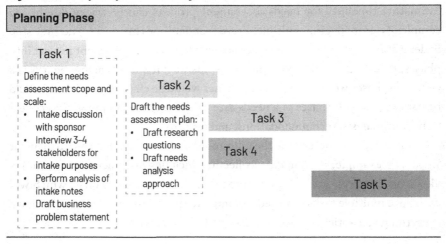

Once you have broken down the work into phases, milestones, and tasks, revisit each task and add additional details, including a task description, priority, any required prep work, estimated time for completion, required resources (including other people), and any required approvals or collaborations. Look at the Example Task Details tool in appendix A. The task is listed at the top and additional details are documented below it. Note that estimated time includes the time required to complete the task and the time required to complete the prep work beforehand. This task information will be helpful in the next step of project scheduling and for delegating tasks as needed.

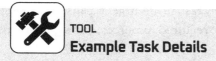

TOOL
Example Task Details

Capturing the details of each milestone task will help you more accurately gauge the time needed to complete each task. You can use the task detail notes provided as an example and modify the details you want to capture as needed for your project. The details can be tracked in project management software, a spreadsheet, or even on index cards. Appendix A includes a blank version you can use for your own projects.

- **Phase:** Planning
- **Task:** Intake discussion with sponsor
- **Task priority:** High
- **Description:** I need to meet with the sponsor to review basic project intake questions so that I fully understand the request for the needs assessment. After this meeting, I will be able to start making plans.
- **Prep work:** I need to review the initial request email, which included links to several intranet sites. Review the list of standard intake questions and add more to fit this particular need.
- **Estimated time:** Prep + meeting = 2.5 Hours
- **Required resource:** Project sponsor
- **Collaborator or approver:** Not applicable

Documenting additional task details helps clarify the work so you can better estimate time requirements and delegate more efficiently. Once the task details are outlined, you can group all tasks within each phase to create a timeline, and then combine them all to estimate the timeline for the overall project.

Identifying task priority is an essential part of estimating the project timeline, especially when operating on a shoestring. Try to determine a priority level for each task—high (must complete), medium (should complete), and low (would be nice to complete)—and then ensure the high priority tasks are completed first. Every task cannot be urgent. An overall sense of urgency can be helpful when keeping a team focused on an important business problem, but if every task is considered a high priority, it will lead to confusion, burnout, and missed deadlines. If every task seems urgent, pause and realign with stakeholders to clarify priorities, required resources, and expectations.

More Than a Best Guess: Making Informed Timeline Estimates

The first time a project manager asked Kelly to assign timelines for a needs assessment, she was truly stumped. Needs assessments are complicated! They take as long as they take! (Imagine the LOL emoji here. To be fair, she was fairly new to the field, had never seen a project management system, and had no clue how to estimate timelines.) With many years of experience, you'll develop your own estimates for the time required to complete needs assessment tasks, but we want to share some tools to help you in the meantime. We recommend three strategies: rule-of-thumb percentages, benchmarking, and data-based estimates.

You will probably use a combination of these strategies to create your needs assessment timeline. With experience, you will get a better sense of how long the work takes within your organization. Some groups move faster than others, and you will need to anticipate the pace of work as best as you can. If needs assessments are new to you or your team, give yourself time to learn and adjust.

Rule-of-Thumb Percentage Estimates

Albert Einstein once said, "If I had an hour to solve a problem, I'd spend 55 minutes thinking about the problem and five minutes thinking about solutions" (Michalko 2001). We agree with the spirit of this quotation, but suggest more time for designing needs assessment solutions. While each project will be unique, the percentages in Figure 7-3 are a good rule of thumb for timeline estimates.

Our recommendation for phase time percentage may be surprising, but a significant amount of time is needed to plan the needs assessment strategy, analyze data, and build recommendations based on the results of the analysis. In our experience, practitioners do not allocate enough time for strategic planning, analysis, or brainstorming and evaluating solutions. Don't undercut your needs assessment by failing to allocate the appropriate amount of time to plan the project scope, synthesize the data, develop findings, come to factual conclusions, and work with stakeholders to make informed recommendations.

Figure 7-3. Rule-of-Thumb Percentage Estimates for Needs Assessment Timelines

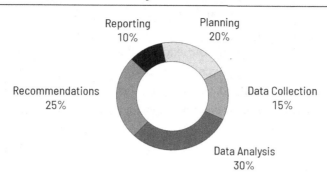

Reporting
10%

Planning
20%

Recommendations
25%

Data Collection
15%

Data Analysis
30%

Benchmarking Estimates

Timeline estimates can be created by benchmarking, but this method is tricky because it requires examples from completed needs assessment projects, including the project scope and timeline. The first step is to identify a benchmarking source—usually a case study—similar in scale to your project and base your timeline estimates on those reported in the case study. Keep in mind that all the details of the benchmarked needs assessment may not be included. However, despite these unknown points, you can use deductive reasoning to come to conclusions. You can also create benchmarks by asking other practitioners how they estimate timelines or if they have any needs assessment project timeline data they could share. A few examples will give you a starting place for building your own timeline estimates.

To aid timeline estimating for future projects, and to possibly be an estimation resource for your peers, *always* track the time of your completed needs assessment projects. The more you do, the more of your own benchmarking data you will create. We wish we could give you clear benchmarks to estimate the time demands of your needs assessment projects, but it's just not possible. We can share a go-to strategy, though!

Kelly often uses a form of internal benchmarking to gauge the complexity of a needs assessment project—knowing the level of complexity can provide some guidance for estimating time. This benchmark metric is simple and only requires you to find the answer to one question: How long did it take to create this problem? You can phrase this question in different ways: "When did this problem start?" or "How long has this problem been occurring?" If the problem has been ongoing for two years and the stakeholders are asking you to complete the needs assessment in a week, you can bet their expectations are unrealistic. If possible, dig a little deeper to find an example of a problem similar in scope, and find out how long it took the organization to solve that problem. Internal examples will give you additional data points for this shoestring version of benchmarked data. The longer a problem has existed, the more time will be required for a needs assessment.

Data-Based Estimates

The best time estimates will likely be the ones you derive from your own experience. You have probably conducted interviews, facilitated a focus group, performed data analysis, and created reports. Review your previous projects and take note of the time required to complete the work. This is the best way to know how long it will take you to complete similar tasks in the future. If you do not currently track your project task time, consider starting this practice to inform your future work. You will also want to track the time involved for stakeholders and participants.

When you track time, you can designate the time into workflow sections, which will help with future project estimates. For example, initial meetings to discuss the problem, time spent identifying stakeholders, and meetings to determine project scope can be grouped as "planning." Time spent designing, pilot testing, and administering surveys; conducting focus groups, interviews, or observations; and collecting existing reports can be grouped as "data collection." Track the time spent addressing delays as well—after several projects, that data will help you build realistic padding into your time budget.

Down to the Hour: Assigning Hours to Tasks

As you break down the work to create your timeline estimates, include the estimated time needed from each team member to complete tasks by project phase. This will help you clarify the ask, clearly explain the expected time commitment of each contributor, and help you estimate the cost of hidden expenses—the total time investment of internal resources.

Table 7-3 is an example of time estimates for a needs assessment project broken down by phases and role. You can create a similar spreadsheet or table with your timeline estimates and adjust it as needed during the project. Make a working copy and update it as tasks are completed so you can compare estimated time to actual time spent. This data will give you benchmarks you can use to estimate timelines for future needs assessment projects.

Table 7-3. Sample Time Estimates for a Needs Assessment Project

Role	Planning (20%)	Data Collection (15%)	Analysis (30%)	Recommendations (25%)	Reporting (10%)	Total Time
Timeline	1 week	1 week	2 weeks	1 week	1 week	6 weeks
Estimated Project Hours						
Project lead	16	16	20	14	12	78
Sponsor stakeholder	6	2	4	10	2	24
Additional stakeholder	4	2	4	8	1	19
SME	6	2	10	8	1	27
Data analyst	1	0	8	0	0	9
Total hours	**33**	**22**	**46**	**40**	**16**	**157**
Percent	21.02%	14.01%	29.30%	25.48%	10.19%	

Visualize the Timeline

Throughout the project, you should stay in communication with stakeholders about the timeline. Status reports are a great way to keep stakeholders informed. However, status reports may not always be the best choice because they can take too long to create or be too formal. You may want to set up a Slack or Microsoft Teams channel specifically for the project, which you can use to collaborate and communicate on a more frequent but informal basis. You can also post frequent updates to the channel that are targeted to stakeholders to keep them apprised of the current work in progress.

In Figure 7-4, the progress status of data collection interviews for a needs assessment project is presented visually using a pie chart.

Figure 7-4. Timeline Visualization With a Pie Chart

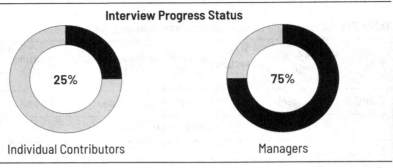

Gantt charts are a great way to visually summarize work that's been scheduled and completed on the project timeline. Project activities are listed by rows in the left column, and the timeline is chunked in sections across the top. The progress of each activity is represented by a bar—place the location of each bar at the point when that activity occurs on the project timeline, and adjust the size of each bar to represent the amount of time scheduled for that activity. Color code the bars to communicate the status of each activity. You can organize the activities by milestones or tasks, and structure the timeline by months, weeks, days, quarters, or another timeframe that makes sense for your timeline.

Most project management software includes Gantt chart tools, which will create a visual chart for you based on the tasks you list in project boards, and even automatically update the visual Gantt chart as work progresses. Figure 7-5, on the next page, provides an example of a simple Gantt chart.

Get creative with how you update your stakeholders on project progress. Dashboards and other visuals make the updates easy to read and can convey progress at a glance. Use color coding to quickly communicate the status of project tasks—green for completed or on schedule, yellow for approaching deadline or risk of delay, gray for not yet started, and red for behind target date. Project management programs can create color-coded status charts for you, and these are also easy to create in any spreadsheet program.

Figure 7-5. Timeline Visualization With a Gantt Chart

Needs Assessment Project Timeline

	Month 1				Month 2			
	Week 1	Week 2	Week 3	Week 4	Week 1	Week 2	Week 3	Week 4
Build the strategy	▬							
Build the case		▬						
Methods design			▬					
Data collection				▬	▬			
Data analysis							▬	
Build the recommendations								▬

ON THE CHEAP
Visual Tools

To create visuals, check out project management systems or make your own using PowerPoint or Google Slides, Excel or Google Sheets, or one of many free online tools such as:

- **Canva** (canva.com) is a website that makes designing graphics easy by providing hundreds of templates for presentations, print media, tables, charts, and more.
- **Lunacy** (icons8.com/lunacy) is a graphic design app with templates powered by AI to make your work more efficient and creative.
- **The Data Viz Project** (datavizproject.com) is a collection of sample data visualizations to help you consider alternatives for data display.
- **Piktochart** (piktochart.com) provides access to customizable templates for infographics, flowcharts, and reports.

Project Management Tools

A good project management software can be incredibly beneficial for your needs assessments. These programs provide powerful tools for collaboration, task management, visualization, communication, and analytics. Many of them offer mobile apps that allow you to use the program seamlessly across a computer, phone, or tablet. It takes time to find the right program to best fit your ways of working, though, and even more time to learn how to use it well. Unless your organization uses a company-wide project management system, it's unlikely that most people on the team will know how to leverage all these tools—and that's OK! You can still leverage programs to help you with this work, and having that program and know-how ready ahead of time is a smart strategy. The best time to learn a project management software program is long before you need to use it.

If you are not familiar with project management programs, reach out to a project manager in your organization and ask them for recommendations. Not only can they offer some ideas, but if you use a tool they are familiar with for your project, you will have someone in the organization you can reach out to for help. Teach yourself the platform by using a previous needs assessment (or a case study example if you've never conducted one), and set it up in the program as if it were a current project. Even if you're the only person on the needs assessment team leveraging a project management system, you'll find value in tracking the time spent completing tasks, and you'll probably find tools and shortcuts in the program to help you work smarter and faster.

ON THE CHEAP
Project Management Tools for Teams of One

Many project management tools are free for individual use, including:

- **Microsoft Office Planner** is a visual planner app found within Microsoft Teams. In Planner, you can create tasks, assign people, and set due dates. It is a light-weight option with just enough features, and it is also included in most Office 365 business subscriptions.

- **Trello.com** is a kanban-style tool that makes task lists and other work more visual. This tool can be useful for teams as well as individuals. Jody used the kanban lists to support her dissertation project. The simple lists (to-do, in process, on hold, and done) helped her stay organized and on track. She has also used it with work teams to make tasks transparent and handoffs a breeze.

- Kelly's favorite collaborative project management system is **Monday.com**. Her team uses it to manage all their projects, connect request forms from the employee intranet system directly to task boards, and manage a digital asset content library. Monday.com offers numerous widgets and automations for any kind of project you might tackle, and it also has tools for tracking various types of data points.
- For projects outside work, Kelly loves **Notion**. It's the most intuitive "second brain" project management system she's ever tried—and there is a free version available for individual users.

After Action

Let's shift gears from project management tactics that help you manage the project at the outset to a tactic will help you improve your next project: after-action reviews. A great project management strategy for you and your team, an after-action review can be an informal discussion of what worked well during the needs assessment and what might be improved for the next project, or it can be a more formalized continuous improvement rubric that your team uses to evaluate the work it completed. In Agile work arrangements, retrospectives are held after each sprint to take a critical look at the work process. This idea is grounded in process improvement and conflict resolution.

For your own professional development, try to identify opportunities throughout a needs assessment project where you can improve your process or approach. *Ongoing periods of reflection*, an Agile project management concept, can be helpful, even if you are a team of one. Consider improvement opportunities after you conduct your first focus group or following your first meeting with stakeholders. Here are a few questions to reflect on:

- What worked well? Why?
- What parts of the work did I enjoy most? Why?
- What parts of the work did I struggle with? Why?
- Did anything fail? Why?
- What parts of the work do I feel proud of? Why?

Once you jot down your responses, read the complete list and pick one thing to do differently. Just one. At the next opportunity, do that one thing. Then, when you repeat this reflection exercise, check in with yourself about that one thing. Did it help? Imagine the improvements and potential efficiencies you could gain if you were to change one thing for the better, several times for the duration of a project. Sometimes, self-reflection is the best detective work you can do.

You Are Your Most Critical Resource

Completing a needs assessment requires you to effectively budget and manage time—but can you really *manage* time? The most likely answer is—no. So, what *can* you manage? You can manage your decisions, focus, tasks according to priorities, energy, attitude, communications, and business acumen. You can effectively estimate and allocate time for needs assessment work based on business priorities to deliver the best results as quickly as possible.

Every task you choose to complete, the order in which you complete them, the ways you complete them, your ability to activate others to get things done, and the ways you communicate all add up to many decisions that ultimately determine the timeline of your project. Never underestimate the power of effective decision making. *You* are your most important resource in any needs assessment. Give two talent development professionals the same project scope, stakeholders, budget, timeline, and resources, and they will likely produce very different results. Their ability to manage time is really their ability to manage themselves, resources, expectations, and tasks by making effective, informed decisions.

Work fast, but first, think slow. Invest the time needed to make good decisions early—collect the information you need to gauge the project scope; consider alternatives, risks, and potential outcomes to determine if the needs assessment project merits completion; and if it does, proactively begin to estimate the tasks and milestones for each project phase. Your ability to work through these steps quickly will help you face tight deadlines and complex situations.

As previously mentioned in chapter 3, when Jody is working on complex projects that require her to work for significant periods of time, she sets up recurring calendar blocks that allow her to focus on one thing deeply. Jody also knows that she must do this type of deep work in the morning. She prefers to work in the morning because she simply has less on her mind and is able to focus without other distractions. She has learned to give herself the time and structure needed to *manage* her time effectively. When Kelly is tackling a tedious or frustrating task, she uses the Pomodoro technique to break it down into short time blocks. She sets a timer for 20 minutes and commits to staying focused on the task until the timer goes off. After the timer sounds, she takes a quick break and steps away from the work. If the task is tedious or frustrating, she sets the timer for five- to 10-minute periods and completes multiple Pomodoro sessions over the course of an hour, with five- to 10-minute breaks between each one.

Consider your calendar demands, preferred ways of working, and competing priorities so you can set yourself up for success. Taking on a needs assessment project will usually require you to postpone, delegate, or reprioritize other projects. Make sure you and your team have the bandwidth for the work. Ask for the resources you need, and explain to your stakeholders and leaders the penalty costs of operating without those resources.

A Shoestring Summary

Every needs assessment project requires you to manage the iron triangle—the balance between time, cost, and quality:

- Align with stakeholders on these priorities early and keep the top priority consistent throughout the project.
- Break down the project timeline into manageable parts within each of the five phases: planning, data collection, data analysis, recommendations, and reporting. Each phase includes tasks that roll up to major project milestones. You can estimate the project timeline by outlining the details of each task.
- Collecting data to measure time on task is a great strategy for managing current and future needs assessment projects, so your time is well spent learning about project management programs and strategies that will help you be more efficient.
- Knowing how you work best, developing strategies for blocking time to complete the work, managing expectations, and communicating project progress are key skills you need for success.

8
Buying Smart

Imagine the thrill of detective work—the adrenaline of the chase, ingenuity of piecing together the final clue, and satisfaction of stamping the case closed. If you visualize a scene from your favorite mystery story, are you thinking about the detective's budget? Well, it's a good bet that they are. Which investigations merit overtime expenses? Which forensic tests are worth the cost? Which cases warrant hiring expert consultants? Detectives have expenses and must manage a budget for each case. You'll have to make similar decisions when budgeting for needs assessments and estimating the costs of potential solutions.

There are probably a dozen requests for every dollar available in an organization's budget. Being a good steward of funds will help you grow as a talent development leader and trusted partner, and increase your awareness of the investment you're asking company leaders to make in a needs assessment and recommended solutions. Before requesting funding, do your homework so you can fully justify the expense. Account for hidden costs, including the time investment of internal resources. If you owned the company, would you invest funds and spend resources on this needs assessment? Being able to answer that question with a confident yes and a clear reason why will help you secure funding and resources for any project.

Even if there's no funding available for needs assessment work, considering the cost-benefit analysis and developing your own financial savvy are always smart strategies. If the project you're currently working with has no budget whatsoever, what you'll learn in this chapter may apply to future needs assessment projects.

Before You Buy: Building Your FQ (Financial Intelligence)

After completing a master's degree and a doctorate, Kelly learned a lot about needs assessments, but her coursework did *not* include two of the most important skills for conducting needs assessments in corporate settings: project management and financial acumen. She had to learn how to quantify costs, create and manage budgets, analyze cost-benefit estimates, justify expenses, allocate spending, advocate for resources, and manage vendors. One challenging real-world lesson Kelly learned was about hiring vendors to outsource needs assessment projects, including creating RFPs (request for proposals), evaluating proposals from vendors, negotiating contracts, and managing vendor relationships. Now, she advises talent development professionals to start building these skills as early in their careers as possible.

You may know the value of IQ (intelligence quotient) and EQ (emotional intelligence), but it's also important to build your FQ (financial intelligence). FQ is part of business acumen, which includes financial literacy, analytics, and strategic thinking; essentially, knowing how companies make money and how your company, specifically, makes money. Your financial intelligence shows your understanding of:

- Financial metrics
- Your company's industry and business ecosystem
- Your company's market, customer segments, and competitors
- Shareholder value
- How the company produces and sells its products and services and delivers them to customers
- Supply chains
- How the company determines its business strategy

Every business activity can be categorized as a cost, profit, or investment (Pangarkar and Kirkwood 2022). Most talent development professionals (including us) would classify a needs assessment as an investment, but in terms of the business ledger, it's a *cost* because it does not generate revenue. Most support centers in an organization are cost centers, including human resources, L&D, and IT, for example. These support centers aren't expected to produce a profit; rather, their purpose is to improve organizational performance so that operational costs are reduced and profit centers are more profitable. Business leaders and stakeholders expect the investment in cost centers to deliver valuable results; this concept is known as a "cost-benefit analysis." Those expectations inform forecasting and budgeting.

Forecasting is strategic financial planning for long-term growth. *Budgeting* is the process of allocating and tracking expenses annually, quarterly, or for specific short-term projects like a needs assessment. Managing a budget, whether for your department or for a project, means eliminating any unnecessary costs, identifying priorities, and justifying expenses by demonstrating value.

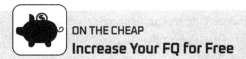

ON THE CHEAP

Increase Your FQ for Free

If you want to increase your financial literacy but don't have time for a college program, book study, or workshop, here are two exercises you can use to learn on the job—free of charge. As a bonus, you'll reinforce what you've learned in this book and practice your needs assessment skills at the same time:

- Practice data collection by interviewing a member of your company's finance team or a leader who's highly skilled in managing a profit and loss (P&L) statement. Imagine that you are conducting a needs assessment to determine the best ways to increase junior employees' business acumen. During the interview, take detailed notes, and, if possible, record the conversation. Then, transcribe the interview and practice coding the data, organizing your findings into categories, and reaching conclusions.
- Browse your company's LMS to find any business acumen e-learning courses that may be accessible to you, and take three of them. If no such courses are available, look for short, free classes from resources like LinkedIn Learning, Coursera, or Udemy. If you were going to conduct a needs assessment to redesign the course, what unmet learning needs would you address and why?

FQ will help you interpret numbers and financial documents (such as P&Ls, balance sheets, and cash flow statements), and understand the story they tell, put numbers into business content, adjust your goals and strategy in alignment with budgets, differentiate *wants* from *needs*, and make more informed budget decisions and more effective budget requests. The higher your FQ, the better you'll be able to work with stakeholders across the company to identify and solve business needs.

DEEPER DIVE
Building Your Business Acumen

Here are three quick resources to help build your financial know-how:

- Ajay Pangarkar and Teresa Kirkwood, "Boost Your Financial IQ," *CTDO*, October 14, 2022, td.org/magazines/ctdo-magazine/boost-your-financial-iq.
- Robert Brodo, "Business Acumen Basics for Talent Development," *TD* at Work (Alexandria, VA: ATD Press, 2018).
- MindTools, "Developing Commercial Awareness: Understanding How Businesses Make Money," mindtools.com/pages/article/developing -commercial-awareness.htm.

Plan First, Budget Next: What Do You Need to Buy?

You can conduct a needs assessment by yourself with nothing more than a trusty notebook and pen (or simple word processing program). You can also conduct a needs assessment with a team of external consultants and cutting-edge analysis software. Your project will probably fall somewhere between these low- and high-cost extremes, although most internal needs assessments are conducted in-house using existing resources with no additional funding.

There is a cost to leveraging existing resources, however, and the biggest expense of a needs assessment is the time investment (productivity and salary costs) required by you, your team, stakeholders, collaborators, and participants. It's important to know how to calculate these hidden costs and ensure that the project merits the investment. Review the "Down to the Hour" section in chapter 7 for strategies on estimating time costs.

Actual expenses (things you might buy) for a needs assessment typically fall into four categories:

- Software or tools to assist with data collection, data analysis, and project management

- Purchasing published research or professional memberships for access to research
- Incentives or appreciation for participants, collaborators, and SMEs
- Hiring an external vendor or consultant (usually for data collection, data analysis, or solutions planning for large, complex, or high-priority needs assessment projects)

Most internally facing needs assessments, especially those conducted on a shoestring, won't warrant hiring external talent. If your project is large in scale, high priority, and urgent, you might consider pricing vendor-provided support when the time and labor requirements of your project outweigh the cost of outsourcing, or when internal resources don't exist and the problem you're addressing poses a high risk for the organization.

You're more likely to estimate costs for solutions than for hiring external talent to conduct the needs assessment. Keep reading for tips and strategies for budgeting your needs assessment project and your recommended solutions.

Building the Budget

Needs assessment budgets fall into two categories: a budget for conducting the needs assessment, and a budget for recommended solutions. The needs assessment budget should be built during the strategy planning phase. The solutions budget should be built during the recommendations phase.

Planning comes before budgeting. The first step is identifying resources you already have. Don't skip this step! Money is wasted when teams invest in a project management software license or survey tool that another department already has in place. Check with your IT team to find out what software licenses are available and how you can gain access to them. Check the benefits of all your professional memberships, and those of your team and company, to determine what research, case studies, or benchmarking data you can access for free or at discounted rates.

Kelly once worked with two departments (at the same company) that each sent a staff member to the same training conference, not knowing that there was a $500 discount available for organizations that registered more than one employee. While $500 may not sound like a huge miss, imagine finding an extra $500 in your budget for professional development, a new survey tool subscription, digital recorders with transcription software, or other needs assessment tools. Small oversights in planning add up—don't squander your resources.

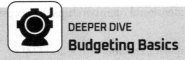

DEEPER DIVE
Budgeting Basics

Want to learn how to budget from the perspective of a talent development professional? Check out this book:

- Lianabel Oliver and Eduardo A. Nin, *10 Steps to Successful Budgeting* (Alexandria, VA: ATD Press, 2019).

Budgeting for Conducting Needs Assessments

Budgeting for a needs assessment includes identifying the resources you'll need to complete the work and estimating the costs of those resources. It helps to breakdown your project work by phase (planning, data collection, data analysis, recommendations, and results) and ask, "What do I need to get the work done?" for each phase. You may already have all the tools on hand. Stakeholders may be able to help you identify resources that you didn't realize were available.

List everything you require for each phase of the project, including what you already have. For each required resource, note how you can access it and potential additional uses—remember—*buy once; use often*. And make sure you're clearly differentiating *wants* from *needs* when requesting funding so that you only need to request funds for critical tools.

The best way to encourage participation in a needs assessment is through clear communication so everyone understands the purpose and how their input will help. But it never hurts to incentivize or reward participation. Depending on your budget and company policies, you may be able to offer a small token of appreciation for focus group participants or a prize drawing for survey participants. Here are a few ideas you might want to budget for:

- Company swag can be a good incentive and your marketing department may be able to provide items for you to give away.
- Serving lunch or a cookie tray during a focus group is a relatively low-cost way to thank participants.
  - If you send a presurvey before holding focus groups or interviews, include a "just for fun" question at the end asking participants to choose their favorite candy (or healthy snack) from a list of options, and then greet them at the focus group or

interview with their selected choice. (Be sure to bring extras for anyone who didn't answer the survey question.) This exercise is a low cost, welcoming icebreaker that you can use to emphasize that you're listening to participants' feedback.

- Sending thank-you cards with a small token of appreciation to stakeholders after a needs assessment helps build relationships and is a good practice to follow.
- If the culture of your organization supports employee recognition, sending a note to stakeholders' managers to express thanks for their support and work during a needs assessment is a fun way to acknowledge these partners. (Bonus: This one is free!)

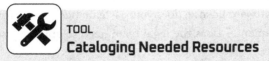

TOOL
Cataloging Needed Resources

Here's a tool you can use to track what resources you might need for your needs assessment project. In this example, the L&D team has identified the need to purchase a survey tool, and after researching options, included a request for $450 for a two-month team subscription as a line item in their project budget. Refer to appendix A for a blank version you can use.

Resource or Tool	Already Have	Need to Buy	Options and Cost	Additional Uses
Project management system	X		• $0 • IT dept will provide access for 3 users	• The L&D team will begin using this system for needs assessments and training projects. • The data analytics team currently uses it.
Survey tool		X	• Survey "Team Premier" plan • $75 per user per month (3 users for 2 months = $450)	• Potential enterprise license for the entire organization

You're asking people to share their time, expertise, opinions, challenges, and honest feedback, and it's important to recognize their participation. Include a modest line item for incentives and appreciation in your project budget and be sure to track those expenses.

If you're not already familiar with your department's cost structure and budgeting process, this is a good time to learn. Questions to consider include:

- Can the needs assessment project expenses be included in current department budget lines?
- Which purchases can be made on a company credit card?
- Which purchases require a PO (purchase order), and what is the process for PO submission and approval?
- Who needs to provide final approval for purchases?

If you're purchasing a software license, does your IT team need to approve it or confirm system requirements? Does the legal team need to approve user agreements or contracts?

Budgeting for Recommended Solutions

As you identify potential solutions with stakeholders (after completing your data analysis), you'll want to determine the costs for each recommended solution. Many business problems can be solved by changing processes, providing information resources, or delivering training in-house, and they don't require additional expenses. For solutions that do come with a price tag, work with stakeholders to conduct a cost-benefit analysis. In your recommendations report, include the estimated cost of each solution, along with the projected positive impact. Work with stakeholders to determine answers to the following questions:

- How many employees (or customers) are currently affected by the problem, and how many will benefit from this solution?
- What does the recommended solution cost?
- How long will the solution be used?
- What internal resources will be required to implement and support the solution?
- What financial and productivity benefits or savings are expected from this solution?

To provide options for stakeholders, include recommendations that range from low cost to higher cost, with the pros, cons, and potential impacts for each.

When a recommendation is selected, you'll work with stakeholders to determine which department cost centers and budget lines will be used to manage the solution's costs.

Thrift Shop Like a Boss: Bargains and Best Buys

There are many practical, inexpensive (or free) tools that can help you conduct needs assessments. Before you settle on something, test it first. Most software tools provide a trial period so you can try before you buy. When selecting data collection programs, Jody likes to test a few using the same sample survey questions to compare the interface and user experience and examine how easy it is to set up questions.

ON THE CHEAP
Data Collection and Analysis Tools

Here are a few of our favorite free or low-cost data collection tools:
- **Google Forms** is part of Google's suite of tools. You can use one of the many available templates or you can create a custom form.
- **Microsoft Forms** is a survey tool in the Office 365 stack that offers templates and customization options. The data works well with other Office products, such as Excel.
- **Qualtrics** (qualtrics.com/free-account) has many great resources including a free survey account. (Their blog is great too.) The free account has templates, eight question types, and up to 500 submissions. It may be too restrictive for your needs assessment, but you can upgrade to unlock additional features.
- **Survey Monkey** (surveymonkey.com) may have a silly name, but it is a seriously powerful survey tool. The free account does have some limitations, such as 10 questions per survey and 40 responses, but individual and team plans are available for purchase.
- **Slido** (slido.com) has a clean and easy-to-navigate participant interface. The tool allows for live polls and surveys that can stand alone or be integrated into meetings. The free version will allow you to try some of the more popular functions.

There are a few things to consider when testing software for usability:

- Is it easy to use?
- Does it include the features you need?
- Does it integrate with other tools you'll be using regularly?
- Does it provide the question formats you need, such as branching?
- Can you export data in the formats you need?

That last question is especially important. Sometimes, free tools limit your ability to export data, which can cause frustration during data analysis, so review each function of the platform before selecting your tools.

Buying External Talent and Solutions

In some situations, organizations elect to hire external resources to conduct or support need assessments or to provide solutions based on needs assessment recommendations. You may end up working with an outside consultant—or you might find an opportunity to work as an outside consultant. The roles in a needs assessment project that are commonly outsourced are the project manager (to design and oversee the needs assessment), researchers (to collect and analyze data), and data analysts (to conduct analysis on large or complex datasets).

Hiring the right external consultants is as challenging as hiring the right full-time employees. Always ask for references, and then ask them good questions about their experience working with the consultant. If you're seeking external talent and are unsure where to look, search Google or LinkedIn for organization development consultants in your area. Depending on the topic of your needs assessment, you can search for experts with specific certifications like the Prosci Certified Change Practitioner (change management), a PMI certification from the Project Management Institute, or the Certified Professional in Talent Development (CPTD) from ATD. Some professional associations include vendor directories on their websites that you can use to search for needs assessment practitioners. You can find consultants at industry conferences and expos too.

Table 8-1 identifies some pros and cons to consider when buying outside talent and services.

Table 8-1. Benefits and Limitations of Buying Help

Benefits	Limitations
• **Cost:** If an organization doesn't have the internal resources required for conducting needs assessments, it may be more cost effective to outsource the work than to hire employees. • **Specialized expertise:** Consultants and vendors may be able to provide expertise that you don't have the time or resources to develop in-house. • **Objectivity:** Consultants and vendors are free from office politics and can provide objectivity and an outside perspective for needs assessments. • **Flexibility:** Consultants and vendors may be able to work on your schedule, at your location, or meet your deadlines with more flexibility than current internal teams.	• **Cost:** Consultants and customized solutions can be expensive. Measure results so that you can determine the ROI of these costs. • **Lack of organizational knowledge:** While consultants and vendors provide expertise, they don't know your organization. Building that understanding takes time. • **Trust:** Employees may not be willing to talk openly with external partners, and it can be challenging to build a sense of trust with outsiders. • **Availability:** Consultants and vendors may have other projects lined up that require a later start date or more limited availability than you'd prefer for your project.

If you decide to explore options for hiring third-party services, you may send out requests for proposals (RFPs) or work with a sales rep or account manager at a vendor company to develop a proposal. The RFP initiates the process for external companies to bid for the work. It starts with a clear explanation of the problem you want them to solve and any associated project requirements. Other RFP components include:

- **Nondisclosure agreement (NDA).** Ensure privacy and confidentiality expectations are met, and your company's information is protected, by having vendors sign an NDA before sharing information. Consult with your company's legal team before sending or signing an NDA.
- **Project scope and requirements.** Include a description of your company, the goals of this project, details of the services you're requesting, and expected results. Does the consultant need to work on-site at your location? Is other travel involved?
- **Budget.** Many vendors will request your working budget up front. This can be a tricky discussion—if you disclose that you have more to spend than what they'd charge you, you'll end up losing money without

knowing it. Ask them for estimates before committing to numbers, or lower your actual budget threshold to make room for negotiations later.

- **Availability.** How soon are they able to start the work? How much time can they dedicate over the course of your project?
- **Timeline.** Be very clear about the timeline for the project and key milestone deadlines. Note: Just like with your own project timeline estimates, we recommend adding 20 percent to third-party cost estimates for your own internal use, approvals, and project management planning. The risk of increased cost is real and constant, so you're better off budgeting for it ahead of time.
- **Deliverables.** What products and services are you expecting them to deliver? Reports? Plans? Training?
- **Communication.** What are your expectations for communication throughout the project? Who will you be able to reach out to quickly if issues need to be resolved?
- **Payment.** How does the vendor expect to be paid? For example, net 30 and net 45 are common payment terms. Do they have an online payment system? Can you pay invoices with a credit card?
- **Intellectual property.** Make sure your legal team reviews all contracts and agreements. IP issues need to be discussed up front. For example, who owns reports or content created by the consultant?

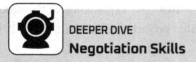

DEEPER DIVE
Negotiation Skills

You get what you pay for, but don't overpay. If you hire external talent or purchase solutions, you will likely need to negotiate rates and contract terms. Kelly recommends *Never Split the Difference* by Chris Voss—she has used it for training programs with sales teams, managers, marketers, and L&D professionals. This book is consistently recommended by and for business leaders—chances are, it will pay for itself the first time you apply what Voss teaches you.

If your company has processes and policies for RFPs, make sure you follow them. Once the RFP is posted externally, be prepared to evaluate the responses.

Your goal is to receive a selection of diverse vendor options offering the right type of services. Use a consistent approach for evaluating proposals.

TOOL
Evaluating Vendors Worksheet

We suggest using a simple scoring rubric to compare responses and options across multiple vendors. A good practice is to compare at least three options to ensure you're identifying the best solutions at the best prices. A *scoring rubric* is a fancy way to describe a table or spreadsheet that captures the same information from multiple vendors. Appendix A includes a blank template you can use.

Vendors may request the opportunity to discuss their proposal and provide more explanation about their services. These conversations can be helpful, but beware the sales pitch! Sales pitches can be very convincing but, unfortunately, often fall short of the final promised results. Ask for work samples, case studies, or customers you can contact to learn more about their experiences with this vendor.

Outsourcing can be a fantastic way to manage workload and deliver results quickly, but vendor expectations and relationships must be carefully negotiated and managed. Whether you need to hire external consultants or only need to purchase a few items and pay for refreshments, remember the *invisible* costs of needs assessments: employees' time (salary and productivity costs). You'll probably need to advocate for all required resources, whether they have a visible price tag or not.

Advocating for Resources

When it's time to request resources, you'll need a strategy so you can present a strong business case and advocate effectively. Having an executive champion is invaluable during this process, as they may be able to provide data or help you frame expenses within larger budget frameworks and company initiatives. You can build a business case for needs assessment resources by identifying the following:

- **Additional use.** What can be used again? Investing in tools such as transcription or analysis software may be worth the cost if those tools will be used again for future needs assessments or other projects.
- **Savings.** Identify the cost of the business problem so that you can calculate the potential savings that will result once the problem is solved.
- **Percentage of the problem.** If you know the cost of the business problem, you can compare the cost of the needs assessment project as a percentage. For example, if a current process has been identified as costing the company $225,000 a year, and the cost of your proposed needs assessment project is $5,000, you're asking the company to invest 2 percent of the current problem's cost into solving the problem.

You'll also want to identify ROI measures of the actual needs assessment. The results are valuable learning opportunities for the company, and quantifying this information can professionalize the talent development function within the eyes of your organizational stakeholders.

Measuring Needs Assessment Value

It's important to note the difference between a needs assessment's ROI and the ROI of the recommended solutions that are implemented as a *result* of the needs assessment, but you'll need to know how to evaluate both. To show the value of the needs assessment, you need to capture (and quantify, if possible) the value of what was learned, cost savings identified by conducting the needs assessment, efficiencies gained by identifying root causes, or other value criteria that you're able to measure.

You can calculate the ROI of your needs assessment if your project has clear financial costs and gains. The ROI formula is:

$$\text{ROI} = \frac{\text{Net income}}{\text{Cost of investment}} \times 100$$

or

$$\text{ROI} = \frac{\text{Investment gain}}{\text{Investment base}}$$

In Kelly's experience, the textbook examples of ROI are harder to calculate for real-world needs assessments, especially for learning and development projects. To identify the value measures of your needs assessment project when your results aren't easy to quantify, consider these questions:

- What did we learn, and how are those findings relevant for the business's bottom line?
- How quickly and efficiently were we able to complete the needs assessment?
- What would it have cost, and how much longer would it have taken, to outsource this needs assessment?
- What opportunities might we have missed, or what investments might we have made in the wrong solutions, if we had not completed this needs assessment?
- How long has the problem been occurring, and what would it cost if the problem continued?

Ultimately, the value of the project is determined by the cost (time, effort, and expenses) compared with the benefits gained by investing in the work of conducting the needs assessment. Value measures answer the question, "Was this needs assessment worth doing?" The value of the solutions implemented based on a needs assessment's recommendations can be evaluated once they have been implemented and enough time has passed to measure the expected results. Refer to chapter 1 and chapter 4 for strategies on planning those evaluation metrics.

Managing the Budget

If you spend any money on a needs assessment project (outside of salary costs from staff time), it's important to plan carefully for budget processes so you can track spending and manage budget lines. Here are some things to consider for your spending planning and tracking:

- **Plan the spending:**
  - What budget systems should your department use? Are there specific cost centers or budget lines you should use for the needs assessment project expenses?
  - What specific software systems or tools should you use to report and track expenses?

- What purchasing systems should your department use? Work with your procurement and accounting teams to ensure vendors are set up properly in the system, and know the process for issuing payments.
- What processes should you follow to track all spending until the project is completed?
- How have you spread costs out over the project phases and milestones? We recommend completing a detailed budget review after each phase is complete, and then conducting a holistic budget review at the end of the project.
- **Track the spending:**
  - How should receipts be stored and submitted?
  - Who should you reach out to in the case of errors on an invoice?
  - What should you do if the project runs over budget, or additional expenses need to be approved?
  - If the project falls under budget, can those unused funds be applied to future projects or used to purchase tools for other needs assessment work?
  - Do you need to conduct regular budget reviews, and, if so, who do those budget reports go to?

Follow all processes and requirements for your company's budgeting systems and processes. If you work in a small organization, this might be an opportunity to help codify processes for the next time you'll need to use them. Review invoices carefully to avoid overpayment due to billing mistakes. We also recommend that you create your own spreadsheet to track all needs assessment project expenses and save copies of all contracts, invoices, and receipts. The insight you gain from tracking the project's budget will help inform your planning for future projects.

A Shoestring Summary

If you have a project budget for your needs assessment, you'll have to plan and advocate for funding, as well as manage and track expenses:

- Break down costs by project phase to help with planning and tracking.
- Only ask for the resources and tools that are absolutely required to complete the work and align with stakeholders on costs.

- Understand your company's processes, policies, and systems for budgets, spending, tracking expenses, and working with vendors.
- Keep track of each expense, receipt, and invoice.
- Operate like an internal consultant, and be a good steward of company funds.

9
Buy-In

When detectives hunt for answers, they have institutional authority and tools to ensure cooperation with the investigation. They can request warrants, make arrests, interrogate, intimidate, and conduct searches—and they don't need to build ongoing relationships with suspects, although it can make their job easier. As a talent development professional, you can't flash a badge or deploy a SWAT team to pave the way for a needs assessment project, but you can gain (and maintain) buy-in from stakeholders by leading through influence and building a strong business case. Buy-in from stakeholders can be hard to win, so you'll need to leverage effective interpersonal skills.

What You Need Most Can't Be Bought

Early in Jody's career, projects would usually come her way from a manager who insisted their team needed training. She would proceed with developing the training course, even though she knew that a needs assessment was a better first step than jumping into designing a training program. Why didn't the needs assessment occur? Looking back, most of the time it didn't happen because she didn't seek the buy-in needed to do one. Those managers who came with a request for training assumed they were doing the right thing by providing the suggested solution to their problems. Jody missed the opportunity to explain the value of conducting a needs assessment and gain the buy-in of someone to sponsor the work.

After 20 years as a talent development practitioner, Kelly has learned the value of asking why instead of saying yes. That may sound like a simple shift, but like many talent development professionals, Kelly got into this field because she believes in lifelong learning, loves curriculum development, and wants to help people. For many years, she thought she brought value to organizations by working hard to say yes—meeting requests creatively, thoughtfully, and thoroughly. A CEO once asked her to justify a needs assessment, and she argued (passionately) for the best practices of quality instructional design. (This is not an approach she recommends today!) A few tough lessons and excellent mentors taught her to critically evaluate learning projects to understand the business case before saying yes, advocating for a yes from others, or counting a yes as a success. The best advice she received from another CEO was "Don't confuse activity for results." Now, she works to determine the business value of a project before beginning the work of a needs assessment.

Needs assessment projects will compete against other initiatives for priority, resources, and support. Part of your job as the project lead is advocating for the project (after you've determined that it's worth the investment) so that you can secure the backing needed to start it. Your leadership work doesn't stop there, though. Even if you gain initial approval for a needs assessment project, continued support is not guaranteed. It can shift as business priorities, perceptions, and opinions shift, and these things may be outside your control. The secret to success is consistently demonstrating value in ways that are valuable to your stakeholders. You can't buy buy-in, but you can earn it. To do that, think like a CEO.

Think Like a CEO

Imagine your company's investors show up at your needs assessment kickoff meeting and ask you to justify the time, effort, and expense of the project. Can you make a convincing business case? If your roles were reversed, would you vote to approve this project?

Talent development professionals usually serve in support roles. And in these roles, our focus is usually supporting people, not profits. Ultimately, businesses invest in talent development because performance improvement increases productivity and profitability. And that's not a bad thing! CEOs are responsible for the financial wellbeing of their organizations, and while many do genuinely care about the professional development of their employees, their priorities must be driven by the business's bottom line. They must determine the value of departments, products, processes, and strategies so that they can make informed decisions. Considering the value of needs assessments from a CEO's perspective will help you align your work with business goals, so frame your needs assessments as strategic planning tools.

Needs assessment results can be powerful strategic planning tools, even if "needs assessments" aren't typically listed in strategic planning frameworks. For example:

- **SWOT analysis**—strengths, weaknesses, opportunities, and threats—the "weaknesses" describe high priority business needs.
- **SCORE analysis**—strengths, challenges, options, responses, and effectiveness—the "challenges" describe high priority business needs.
- **NOISE analysis**—needs, opportunities, improvements, strengths, and exceptions—the "needs" describe high priority business needs.

Each of these strategic analysis models has parallels with needs assessments. Often, needs assessment work is coordinated with an organization's annual strategic planning cycle. Many organizations set strategic goals for the upcoming year during the third or fourth quarter of the current year. Jody likes to work backward from these dates and consider how any needs assessment work she's done might connect with strategic goals. She determines who she should make aware of relevant needs assessment projects (check the stakeholder list) and then connects her needs assessment reports as inputs for those stakeholders' upcoming strategic planning process. Many times, after those connections have been made, the planning team will use needs assessment data and recommendations to make decisions about training and other organizational initiatives. This strategy helps Jody continuously communicate the value of needs assessment projects long after they're complete.

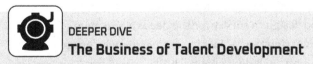

DEEPER DIVE
The Business of Talent Development

Want to keep your passion for talent development close to your heart while developing business sense? Check out these resources:

- Terry Bickham, ed. *ATD's Talent Management Handbook* (Alexandria, VA: ATD Press, 2021).
- Beverly Scott and B. Kim Barnes, *Consulting on the Inside: A Practical Guide for Internal Consultants* (Alexandria, VA: ATD Press, 2021).
- John Zorbini, "Be a Planner," *CTDO*, April 15, 2022, td.org/magazines/ctdo-magazine/be-a-planner.

Practice seeing things from a CEO's perspective by challenging yourself to consider multiple priorities, complexities, costs, risks, and impacts to provide strategic support to your organization. This doesn't mean devaluing the capabilities you have as a needs assessment practitioner—you're just adding to them. Your interpersonal skills are essential, and you'll leverage them as you gain and maintain buy-in for a needs assessment.

The Platinum Rule: Managing Communications

By our estimates, 75 to 90 percent of your time as a needs assessment practitioner will be spent communicating. Communication spans every phase of your project. You will almost always be messaging, emailing, or calling someone—stakeholders, SMEs, collaborators, and participants. Remaining friendly while keeping everyone informed and on task requires constant, thoughtful effort on your part. Clear and effective communication is a full-time requirement for the entire needs assessment.

Needs assessments can quickly become large-scale initiatives, but regardless of the size of your project, you need a system for keeping track of everyone involved and ensuring they each understand their role and the project's interdependencies. We recommend a RACI chart to track who should be *responsible* for, *accountable* for, *consulted* about, and *informed* of each aspect of the needs assessment. Set up a table or spreadsheet as a RACI matrix and assign each role:

- **Responsible.** Assign the "R" label to the person who is directly responsible for completing the task, such as the talent development specialist who designs a survey for the needs assessment.
- **Accountable.** Assign the "A" label to the person who ensures the task's completion, including quality checks or reviews. This person may also be the one who delegates tasks to others, such as the talent development director who is supervising the survey.
- **Consulted.** Assign the "C" label to those individuals who have expertise or leadership in the task area. These are the people who should be consulted on questions or decisions as needed, such as an analytics manager who needs to review the survey before it is sent to employees.
- **Informed.** Assign the "I" label to anyone who should be communicated with during the task, such as the project's key stakeholders.

Once you've built your RACI chart, use these strategies to keep communications frequent while minimizing the time required to do so:

- **Status reports.** Send a status report regularly to provide information to stakeholders. Traditionally, status reports include progress, schedule, and budget updates. However, you can adjust these to cover any topics you need to discuss with your team, such as resource challenges.
- **Summarize, and then explain.** When you send status reports, put the major highlights at the top—a few short bullet points with the most important updates. Then provide more detailed information after the headline-level summary. This will give others the option to skim or dive deeper while keeping everyone informed.
- **Use visual cues.** Simple visual strategies work well for status updates if you use them consistently. For example, color-code tasks and milestones—green for on schedule, yellow for minor delays, red for major delays or roadblocks, and blue for complete.
- **Spread the word.** Consider multiple ways you can spread the word about the needs assessment. Trust us; sending one email at the beginning of the project is not enough! Consider adding the needs assessment work to existing meeting agendas. Sharing a quick update during routine department meetings is a great way to update a large audience on a regular basis without adding another meeting to the calendar.
- **Create a virtual project headquarters.** Put all the information needed by the team in one place, bookmark or pin key files, and follow a file management process so everyone can quickly and easily see additions and edits, status reports, the RACI chart, and the project management task page.

TOOL
RACI Chart

In the "Team Expectations and Communication" section in appendix B, we use the customer service needs assessment scenario to provide a worked example of multiple RACI charts that define roles and set communications expectations.

To ensure you are sharing the right information at the right time to the right people, ask for feedback about the communications you're providing. You might be surprised by the communication preferences you receive. Jody has worked with stakeholders who asked her to provide less information, including reducing a full-page report to a single paragraph. Another time, a stakeholder asked Jody to partner with the department's project manager, who provided the status update for her. Kelly has worked with sponsors who asked to be contacted only when something went wrong, as well as others who insisted on weekly meetings with recorded agenda notes. The golden rule says to communicate with others the way you want them to communicate with you, but when you're leading a needs assessment project, follow the *platinum rule* instead: Communicate with others the way they want to be communicated with.

The Good, the Bad, and the Inevitable

If needs assessment project communication only required efficiency and congeniality, our jobs would be a lot easier. However, your communication strategies are only effective if they work for hard conversations. We can almost guarantee that you will have to communicate bad news, mediate conflicts, hold others accountable, explain delays, and follow up on tasks and requests many more times than you might expect. Recognize communication challenges as part of the process, and you'll be ahead of the game. Prepare for tension the way you would for an oncoming storm—get ready in case it hits. If you make a plan *before* the warning alarms blare, you'll be able to handle the hard parts with calm professionalism.

There will come a time when you need to communicate project delays. We have both needed to deliver news about broken data collection tools, resources lost due to job changes, and the cancellation of focus groups due to changing business priorities. We've each had to share results that showed risks and vulnerabilities that required immediate action, including HR initiatives and disciplinary actions. In these situations, double check your findings *before* sharing them. If the issues you uncover are sensitive, and you're unsure about appropriate next steps, take the data to your HR director and ask for guidance.

We suggest asking your sponsor or champion how they want you to reach communicate about serious challenges or conflicts if they arise. It's also a good idea to designate a backup—whom should you contact if something goes off the rails and your sponsor or champion is offline? It's better to align early than to panic later. Uncertainty makes stressful situations worse, so knowing what to do when communications get tough is a great strategy for every needs assessment project.

Knowing how to communicate during difficult situations is crucial, but it's equally important to share good news! Celebrate wins along the way, send kudos as milestones are reached, and express appreciation generously. And don't worry—we keep warning you about hard things, but there will be fantastic things, too. Reflect on the positive as much as you do the negative and remember that every step toward solving a problem is a step that makes your organization better.

The Currency of Trust

Detectives focus on finding facts, no matter the consequences for the perpetrator. Needs assessment practitioners also uncover facts but must manage these efforts while maintaining positive relationships. When you conduct a needs assessment, you may encounter colleagues who perceive you as an unwelcome or threatening investigator instead of a partner striving to help your organization solve a pressing problem. Some employees may worry that you're operating undercover or secretly evaluating their performance. Managers may think that you're overstepping and tell you to stay in your own lane when you start asking questions. Others may be concerned about data being manipulated in ways that make them look bad.

How can you possibly manage the demands of a needs assessment when the people you're trying to help don't want your interference? You can bulldoze ahead and leave damaged relationships in your wake, or you can do the work required to build and maintain trust. You don't need a detective hat to guess the right choice. Needs assessment practitioners must be trustworthy. You can't prevent everyone from doubting your motives, but you can ensure that your methods are beyond reproach.

Always remember that when the needs assessment is over, you will still work with all the people involved. Most of the needs assessment should be built or borrowed from a foundation of trust. You need to establish and maintain relationships with stakeholders, SMEs, leaders, collaborators, peers, and participants—so you must establish and maintain trust. Researchers have cited the value of trust so much that they refer to it as *currency* in business (Botsman 2012). You want to be someone people are willing to spend their money on. Each interaction is an opportunity to either make a deposit (build trust) or risk a withdrawal (damaged trust) from your relationship "bank."

DEEPER DIVE
Trust

Here are two of our favorite videos about building trust and learning how to repair it when relationships become strained:

- Rachel Botsman, "The Currency of the New Economy is Trust," TED, June 2012, video, ted.com/talks/rachel_botsman_the_currency_of_the_new _economy_is_trust.
- Frances Frei, "How to Build (and Rebuild) Trust," TED, April 2018, video, ted.com/talks/frances_frei_how_to_build_and_rebuild_trust/transcript.

If you want to read about trust, we recommend:

- Stephen M.R. Covey and Rebecca R. Merrill, *The SPEED of Trust: The One Thing That Changes Everything* (New York: Free Press, 2008).

Establishing trust takes time and many consistently positive interactions. The best way to build trust is simple: Do what you say you're going to do. Needs assessments are especially challenging because they require trust *before* work begins. You may not have the time required to build deep and lasting trust during a needs assessment project, but you can demonstrate trustworthiness through your behavior:

- **Be confident.** Step into the needs assessment with confidence so you can lead others through the process.
- **Be confidential.** Maintain confidentiality, treat data ethically, and keep sensitive needs assessment situations under your hat.
- **Be collaborative.** Encourage others to share their ideas and perspectives.
- **Be considerate.** Look for opportunities to add value. How can you make tasks easier for stakeholders to complete? Where can you share

the needs analysis results within your organization? How can you support someone else's needs assessment project?

- **Be consistent.** Have a plan for each interaction. Come to meetings prepared with an agenda, a clear purpose, a plan for the time together, and next steps.

Your needs assessment's success depends greatly on your ability to gain the cooperation of stakeholders, SMEs, collaborators, and participants. The more they trust you to conduct the work, the better your results will be.

A Shoestring Summary

Buy-in is a shortcut term for describing support, sponsorship, commitment, cooperation, and trust, and it's the key ingredient in any needs assessment. It is how the best work gets done—in any needs assessment, it's impossible to do all the work alone. Buy-in can't be bought. It can only be earned, and you earn it by:

- Building trust
- Developing and maintaining positive relationships
- Considering multiple perspectives
- Planning strategically
- Communicating effectively
- Behaving ethically

Bringing It All Together

Congratulations to you, gumshoe! You now have enough knowledge, tools, and strategies to build, borrow, and buy your way through the challenges and rewards of conducting a needs assessment on a shoestring. You've reached the end of this book, but it's just the beginning of many new opportunities to continue developing your skills. Every needs assessment experience will help you hone your approach, improve your techniques, and find effective and creative solutions to complex problems.

Key Takeaways

Needs assessments start with questions and end with answers. They're triggered by problems and resolved by solutions. No two needs assessments are ever the same, and the road to completion is paved with ambiguity and complexity. You will steer around delays and detours, and, sometimes, you will need to keep driving without GPS. Needs assessments are hard work. So why do we keep conducting them and encouraging you to do the same?

We believe in the value of needs assessments because we've seen the value they bring to companies, teams, and training programs. By conducting needs assessments, we're able to figure out how to fix what's broken, improve processes, empower others, encourage growth, and deliver recommendations that make organizations better. The needs justify the means—it's worth the hard work because the results have real impact. A small needs assessment might result in a more engaging onboarding program for new employees, while a large project might result in the digital transformation of the entire employee experience. Regardless of scale, every needs assessment has the potential to facilitate positive change.

Also, solving mysteries is fun. Finding clues, cracking codes, recognizing patterns, and getting to the root cause keeps our inquiry and critical thinking skills sharp. We hope that you also experience the rewards of this work and that this book becomes a helpful guide for many future needs assessment projects.

What's Next?

You've learned the process from start to finish—planning, data collection, analysis, recommendations, and results reports. So, what's next? When you wrap up a needs assessment, there's a lot you can do to keep the momentum going:

- **Collect the lessons you learned from the experience.** Use reflection exercises, retrospectives, after-action reviews, or simply journal a few things you want to keep in mind before your next project. Reflection encourages continuous learning.
- **Seek opportunities to share your work with others who may benefit from the information or learn from your experience.** Jody calls this a "double coupon" opportunity—get more for your investment in your own work by helping others with theirs. Look for colleagues who are interested in training, research, or continuous improvement. Share your process and end product with internal training and business performance groups.
- **Ask the sponsor to champion your needs assessment by sharing the results.** The outward expression of support can lend energy to the next phase of work when solutions are implemented, as well as create an organizational appreciation for needs assessments. Even a reluctant sponsor can become a champion after they see needs assessment results in action.
- **Lead or contribute to kick-off activities for the recommended solutions.** If you have the opportunity, participate in the implementation and evaluation of the solutions you recommend.

Needs assessments can be a starting point for learning data analytics and program evaluations. If you enjoy conducting needs assessments, you might also enjoy conducting evaluations. Needs assessments measure problems; evaluations measure the results of solutions and identify opportunities for continuous improvement. Needs assessment data provides baselines for measuring current and future performance. It can also serve as the foundation for annual systematic inquiry (program evaluation), which monitors the outcomes of training, development, and change management programs and provides insights for continuous improvement. As a savvy practitioner, you can guide efforts for change from a needs assessment through solutions to program evaluation. Keep wearing your detective hat, follow the data, and bring it all together.

DEEPER DIVE
Capabilities

Needs assessment projects are a great way to have a positive impact on your organization by developing your capabilities as a talent development professional (and a detective). ATD's Talent Development Capability Model illustrates the key capabilities you need to succeed. Check it out at td.org/capability-model.

APPENDIX A
TOOLS AND TEMPLATES

Use the following templates to create tools to help you conduct your needs assessment project:

- Needs Assessment Strategy Worksheet
- Data Collection Plan Template
- Data Analysis Plan Template
- Dataset Summary Template
- Data Keep Pile Template
- A Visual Summary of Needs Assessment Results
- Root Cause Category Template
- Results Report Template
- CCA+ Framework Tool
- Graphic Organizer for Selecting Participants
- Breaking It Down Into Phases, Milestones, and Tasks
- Task Details Template
- Cataloging Needed Resources
- Evaluating Vendors Worksheet

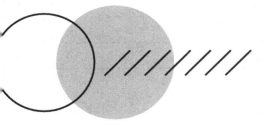

Needs Assessment Strategy Worksheet

Use this template for capturing all the components of your needs assessment strategy, and as a big picture view of the process. Refer to these details to save time and effort when you're ready to write the results report.

Kickoff		
Start date:	Milestone dates and notes:	
Estimated completion date:		
Strategy		
Problem:		
Business impact:		
Current state:	Goal state:	Known gaps:
Stakeholders:		
Research questions:	Data collection:	Analysis plan:
Project scope notes:		
Timeline:	Budget:	Available resources:
Plans for sharing results:		
Constraints (limitations and delimitations):		
Success metrics to evaluate solutions:		
Needs assessment value measures:		
Results		
Findings:		
Conclusions:		
Recommendations:		
Results deliverables:		

Debrief
Actual completion date:
Benchmarks:
After-action review and lessons learned:
Next steps:

Data Collection Plan Template

Use this template to build your data collection plan. Start by listing the primary research question and related subquestions—one question per row. Then, consider where you might find the information you need to address each research question, and list those ideas in the "Data Source" column. Once you confirm the sources, determine which data collection methods are the best choice for each source. Remember, the five most common data collection methods are existing documents and work products, surveys, focus groups, interviews, and observations.

If you collect additional opportunity data during the needs assessment, add it to your data plan. This allows you to track the opportunities that were truly spontaneous, as well as those you should plan for during your next project.

Primary Research Question:		
Subquestions	**Data Source**	**Data Collection Methods**
Data collection constraints:		
Participant-facing research questions (for surveys, focus groups, and interviews):		

Data Analysis Plan Template

Use this template to build your plan for analyzing all the data you collect. Start by listing your research questions and sources. List one question per row, and then include each source you collected data from to address that question. Next, decide what steps you need to take to analyze the data. As you list your analysis tasks, identify any that you will need assistance with or support for so you can start working with collaborators. Finally, note the application of data analysis for each research question—how will you use the results? For example, you may create a visual summary of trends over a specific time, a chart comparing two datasets, or a list of key themes you identify during qualitative analysis. Having a plan for a practical way to use each dataset will help you apply what you learn from the analysis as you identify root causes and potential solutions, build recommendations, and create your results report. If you collect additional opportunity data during the needs assessment, add it to your analysis plan.

Primary Research Question:			
Subquestions	**Data Source** *(What was collected?)*	**Data Analysis** *(How will the data be analyzed?)*	**Application** *(How will the analysis results be used?)*

Dataset Summary Template

As you collect data, you'll need to organize it all by dataset. Remember, if you collected existing documents, conducted two surveys, facilitated three focus groups, and completed several interviews, you would have four datasets—document data, survey data, focus group data, and interview data. Each dataset also includes subsets—two surveys would result in two subsets within the survey dataset. It's important to organize datasets so you can compare findings across data collection methods, within subsets, and across datasets. A dataset summary will help you stay organized, check for quality assurance, define follow-up action items, capture important notes, identify gaps, and ensure you have the tools and resources you need for analysis and quality assurance. If you collect additional opportunity data during the needs assessment, add it to your dataset summary.

	Dataset 1 (Data collection type)	Dataset 2 (Data collection type)	Dataset 3 (Data collection type)
Data type			
Subsets and data quantity			
Data location			
Dataset contents			
Errors and usability			
Important notes			

Data Keep Pile Template

Use this template to keep track of the existing research sources that you referenced for each needs assessment project (for example, an annual industry report). If you're using a project management program, we suggest tracking this information along with your project tasks so you can find it easily if you need to revisit it for future projects.

Source *(Title, author, and publisher)*	
Summary *(Key findings or notes you want to remember)*	
Research method and publication date *(Type of study and date completed)*	
Application *(Relevance to your project)*	
Cost *(If applicable)*	

A Visual Summary of Needs Assessment Results

Use this visual summary to organize your key findings, conclusions, and recommendations to ensure they align.

Findings
The most relevant
results of data analysis

Conclusions
The significance
of key findings

Recommendations
Potential solutions
to solve the problem

This is a great tool to use with the What? So What? Now What? model because your findings answer the question, "What?"; your conclusions answer the question, "So what?"; and your recommendations answer the question, "Now what?"

What? *(Needs assessment findings)*	So What? *(Needs assessment conclusions)*	Now What? *(Needs assessment recommendations)*
• What is the real business problem? • How do we know this is the real problem?	• How is this problem affecting the organization? • What will happen if we do not solve this problem?	• What is needed to solve the problem? • How will we know that the problem is solved?

Root Cause Category Template

Use this template to categorize the root cause of problems and their potential solutions so you can ensure your recommendations align with the type of problem you're trying to solve.

Problem Types	Key Findings	Possible Solutions
Knowledge problems (*Information gap*)		
Skill and behavior problems (*Performance gaps caused by a lack of ability or know-how*)		
Resource problems (*Due to a lack of time, people power, materials, hardware, or other resources*)		
Process problems (*Due to a lack of standardized processes*)		
Leadership and culture problems (*Due to misalignment of values and actions*)		

Results Report Template

Use this template to create the results report for your needs assessment project. Refer to your strategy worksheet to capture details as needed for your report. We recommend writing the executive summary last. It comes first in the report, but it's much easier to write after all the other report sections are complete.

Executive Summary • Purpose, background, and methods • Conclusions • Recommendations
Introduction
Background
Methods
Key Findings
Recommendations
References*
Appendix*

If applicable

CCA+ Framework Tool

The CCA+ framework is a great tool for facilitating conversations when stake-holders or team members disagree about the key problem, findings, conclusions, or recommendations. It's also great to use when you're clarifying the key problem at the beginning of a needs assessment. Modify this template as needed to discuss different points for comparison.

	Perspective 1	Perspective 2
Highest priority needs		
Causes		
Consequences		
Difficulty to correct		
Critical rating		
Recommendation		
Measurements		

Graphic Organizer for Selecting Participants

Create a graphic organizer highlighting the business areas and teams connected to the needs assessment problem. Put the problem at the center, and then draw connections to the primary department or departments involved. Then, add connections between other departments or teams that share work, processes, or systems with the primary departments. This visual overview can help you identify potential stakeholders, SMEs, supporters, and participants for your needs assessment project.

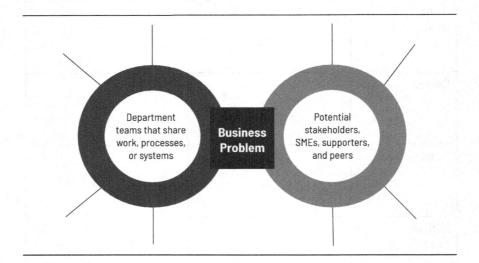

Breaking It Down Into Phases, Milestones, and Tasks

Use this tool to organize a needs assessment project by breaking it down into different phases, milestones, and tasks.

Phase 1: Planning		
Milestones	Task 1	
	Task 2	
	Task 3	

Phase 2: Data Collection		
Milestones	Task 1	
	Task 2	
	Task 3	

Phase 3: Data Analysis		
Milestones	Task 1	
	Task 2	
	Task 3	

Phase 4: Recommendations		
Milestones	Task 1	
	Task 2	
	Task 3	

Phase 5: Reporting		
Milestones	Task 1	
	Task 2	
	Task 3	

Task Details Template

Capture a few details about your needs assessment tasks to estimate the time required to complete them, and then compare that estimate to the time that was actually spent. This will help you create benchmarks for estimating timelines for future projects. Adjust the details you want to track to capture what's most relevant for your project and planning strategy.

Phase
Task
Task Priority
Description
Prep Work
Estimated Time
Required Resources

Cataloging Needed Resources

Use this tool to track what resources you might need for your needs assessment project.

Resource or Tool	Already Have	Need to Buy	Options and Costs	Additional Uses

Evaluating Vendors Worksheet

Use this scoring rubric to compare responses and options across multiple vendors. A good practice is to compare at least three options to ensure you're identifying the best solutions at the best prices. A *scoring rubric* is a fancy way to describe a table or spreadsheet that captures the same information from multiple vendors.

Vendor	Contact Info	Availability	Deliverables	Cost Estimates	Estimated Timeline	Notes
1.	Contact name, title, email, phone, website	Date available to begin the project	Description of services discussed with vendor	Cost estimate total (include hourly rate or other details if applicable)	Vendor's estimate of time required to complete the project	Additional details to consider
2.						
3.						
4.						
5.						

APPENDIX B
A WORKED EXAMPLE

In chapter 1, you read a scenario about a customer service department that was experiencing significant increases in an already high employee turnover rate. To help improve an urgent problem, the company's "team of one" instructional designer rushed to meet the department director's training demand—to create an onboarding training course—without conducting a needs assessment. Unfortunately, her onboarding program didn't have the desired results.

As you'll see, the real need was complex and required interdepartmental support and new ways of working for the department director. This worked example shows how the needs assessment team was able to identify improvement solutions that could be implemented quickly, within the project scope and budget, and without a lot of resources.

In this worked example, you'll walk through the needs assessment from start to finish and see the team's strategy plan, data collection and analysis methods, findings, conclusions, recommendations, and results report summary. You'll experience a small team's practical approach to tackling a critical business problem with a needs assessment—while operating on a shoestring.

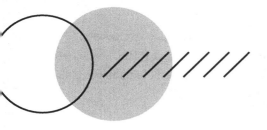

Background

This fictional customer service department is the frontline help center at an employee assistance program (EAP) provider that was founded in 1996 in Knoxville, Tennessee. Company growth was steady until the COVID-19 pandemic, with consistent profit margins from 1997 to 2020. The customer service department provides 24/7 customer support via phone, email, and online chat. The department experienced major setbacks in 2020 due to unprecedented customer support demands for virtual healthcare resources.

Prior to 2020, all employees were required to work on-site. Technology limitations made the shift to unplanned mandatory remote work even more difficult. These challenges resulted in financial losses, and a hiring freeze was implemented between January and September 2021. From 2020 to 2021, the customer service department's employee turnover rate increased by 7 percent while demands for customer support increased by 120 percent. Turnover during the hiring freeze created an even larger workforce gap.

The CEO mandated employees to return to the office in March 2022, but after two years of working from home, the majority of employees were reluctant. As of April 2023, employees continue to request remote work options. Especially for those who joined the company before 2020, frustration with the in-office mandate is building into resentment. Company wide, employee satisfaction ratings have decreased, turnover has increased, morale is low, and performance is suffering.

Historically, the customer service department had the highest employee turnover in the company—around 30 percent—but that rate was on par with industry benchmarks. During the director's first four years at the company (2015–2019), employee satisfaction was measured at slightly above average. However, the department's turnover rate has increased by 13 percentage points since January 2020 and is currently at 43 percent. Business forecasts recommended increasing headcount based on sales volume, but turnover continues to increase the workforce gap. The department is currently failing all key performance indicator (KPI) standards, and the latest customer satisfaction report shows a trend of steep decline.

The director's intervention attempts did not yield positive results, so the problem was escalated to the chief human resource officer (CHRO), who determined that a needs assessment was warranted and assembled a project team.

She directed the team to decide which factors were most affecting retention and to recommend solutions that could be implemented quickly.

Stakeholders

After a financial intervention pilot program including merit increases, KPI incentives, and signing bonuses failed to reduce the department's turnover rate or workforce gap, the director determined that the underlying problem was the large amount of information that new hires had to learn before they could start doing their jobs. He pushed the internal functional training team to create a new onboarding course on an accelerated development schedule and began assigning it to all new hires the day it was published in the learning management system (LMS). But after six months with no improvement in the turnover rate or workforce gap, he deemed the new training course a failure.

During the six months between implementation and evaluation, the instructional designer who built the new course researched needs assessments. She'd learned the basics during her master's program, but realized it was time to learn more after she was asked to build an urgent training solution without conducting a needs assessment. The customer service director told her about the financial intervention pilot program *after* the new onboarding course she designed launched. And she would have responded to his training request differently if she'd known that the financial incentives had failed. She thought the turnover problem was likely more complex than the new hires' knowledge gap. She was disappointed that the new employee training evaluation showed no improvements in the turnover rate, so, when the problem escalated and the new CHRO gave her the opportunity to serve as the needs assessment project lead, she was determined to find a better solution.

As the company's only instructional designer, she'd been a "team of one" in the HR functional training group since 2019. To prepare for this project, she expanded her research by interviewing four practitioners in her professional network about needs assessment best practices. The CHRO, who had joined the company a few weeks prior, immediately planned several company-wide needs assessments to examine employee retention, workplace culture, and remote work. The instructional designer wanted to gain experience and develop her capabilities by contributing to those initiatives.

The CHRO added three members to the team:
- The customer service department's HR business partner, who started his career in a support center
- The employee engagement manager, who would be an advocate for the customer service managers who recently reached out for help
- The HR analyst, who would serve as a research methodology subject matter expert (SME)

The customer service director was assigned as the project sponsor. The instructional designer hoped the effort she put into building the new employee training course would help her build trust with the director.

The customer service director joined the company in 2015. During his first five years, the department met or exceeded its KPIs. He was frustrated that the financial incentives pilot program and the new employee training course failed to improve the retention problem, and he was under enormous pressure to turn things around immediately. The CEO had given company directors a performance grace period due to setbacks beyond their control, but that grace period had just ended—and customer service employee retention, KPIs, and customer satisfaction rates were at all-time lows. A needs assessment seemed like an overly complicated waste of time. He already knew that he needed to reduce turnover and improve performance, but he didn't know how to do that with the less than $15,000 left in his budget for solutions. How could a group of people outside his department solve the retention problem in several weeks when none of his efforts over the last year had worked?

Team Expectations and Communication

The project lead gathered assigned team members for a brief intake meeting to define roles and expectations. She created a RACI (responsible, accountable, consulted, and informed) chart to describe each team member's role (Table B-1). Note: You can create multiple RACI charts for the project overview, key milestones, and important tasks.

The project lead then created Table B-2 to record data collection tasks. (Note: She consulted and informed the C and I stakeholders during the data collection phase.)

Table B-1. RACI Chart: Project Overview

Title	Department	Needs Assessment Role	RACI
Director	Customer service	Stakeholder and primary sponsor	A, C, I
Business partner	Human resources	Stakeholder and cross-functional department partner	C, I
Employee engagement manager	Human resources	Stakeholder, cross-functional department partner, and champion	R, C, I
Analyst	Human resources	Collaborator and research methods SME	R, C
Instructional designer	Functional training team (HR)	Project lead and needs assessment practitioner	R
Chief HR officer	Human resources	Stakeholder and advisor	C, I

Table B-2. RACI Matrix: Data Collection Responsibilities

Team Member	Tasks	RACI
Employee engagement manager	• Compile HR notes and employee retention data; ensure identifying details are removed as needed. • Assist with the design of surveys, focus groups, and interview questions.	R
Analyst	• Synthesize HR notes; conduct retention data analysis and create reports. • Design data collection instruments. • Send survey links to participants, collect and analyze responses, provide results along with response data files.	R
Instructional designer	• Continue to manage the needs assessment project. • Develop questions for surveys, focus groups, and interviews. • Pilot test data collection instruments. • Request documents from the business analytics (BA) team. • Manage schedules and logistics for focus groups and interviews. • Conduct interviews and facilitate focus groups. • Organize data into a shared project folder; document all datasets.	R

Once roles were defined, the team set communication expectations. The CHRO planned to begin a related company-wide needs assessment in six weeks and wanted to build on the results of this project. The employee turnover problem was both a high priority and urgent, so the team would have to operate on an accelerated timeline of four weeks. Team communication was critical for the success of this project. Everyone committed to staying available during the entire project and dedicating the time required each day to keep the work on track. The project lead created a private Slack channel, and the team agreed to use it as the primary method for daily communication and progress updates. She also created a board in the project management system and a shared drive for all project files. Stakeholders requested a kickoff meeting to formalize the project kickoff, regular status updates, and a results report. In addition, the project lead requested an after-action review. Table B-3 presents a summary of the team's communication expectations.

Table B-3. Communication Plan

Communication	Audience	Purpose and Content	Method
Project kickoff	Full project team	• Discuss needs assessment purpose, scope, success measures, and resources.	Meeting
Progress updates	Stakeholders	• Communicate progress updates. • Request support if needed; discuss roadblocks if applicable.	Project lead will send a brief update report via slack
Results report	Stakeholders	• Share needs assessment results and recommendations. • Discuss next steps for implementing solutions.	Meeting (results report presentation and delivery)
After-action review	Full project team	• Review successes, lessons learned, and improvement opportunities. • Determine how the project's results further serve the organization. • Discuss next steps.	Meeting

During the initial intake conversation, the project lead facilitated the team's discussions to align on roles, responsibilities, and communication expectations, and then she scheduled the project kickoff meeting for the following day to officially begin the needs assessment.

Aligning on Strategy and Mitigating Bias

The needs assessment team had to align on strategy immediately to meet their tight deadline. Stakes were high, time was short, and everyone was new to the needs assessment process. Complicating matters, the sponsoring stakeholder was skeptical of the project and unwilling to consider the impact of employees' increasing frustrations with the company's return to the office mandate as a factor in contributing to the retention problem.

He told the team that he thought demanding to work from home was ludicrous. When the department was working remotely during the pandemic, he found it impossible to know if employees were working or not. Also, the CEO told everyone to come back to the office, so he didn't understand why employees kept arguing about working from home. He wanted to find a solution to improve retention for people who were willing to come to the office to work.

The project lead believed that remote work options were a crucial need for the entire company. She thought that the director's attitude showed a lack of awareness and concern about his employees' realities, especially those who still needed to manage virtual school during work hours while they were isolated at home with their children. However, she had learned enough about needs assessments to know that strategy planning was not the time to debate solutions. And that even if the sponsor did not like her response, it was important to be honest and explain that the team could not ignore the remote work issue if it was relevant to the retention problem. She explained that data collection would likely include asking employees about remote work as a retention factor because it was necessary to include known or assumed factors when trying to identify the unknown ones. She assured the sponsor that while the team probably would recommend a company-wide solution related to remote work, 90 percent of their recommendation efforts would be spent identifying other solutions that he could implement quickly for his department. She asked if he would be willing to consider key findings related to remote work after the team provided him with other recommendations, and he reluctantly agreed.

The project lead knew that the CHRO was planning a needs assessment to address remote work, so any relevant data collected or insights gained during this project could be applied to that upcoming initiative. It was her job to keep the current team focused on the immediate need to improve employee retention in the customer service department, so she redirected the conversation to project scope and research methodology. The kickoff meeting started off shaky, but by effectively mitigating biases—the sponsor's as well as her own—she was able to keep the team on track.

Needs Assessment Strategy

After the kickoff meeting, the project lead created a strategy plan for the needs assessment (Table B-4). The project lead added value measures after the work was complete, and she continued to refer to this strategy plan as she later wrote the results report and prepared for the next needs assessment project.

Table B-4. Strategy Plan

Problem
The primary problem is employee retention. The department needs to improve their employee turnover rate by at least 13 percent and close the current workforce gap so they can meet customer service demands and KPI standards.
Business Impact
Turnover is causing the existing workforce gap to grow; this gap will continue to increase until turnover decreases. The cost to recruit and hire each new employee equates to 6 to 9 months of the role's salary. High employee turnover is causing steep performance declines. Service level KPIs have not been met since January 2020. Customer satisfaction rates have decreased from 86 percent in January 2020 to the current rate of 68 percent (17 percent below KPI standard of 85 percent).
Current State
The current employee turnover rate is 43 percent. The workforce gap (15 percent) did not exist prior to 2020. Current headcount is 131 (1 director, 9 managers, and 121 frontline employees). The forecasted headcount recommended to meet customer support needs is 153 (1 director, 12 managers, and 140 frontline employees). HR is actively recruiting for 3 managers and 19 frontline employees.
Goal State
The turnover rate will be 32 percent or less and continue to stabilize at that rate or below. The department will be fully staffed within 12 to 18 months (the workforce gap will no longer exist). Employee satisfaction rates will increase. Department KPIs and customer satisfaction rates will meet or exceed standards.

Table B-4. (Cont.)

Known Gaps The department's turnover increases and workforce gap began in 2020 and were compounded during a hiring freeze in 2021. Employees have been requesting remote work options since the return to the office mandate was implemented in March 2022. Over the last year, the department has implemented 4 intervention solutions—signing bonuses, merit increases, KPI incentives, and new onboarding training—but these solutions have not improved employee retention.
Project Team • Director, customer service department (sponsoring stakeholder) • HR business partner (key stakeholder and customer support center SME) • Employee engagement manager (key stakeholder and champion) • Chief human resource officer (advisor) • Instructional designer, functional training team (needs assessment project lead) • Analyst, human resources (research methodology SME)
Primary Research Question What factors, in addition to remote work options, are contributing most to the increasing employee turnover rate?
Data Collection • Documents: Employee data and HR notes, KPI reports, and customer satisfaction reports • Surveys: Frontline employees and managers • Focus group: Frontline employees • Interviews: Director, managers, HR business partner, and employee engagement manager
Analysis Plan • Documents analyzed by the project lead, HR analyst, and stakeholders • Survey data analyzed with Excel and the tools in the survey tool (HR analyst) • Qualitative data transcribed, coded, and synthesized (project lead and stakeholders)
Scope Determine which factors, in addition to the known factor of remote work preferences, are contributing most significantly to the increasing employee turnover rate. Determine solutions (in addition and unrelated to remote work options) to mitigate employee turnover.

Timeline	Budget	Resources Available
4 weeks	• $400 for focus groups refreshments • Solutions budget: $12,000	Survey platform with built-in analysis tools

Plans for Sharing Results Results report delivered to stakeholders

Table B-4. (Cont.)

Constraints (Limitations and Delimitations)
The department is responsible for providing 24/7 customer support, so employee time away from support calls must be scheduled at least a week in advance and approved by the manager. Given the accelerated timeline limitation of 4 weeks to complete this project, any interviews or focus groups need to be scheduled immediately. The needs assessment project lead will prioritize data collection to begin as quickly as possible.

Success Metrics to Evaluate Solutions
• Some improvements made in employee turnover within 3 months. • Continuous improvement measured at 6, 9, and 12 months. • Goal reached within 12 to 18 months. • Solutions budget cannot exceed $12,000. • We expect that employee retention improvements will result in a workforce gap reduction, KPI improvements, and increased customer satisfaction rates.

Needs Assessment Value Measures
• Analytics from HR and BA teams leveraged quickly and effectively. • Project completed within 4 weeks (accelerated timeline due to problem urgency). • Mitigating factors identified; feasible solutions for improvements recommended. • These results will be used for a company-wide needs assessment launching next month to examine employee retention, company culture, and remote work options.

Insights Exercise

After the kickoff meeting, the project lead realized that she needed a lot more background information—it suddenly dawned on her that she'd never even set foot on the customer service floor. She remembered a needs assessment exercise about insight categories (contextual, organizational, operational, and individual) for considering the big picture of a problem.

She brainstormed a list of insight gaps and then narrowed it down to four categories of 10 insights she could learn about quickly.

Contextual insight

1. Why is a 30 percent turnover rate acceptable in the customer support industry?
2. What strategies have other companies found for reducing turnover?
3. When you quit a customer service job, can you find another one easily? With such high turnover, are there stigmas or tolerances if you've resigned or been let go?

Organizational insight

4. What skills and experience are required for a customer service associate at our company? Who are we trying to hire?
5. What is the hiring process, and what is that experience like for candidates?
6. Why did our CEO mandate in-office work when most employees want to work remotely? Does he have a good reason for enforcing such an unpopular decision?

Operational insight

7. How does the customer service department manage 24/7 coverage? I know they work in three shifts, but how do they handle all the operational demands?
8. How many calls, emails, and chats does an employee usually answer every day?
9. What is the physical work environment like?

Individual insight

10. Answering support calls for eight hours a day, five days a week sounds tedious and draining, especially for people on the night shift. What are the pros of this job? What parts do people enjoy?

For questions 1 through 10, the instructional designer would meet the customer service director on the department floor for a tour and a short coffee chat. Then, she'd compare his thoughts with the HR business partner's thoughts (which she'd get after the customer service visit). For questions 1, 2, and 4, she planned to request 15 minutes with the CHRO to discuss. Then, she'd compare her thoughts with the employee engagement manager's ideas.

The customer service tour helped her understand the physical work environment, and the director appreciated her asking about department operations instead of only asking about turnover. She gained a lot of background knowledge through a few quick meetings with stakeholders. After this insights exercise, she was better prepared to start the data collection plan.

Data Collection

Table B-5 is a worked example of the team's data collection plan. For each research question, they identified where they could find the information (data sources) and a strategy to gather that information (data collection method).

Table B-5. Data Collection Plan

Primary research question: What factors, in addition to remote work options, are contributing most to the increasing employee turnover rate?		
Subquestions	**Data Source**	**Data Collection Methods**
How has the turnover rate changed over time? How does the rate increase compare to other departments? Are there relevant trends or mitigating factors?	**Human resources:** Employee retention data, exit interview notes, training records, job descriptions, recruiting notes, performance improvement plans, and observations	• The HR analyst will compile a data report and upload it with any additional relevant files to the project's shared drive.
What aspects of customer service work are the most difficult, frustrating, or demoralizing? What would help improve the day-to-day job experience?	**Business analytics:** KPI reports and customer survey reports **Customer service:** Recorded customer calls, emails, and chat logs; QA checklist and job aid **Human resources:** HR data summary report (analyst will upload)	• The BA team manager will email department KPI reports and customer satisfaction reports. • The customer service director will upload QA samples and job aids to the shared drive. • These will be used as participant-facing questions in the surveys, focus groups, and interviews.
What do the department director, managers, frontline employees, and HR team believe is contributing to the turnover rate?	**Project stakeholders, customer service staff, and human resources:** HR data summary report (analyst will upload)	• Surveys will be emailed to managers and frontline employees. • There will be 3 focus groups (1 per shift) with 6–9 participants in each and a purposeful sampling of frontline employees. • Interviews will be conducted with the HR business partner, employee engagement manager, department managers, and director.
Data collection constraints: To focus on employee data trends since the hiring freeze was lifted, employee data from prior to October 2021 will not be included.		

The needs assessment team planned to use surveys, focus groups, and interviews, so they had to develop *participant-facing* questions—the questions they would ask participants to address the *project-facing* research questions. Table B-6 provides some examples of participant-facing questions the team used for the frontline employee focus group and survey.

Table B-6. Participant-Facing Research Questions

Research Question What do frontline employees believe is contributing to the turnover rate?
Focus Group Questions • What things do you look forward to when coming to work? • Tell us about a time when you were recognized for your contributions. • What do you like least about your job? • What's the most difficult part of your job? • How do you measure success in your role? • What support or resources do you need most to succeed in this role? • If you could change one thing about how things work in the department, what would it be and why? • What's one thing you'd like your managers to know? • What additional comments would you like to share today?

Survey Question Examples
• In the last 30 days, how many times have you considered searching for a new job?
  ☐ *Never*   ☐ *Once*   ☐ *Twice*   ☐ *Three times or more*
 	
• How would you describe your usual stress level at work over the last 30 days?
  ☐ Very high stress   ☐ High stress   ☐ Moderate stress   ☐ Low stress
 	
• How would you currently describe employee morale in your department?
  ☐ Very high morale   ☐ High morale   ☐ Moderate morale   ☐ Low morale
 	
• What do you believe contributes to employee morale?
 	
• To what extent do the following factors contribute to your current job satisfaction?
(Likert Scale: Very important, important, slightly important, or not important)
  ◦ Company mission   ◦ Remote work options   ◦ Performance goals
  ◦ Department culture   teammates   ◦ Workload
  ◦ Salary   ◦ Managers
  ◦ Benefits   ◦ Training

Data Analysis

The team's data analysis plan summarizes the actions they decided to take to analyze the data they collected for this needs assessment project (Table B-7).

Dataset Summary

The project lead created a simple dataset summary to keep track of all the data that she and the team collected for this needs assessment (see Table B-8 on page 226). A dataset summary can help you stay organized, define follow-up action items, capture important notes, identify gaps, and ensure you have the tools and resources needed for analysis and quality assurance. If you collect additional opportunity data during the needs assessment, add it to your dataset summary.

Table B-7. Data Analysis Plan

Research Questions	Data Source (What was collected?)	Data Analysis (How will the data be analyzed?)	Application (How will the analysis results be used?)
• How has the turnover rate changed over time? • How does the rate increase compare to other departments? • Are there relevant trends or mitigating factors?	Reports containing numerical data: • KPI reports • Customer satisfaction reports • Employee retention data	HR analyst: • Excel and Qualtrics • Data will be compared with other findings to examine the why of trends.	• Create visual charts to show trends over time. • Include notes relevant to trends from the survey, focus groups, and interviews.
• What aspects of customer service work are the most difficult, frustrating, or demoralizing? • What would help improve the day-to-day job experience?	• Data reports • Recorded customer calls, emails, and chatlogs • QA checklist and job aids • HR data summary report	• Documents and audio recordings will be reviewed and coded multiple times to identify themes.	• Themes are illustrated and will be compared with quantitative data to explain causes and trends.
• What do the department director, managers, frontline employees, and HR team believe is contributing to the turnover rate?	• HR notes summary document • Interview and focus group notes • Employee survey responses	• Document will be reviewed, coded, and compared with other datasets. • Focus group and interview notes will be reviewed and coded multiple times. • Survey results will be analyzed using the software's tools; qualitative responses will be reviewed and coded multiple times.	• Identify themes, patterns, or other meaningful data points related to the participants' experiences and department's history, as well as any challenges, gaps, and key needs.

Table B-8. Dataset Summary

Project Folder Link	Dataset 1 (4 work product sets)	Dataset 2 (2 surveys)	Dataset 3 (12 interviews)	Dataset 4 (3 focus groups)

Dataset contents	• Department KPI reports (last 12 months)
	• Customer satisfaction reports (last 12 months)
	• HR data summary (since October 2021)
	• Customer service QA review calls and job aids
		• A copy of each survey and invitation email
		• Employee survey:
		  ○ 121 sent
		  ○ 65 started
		  ○ 47 complete
		• Manager survey:
		  ○ 9 sent
		  ○ 7 started
		  ○ 6 complete
		• Consolidated responses compiled in a .csv file
		• Individual responses (53 .csv files)
			• Participants' contact info and dates of interviews
			• Interviewer guide
			• Notes from 12 interviews (30 minutes each)
				• Participants' contact info and focus group dates
				• Facilitator guide
				• Notes from 3 focus groups (45 minutes each)
				• 22 total participants:
				  ○ First shift: 6
				  ○ Second shift: 9
				  ○ Third shift: 7

Errors and usability	Employee retention records reformatted from YY/MM/DD to MM/DD/YY	Review partially completed surveys for usability.	Interview 4: Only 6 of 7 questions were answered due to time constraints.	N/A
Action items	Do not include data from before October 2021.	Calculate response and completion rates.	Responses must remain confidential; summarize notes so direct quotes or details do not identify participants.	
Important notes	During each focus group, employees expressed concerns about their responses being shared with management. The HR business partners emailed participants to reassure them that their feedback will remain confidential.			

The needs assessment's team research methodology SME, the HR analyst, calculated the response and completion rates for each survey to determine how many of the target participants were represented in the results (Table B-9).

Table B-9. Survey Response Rates and Completion Rates

Target *(The total number of surveys sent)*	Response Rate *(Target ÷ Number of surveys opened × 100)*	Completion Rate *(Number of surveys opened ÷ Number of surveys completed × 100)*
We sent 2 versions of our survey because we had 2 distinct participant groups: • Survey 1 was sent to 121 frontline employees. • Survey 2 was sent to 9 managers.	• 65 of the 121 frontline employees opened or started the survey. The response rate was 54 percent. • 7 of the 9 managers opened or started the survey. The response rate was 78 percent.	• 47 of the 65 frontline employees who opened or started the survey answered every question. The completion rate was 72 percent. • 6 of the 7 managers who opened or started the survey answered every question. The completion rate was 86 percent.

The HR analyst examined responses from each of the target groups—frontline employees and managers. While the response and completion rates were high, according to the survey math, the team only received responses from approximately half the employees they tried to reach. However, this data was still useful for the needs assessment because the survey wasn't the only method used to collect data. The team was able to compare and triangulate survey results to work products and documents as well as interview and focus group responses.

Findings and Conclusions

The team identified themes, trends, and responses from each dataset and then compiled the most relevant findings into one list organized by dataset. To provide a rich description of key findings from the manager interviews dataset, they consolidated responses into an excerpt summary based on the managers' own words. Table B-10 shows a comparison of key findings from three of the datasets the team analyzed for this needs assessment, followed by an example interview excerpt.

Table B-10. Findings

Documents and Work Products Dataset

- The current employee turnover rate is 43 percent:
  - There has been a 6 percent increase in turnover since October 2021
  - "Lack of remote work options" is the most frequent reason given when employees resign or candidates turn down job offers.
- Forecasting based on customer demand recommends a department headcount of 140 frontline employees and 12 managers:
  - Current headcount is 121 frontline employees and 9 managers (15 percent workforce gap).
  - The cost to hire a new employee equates to 6–9 months of the role's salary.
- These service level KPIs have not been met since January 2020:
  - **Call availability.** Average wait time increased from 2 to 4 minutes (100 percent increase). The KPI standard is less than 2 minutes.
  - **Average handling rate.** Call times have increased from 7 to 11 minutes (83 percent increase). The KPI standard is less than 6 minutes.
  - **First-call resolution rates.** These have decreased from 74 percent to 63 percent (14 percent decrease). The KPI standard is 85 percent.
- The customer satisfaction rate dropped from 86 percent in January 2020 to the current rate of 68 percent. This is 17 percent below the KPI standard (85 percent).

Employee Survey Dataset

- 47 of 121 current frontline employees completed the needs assessment survey:
  - In the last 30 days, 39 respondents (82 percent) have considered resigning.
  - 42 respondents (91 percent) reported increased stress levels.
  - 37 respondents (78 percent) reported low department morale. The remaining 22 percent reported moderate morale. No employees reported high morale.
- Respondents were asked to rate 10 factors that contribute to job satisfaction on a Likert scale of importance. Four factors received the highest rating ("very important") from 35 respondents or more (which represents more than 75 percent):
  - **Remote work options:** 43 respondents (92 percent)
  - **Managers:** 40 respondents (86 percent)
  - **Department culture:** 37 respondents (78 percent)
  - **Performance goals:** 36 respondents (76 percent)
- Employees attribute turnover and performance problems to a lack of support from managers. They expressed a need for more help and guidance.
- Employees are unsure if their performance is being measured by accurate resolution rates, total call time, customer hold times, or other QA metrics.

Table B-10. (Cont.)

Manager Interviews Dataset
• Managers report that heavy workload demands prevent them from having enough time to help staff. They cannot assist with HR recruitment interviews and plan 24/7 coverage work schedules while accounting for employees' paid time off (PTO) requests and conducting QA reviews for calls and emails. • Managers do not have access to the department KPI reports and are not sure which items on the internal QA scoring rubric count toward those company KPIs. • Managers also report that they do not have time to collaborate and that time is not available to meet with their director. • Managers continue to receive requests for remote work options, and employees are frustrated and disgruntled by the in-office requirement. Managers want employees (and themselves) to be able to work from home at least 2 to 3 days a week, but they don't know how to support employees in a remote work model. • Managers feel powerless to advocate for their teams.

Interview Excerpt

This interview excerpt example is a compilation summary of all nine managers' responses to interview question 3: "I'm hoping to get a sense of the demands on your time and the things you're responsible for. Can you describe your current workload and pain points?"

"We try to help our teams as much as we can. They need a lot of help—half of them are brand new, some have worked here for about six months, and some have worked here for a couple years. We know they need more help, and they get frustrated when we don't have time, but we don't think they understand how many other things the managers need to do. A lot of employees have quit, so we spend a lot of time reviewing potential candidates and conducting hiring interviews with our HR recruiter. It's so hard to hire people when everyone wants to work from home, and honestly, since we all got company cell phones and the IT systems were all updated last year, there's really no reason we can't work from home. We proved we could during the pandemic, so it seems unfair not to have that option anymore. It's like we're being punished for sticking with the company through the pandemic. Our teams ask all the time when they can work from home again, and they seem to think we're the ones deciding that they can't. We'd love for everyone to be able to work remotely—but we can't convince the CEO and we don't know how to support our employees working remotely when we don't even have time to support them when we're all here in the same place at the office. The managers build the work schedules—we need to cover phones 24/7, plan for employees' PTO requests, and have backup plans if someone gets sick or has an emergency. There are 121 employees and only nine of us, and because managers work in three different shifts, we don't usually get to meet or work together as a group. The nine of us also need to complete dozens of quality assurance review checklists every week—we listen to recorded calls and review customer emails and chat logs with a QA scoring rubric. We all want to know how those scores are used by upper management. We are told that we're not meeting KPIs, but we don't know where we're performing worse than we used to. Managers don't have access to the BA reports, so we don't know how to explain the KPIs and QA scores to our employees. They think we're keeping that information secret and just don't want to help them or explain the scoring. We do want to help them—and we don't want anyone else to quit—but we don't have enough time or information. And we can't tell them that our director puts too much work on us or that he doesn't share the department reports with us. Comments like that sound like gossip or complaining and will make department morale even worse. And none of us have enough time with our director to really know what's going on at his level. We haven't even had time for our one-on-one meetings for the last month. We've all been pitching in on the floor even more than usual because we're so short staffed right now."

Conclusions

After the team identified key findings from each dataset, they grouped those findings into three categories based on the business impact of the turnover problem: employee retention, department performance, and customer satisfaction. They listed the key findings for each category and synthesized those findings into conclusions. Then they checked assumptions and brainstormed solutions for each conclusion. This example shows their conclusions and the key findings they included to support each one.

Employee Retention

The current employee turnover rate (43 percent) and workforce gap (15 percent) are critical business risks requiring immediate intervention. The department does not have the people resources required to meet our company's customer service expectations. Turnover is affecting the company's talent recruitment budget—each new hire costs six to nine months of the role's salary. Department turnover is trending upward, and 81 percent of current employees and managers have considered resigning in the last 30 days.

Employees and managers report increased stress levels, decreased morale, ambiguous performance metrics, and lack of support from leaders. Managers report burdensome workloads and competing responsibilities that prevent them from supporting employees. The most important factors for job satisfaction reported by frontline employees were remote work options, managers, department culture, and performance goals. The most important factors for job satisfaction reported by managers were remote work options, workload, performance goals, and department culture.

Key Findings

From 2020 to 2021, demands for customer support increased by 120 percent; the customer service workforce did not increase as needed to meet current demand. Employee turnover increased during the pandemic, and the company mandated a hiring freeze in 2021. The department has been playing catch up since then.

- The current turnover rate is 43 percent (6 percent increase since October 2021). The target rate is 32 percent or lower based on the BA team's analysis of KPIs, customer demand, and industry benchmarks.
- Business forecasting recommends department staffing levels at 140 frontline employees and 12 managers. Current headcount is 121 frontline employees and nine managers.
- HR is actively recruiting for 19 frontline employees and three managers:
  - Each employee separation offsets a new hire. The workforce gap will continue to grow if turnover does not improve.
  - The cost to hire a new employee equates to six to nine months of the role's salary.

- Department turnover is trending upward:
  - Combined, 81 percent of current staff—82 percent of employees and 79 percent of managers—have considered resigning at least once in the last 30 days.
  - 91 percent of employees reported increased stress levels.
  - 76 percent of employees reported low morale, 22 percent reported moderate morale, and no employees reported high morale.
  - Employees and managers report having ambiguous performance goals. They are unsure of how internal QA scores affect department KPIs and lack clarity about how their performance is being measured.
  - Employees attribute performance declines and decreased job satisfaction to a lack of support from their managers.
  - Managers report demanding workloads and competing responsibilities that limit the time they can spend supporting employees, including on quality assurance reviews, work shift scheduling, and employee recruitment and hiring.
- Frontline employees reported these job satisfaction factors as the most important:
  - Remote work options (92 percent)
  - Managers (86 percent)
  - Department culture (78 percent)
  - Performance goals (76 percent)
- Managers reported these job satisfaction factors as the most important:
  - Remote work options (90 percent)
  - Workload (92 percent)
  - Performance goals (86 percent)
  - Department culture (81 percent)
- Managers and frontline employees both reported the lack of remote work options as the most important factor in turnover, workforce gaps, low department morale, and job satisfaction. The HR team reported this trend across all departments.

Department Performance

Employee turnover (43 percent) and the workforce gap (15 percent) are causing department performance failures. KPIs are not being met. Service level

KPIs (call availability, average handling rate, and first-call resolution rates) are significantly below the acceptable rates. Department workforce headcount is determined by customer call volume and support demand, which has increased by 120 percent since 2020. To meet customer needs, the turnover rate must increase by 11 percent or more and the workforce gap must improve by at least 10 percent.

Key Findings

The department's KPIs have fallen farther below target rates over the last 12 months. KPIs were not met during the previous 12-month period and improvements are expected this year. However, the department is currently failing every service level KPI:

- **Call availability.** Average wait times have increased from two minutes to four minutes (100 percent increase). The acceptable standard is less than two minutes.
- **Average handling rate.** Call times have increased from seven minutes to 11 minutes (83 percent increase). The acceptable standard is less than six minutes.
- **First-call resolution rates.** Resolution rates have decreased from 74 percent to 63 percent (14 percent decrease). The acceptable standard is 85 percent.

Customer Satisfaction

The customer service department is the customer-facing arm of our company, and the department's performance directly influences customer satisfaction, sales, and profit. The department's current performance is negatively affecting customer's perceptions of and satisfaction with the services our company provides. The current customer satisfaction rate has dropped to 68 percent. Solutions are required to improve department performance to improve the customer satisfaction rate to an acceptable level (85 percent or more).

Key Findings

Business analytics correlate declines in sales and profit with a customer satisfaction rate below 85 percent. The current customer satisfaction rate is 68 percent.

Challenging Assumptions

Before the team brainstormed solutions, they summarized their conclusions and checked their assumptions. This exercise helped them identify solutions informed by data. This example provides an excerpt of the team's discussion, including the factors they considered to challenge their assumptions for each conclusion.

Conclusion 1

The current employee turnover rate (43 percent) and the workforce gap (15 percent) are critical business risks requiring immediate intervention. The department does not have the people resources required to meet our company's customer service expectations. Turnover is affecting the company's talent recruitment budget—each new hire costs six to nine months of the role's salary. Department turnover is trending upward, and 81 percent of current employees and managers have considered resigning in the last 30 days.

Can we be certain that employee turnover is increasing as reported in our conclusion? We have a high degree of certainty because we reviewed official HR data reports from the HR analyst and the customer service director.

Was the department's performance decline caused by employee turnover? Although we're not certain, we know that KPIs metrics have decreased during the same period that employee turnover and customer demand have both increased. From performance improvement research, we know that high employee turnover results in financial and productivity costs. New employees need time to learn the job and gain experience in skillfully addressing customer concerns. Managers spend more time hiring and training new employees, so they have less time to provide support and coaching to current employees. Turnover can also lower morale, which can decrease productivity.

Is the turnover problem currently a high risk for the business? We know that BA and HR forecasts are based on KPI data, sales volume, and anticipated demands for customer support, so we are confident that the recommendations to reduce turnover and close the workforce gap are aligned with business needs.

Conclusion 2

Employee turnover (43 percent) and the workforce gap (15 percent) are causing department performance failures. KPIs are not being met. Service level KPIs (call availability, average handling rate, and first-call resolution rates) are significantly below the acceptable rates. Department workforce headcount is determined by customer call volume and support demand, which has increased by 120 percent since 2020. To meet customer needs, the turnover rate must increase by 11 percent or more and the workforce gap must improve by at least 10 percent.

Can we be certain that department performance is causing the decrease in customer satisfaction? Maybe customers are angry about increased fees, or frustrated with product offerings, and reporting low satisfaction after calls with support staff who cannot fix those problems. In the absence of data concerning customers' specific complaints, we made the most reasonable conclusion (based on employee feedback, interviews with the director and managers, and department KPI reports) that increased wait times, increased call times, and fewer first-call resolutions were contributing to customer dissatisfaction.

Conclusion 3

Department performance is causing declines in customer satisfaction. The current customer satisfaction rate has dropped to 68 percent. Solutions are required to improve department performance before the customer satisfaction rate will increase to an acceptable level (85 percent or more).

Can we be certain that department KPIs are not being met? We have a high degree of certainty because we were able to access and analyze KPI data reports and review them with the customer service director. However, if these reports were inaccurate, then our conclusions are faulty. Unless we saw red flags concerning data quality in the KPI reports, though, we assumed that they were accurate.

Recommendations

If the needs assessment team's conclusions are accurate, and effective solutions are implemented, they expect to see improvements in the customer service department's employee retention rate and workforce gap and, consequently, improvements in the department's performance and customer satisfaction. For each solution that is implemented, the team will benchmark the turnover rate, workforce gap, KPI scores, and customer satisfaction rates at the point of implementation and then after three, six, nine, 12, and 18 months to measure impact.

Previous solutions that attempted to improve employee turnover included financial interventions (merit increases, KPI incentives, and signing bonuses) as well as a new onboarding training course that was designed to help new hires learn the key information and skills needed to do their jobs quickly. None of these solutions proved effective, so the needs assessment team brainstormed solutions to address different root causes; they focused on department culture, leadership development, and process improvement.

The team categorized their recommendations as internal solutions, external solutions, and executive leadership solutions. Internal solutions require interdepartmental cooperation to provide *borrowed* support for the customer service department for a short intervention period. The external solution requires *buying* training with a cost of $10,850, which meets the project budget requirement (less than $12,000). The executive leadership solution requires the CEO to reconsider the mandate against remote work and authorize *building* a hybrid work pilot program.

This executive leadership solution encompasses needs outside the scope of this project—remote work issues are a company-wide concern, but our recommendation could potentially improve the customer service employee retention problem, which was in this needs assessment's scope. After reviewing findings and conclusions, the customer service director acknowledged that remote work did appear to be an important factor for employee retention, job satisfaction, and hiring in his department. He agreed to participate in a hybrid work pilot program if the CEO approved.

Table B-11 presents the team's recommendations for improving the customer service employee retention rate and workforce gap through efforts that borrow internal solutions. These are the easiest of the recommended solutions to implement.

These borrowed solutions provide much-needed support for the customer service department, but they cost resources and potential productivity for the HR, functional training, BA, and marketing teams. When recommending internal solutions, be careful not to assign burden without first discussing bandwidth—the resources you're *borrowing* will not appreciate being voluntold to cooperate. Provide those giving (employee engagement and retainment, positive workplace culture, customer service strategies, and stress management) *and* receiving support with clear expectations, details of the request, and a cut-off date. Put limitations in place so no one is borrowed to the point that their own performance suffers.

Table B-11. Borrow—Internal Solutions

Employee Retention	• HR intervention • Functional training team support

- Due to the severity of the business impact of increasing employee turnover, an immediate HR intervention is recommended.
- The employee engagement manager will schedule biweekly coaching sessions with each manager for the next 8 weeks. Coaching will include strategies for managing demanding workloads, supporting employees, and having difficult conversations when employees bring up issues affecting job satisfaction that are beyond managers' control.
- HR will conduct stay interviews and deploy other engagement strategies to retain current managers and frontline employees.
- HR will shorten the time required of customer service managers for evaluating and interviewing potential candidates. The manager will only be asked to participate in final interviews after initial resume reviews, phone screenings, and other hiring assessment steps are complete.
- HR will work with the department director to create a plan for reducing managers' administrative responsibilities so they have more time to support employees. The functional training team can provide 8 hours of support each week for the next 3 months to assist with QA reviews. The HR director will work with the customer service director to implement new responsibility plans with support resources for managers within the next 30 days.
- HR is currently recruiting 3 additional customer service manager roles. We recommend that 2 of those open positions be reposted to hire quality assurance managers instead. This would place more strategic focus on QA and allow current managers to spend more time supporting and coaching frontline employees.
- HR will assess progress after 1, 3, 6, 9, 12, and 18 months. HR will monitor resignations and terminations for the next 18 months, collect exit interview data for each separation, and follow up with department leadership as needed.

Table B-11. (Cont.)

Department Performance	• Business analytics team support • Functional training team support

- The BA team manager will work with the customer service director to review department processes and systems to ensure they are clearly aligned with and providing support for KPIs. They will identify opportunities for easy process improvements within the next 30 days.
- The functional training team will partner with the BA team and customer service managers to create job aids for customer service employees and managers that clearly explain the department's performance metrics and internal QA scores, along with strategies for improvement. These job aids will be completed within 30 to 45 days.
- We recommend a member of the BA team meet with the department director once a month for the next 6 months to review KPIs and customer satisfaction scores. If KPIs don't improve in 6 months, intervention from the CFO is recommended.

Customer Satisfaction	• Marketing support

- We suggest requesting marketing support to gain more insight into the customer satisfaction rate and strategies for improvement.

Table B-12 presents the recommendations that require buying external solutions. These solutions will be harder to implement than the borrowed ones.

Table B-12. Buy—External Solutions

Leadership Training	• Local vendor • $10,850 budget • Three training classes at $3,500 each; $350 for meals

- Provide leadership development training for the department directors and managers focused on employee engagement and retainment, positive workplace culture, customer service strategies, and stress management.
- The vendor will deliver the training classes on-site, which eliminates travel or space rental expenses. The first class can be scheduled within 2 weeks of budget approval and deposit payment.
- The vendor will also include 3 follow-up coaching sessions for each participant at no additional charge.

The company has a dedicated functional training team, but they do not yet have the resources required to deliver leadership development training beyond an introductory course for new and first-time managers. The customer service director and managers need targeted leadership development training to help them lead a team that is understaffed, underperforming, recovering from negative impacts of the COVID-19 pandemic, and facing significant challenges.

We identified and vetted a local vendor who provides leadership training focused on employee engagement and retainment, positive workplace culture, customer service strategies, and stress management. The vendor understands the customer service department's challenges and workforce shortage, and will provide strategies to help department leaders support employees more effectively while also receiving the support they need as leaders. Each training class runs for two days from 8:30 a.m. to 5 p.m. Three classes will be offered to accommodate the department's need for 24/7 coverage; attendees can select the session that works best with their work schedule. Considerations will be made for the two managers who are usually on third shift, as they typically work from midnight to 8 a.m. The maximum budget allowed for solutions is $12,000, so this solution is within scope. We recommend that the customer service director uses the remaining $1,150 on team building activities or employee appreciation activities to boost department morale. The employee engagement manager is available to consult on strategies for spending those funds as effectively as possible.

Table B-13 presents the recommended executive leadership solution. This will be the hardest to implement because it requires convincing the CEO to build a hybrid work pilot program.

Recommending a company-wide solution contradicting the CEO's current stance on the issue was a risk. The pros of a hybrid work pilot program include improving company-wide pain points—increased employee turnover, decreased job acceptance rates for recruits, and employee dissatisfaction and morale. In addition, a compromise is embedded in the solutions—a pilot program, by definition, is an experiment with an end date. If the company tries a hybrid work pilot program and success measures worsen instead of improving, there will be data to validate and explain the rationale for the company's mandate against remote work.

Table B-13. Build—Executive Leadership Solution

CEO and Executive Leaders	• Hybrid work pilot program

- The company's current remote work policy is negatively affecting employee retention, recruitment, and job satisfaction, and these factors are negatively affecting company performance. We are not asking for a full reversal of that policy. However, to meet employees halfway and improve our position as an employer, we recommend that the company implement a hybrid work pilot program that will allow employees to work from home 2 to 3 days a week if performance standards are met.
- Many of our current employees worked here before and during the COVID-19 pandemic and successfully performed their job duties for 2 years while working remotely. We want to retain good employees, and our employees want more flexibility to work from home. A hybrid work environment is not new, experimental, or unconventional; it has become a normal way of working.
- Considering the potential gains—decreased employee turnover and costs required to rehire and retain the same roles, increases in successful employee recruitment efforts, and improvements in morale and our brand as an employer—we expect this pilot program to result in company-wide performance improvements.

Before presenting the idea of a hybrid work pilot program to the CEO, we need to organize a collective appeal from several executive leaders who are aligned on the purpose, benefits, costs, risks, and strategy for implementing the program and are willing to advocate for it. Instead of advocating for that solution now, we will share the results and relevant data from this needs assessment with the CHRO, as she is currently planning a company-wide needs assessment to investigate remote work options. Because the executive leadership solution is sensitive, complex, and large in scale, scope, and risk, we will not include it in our results report, except to mention that remote work is a factor in employee retention, and that the customer service director is willing to participate if remote or hybrid options become available.

Results Report

The team has nearly completed its journey through a needs assessment, but as a final step, the project lead needs to produce a results report that includes an executive summary, which brings everything together into a concise, compelling synopsis.

Executive Summary

What follows is the executive summary of the team's results report. This provides a brief overview of the needs assessment's purpose, background, methods, key findings, and recommendations.

Background

The customer service department provides 24/7 support to our client base via phone, email, and online chat. Customer demands grew exponentially from 2020 to 2021, and during the same period, the department's employee turnover rate increased. Staffing efforts were delayed during the company's hiring freeze. Today, the customer service department has a workforce gap of 15 percent. The employee turnover rate of 43 percent is trending upward as employees report low job satisfaction and low morale. Several attempts to reduce turnover over the last 18 months have not achieved improvements. Department performance is in steep decline; every KPI is below the acceptable threshold. Our current customer satisfaction rate is 68 percent, which is 17 percent below threshold.

Purpose

Employee turnover and workforce gaps in our customer service department have become critical business risks requiring immediate intervention. To meet the demands of our customers and fulfill support expectations based on sales volume, the customer service employee turnover rate must improve by at least 11 percent and the workforce gap must improve by at least 10 percent.

Methods

Over the last four weeks, we conducted an internal needs assessment to determine key factors contributing to employee turnover and to recommend solutions for immediate stopgaps and continuous improvements. Leaders from our human resources, customer service, and business analytics teams compiled and analyzed performance data, employee data, and business forecasts while also conducting surveys, focus groups, and interviews with customer service department employees and managers.

Key Findings

Data analysis resulted in three key findings.

Employee retention is a significant business problem with a high risk of escalation. The department's current employee turnover rate (43 percent) and workforce gap (15 percent) present serious risks for customer support capabilities (Figure B-1). The department is critically understaffed, and high turnover is affecting the talent recruitment budget. Each current employee separation negates a new hire, and the cost to recruit each new hire equates to six to nine months of the role's salary. Sentiment data suggests the turnover rate will remain high and may increase. Also, 81 percent of current employees and managers indicate they have considered resigning in the last 30 days.

Figure B-1. Employee Retention Rates

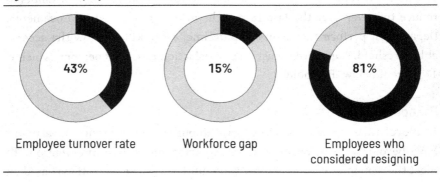

| Employee turnover rate | Workforce gap | Employees who considered resigning |

Department performance failures can be traced to employee turnover and workforce gaps. Current service level KPIs (call availability, average handling rate, and first-call resolution rates) have been below target rates for more than a year. The department's current workforce is insufficient to meet increased customer demand. Prior to 2020, the department met or exceeded all KPIs. Customer demand increased by 120 percent from 2020 to 2021, while the employee turnover rate increased by 7 percent and the workforce gap was created. Turnover has increased by an additional 6 percent, and the workforce gap has increased to 15 percent. To meet KPIs, turnover must improve by at least 11 percent and workforce gaps must improve by at least 10 percent (Figure B-2).

Figure B-2. Key Gaps

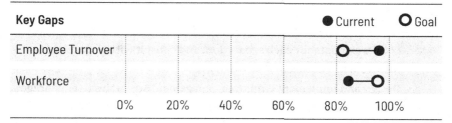

Key Gaps	● Current	○ Goal

Turnover is causing performance declines resulting in customer dissatisfaction. The customer service department is understaffed and underperforming. Most employees reported increased stress (82 percent) and decreased morale (76 percent). The department's KPIs, all of which are currently at failing rates, represent the customer experience, which is currently in steep decline. The current customer satisfaction rate has dropped to 68 percent. Solutions are required to improve employee retention as a driver for department performance to improve the customer satisfaction rate to an acceptable level of 85 percent or more (Figure B-3).

Figure B-3. Customer Satisfaction Rating

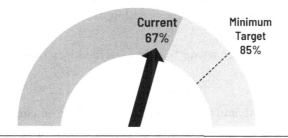

Recommendations

Our recommendations include internal and external solutions to implement immediately and additional recommendations for continuous improvement. Progress will be measured three, six, nine, 12, 15, and 18 months after implementation. Benchmarks include employee turnover, the workforce gap, department KPI scores, and customer satisfaction rates.

Recommended Internal Solutions—Implement Immediately

Human resources:

- Monitor resignations and terminations for the next three months, collect exit data for each separation, and consult with department leadership as needed.
- Design and implement employee engagement strategies to encourage retention. The department's employee appreciation budget line can fund these efforts.
    - The external training solution we recommend can be implemented with the remaining $1,150 in the budget. Consider reallocating those funds to the employee appreciation budget for the HR team to use in these efforts.
- Revise or reassign responsibilities to provide department managers with time to support frontline employees.
- Provide coaching for department managers.
- Repurpose two of the three open manager roles to hire quality assurance specialists instead.

Business analytics and marketing:

- Review department processes to ensure KPI alignment.
- Identify opportunities for operational improvement.
- If KPI measures do not improve within six months, CFO intervention is recommended.
- Analyze customer satisfaction data and identify strategies for improvement.

Functional training:

- Create job aids and reference documents to help employees and managers meet quality assurance standards and performance metrics.
- Provide functional training on QA and KPI expectations.

Recommended External Solution—Implement Immediately

Training for leadership development:

- Vendor solution
    - Solutions budget: $12,000
    - Recommendation cost: $10,850

- The customer service director and managers will benefit from targeted leadership development training. The needs assessment team has identified a local vendor who will deliver a day-long workshop on-site and provide three follow-up coaching sessions for each participant. The workshop will provide strategies and best practices for employee engagement and retention, positive workplace culture, and customer service.

Recommended Continuous Improvement Solutions— Implement for 3–18 Months

Human resources, business analytics, and functional training teams:

- Measure progress after three, six, nine, 12, and 18 months to determine the effectiveness of implemented solutions and identify opportunities for continuous improvement. Benchmarks include employee turnover, the workforce gap, KPI scores, and customer satisfaction rates.
- HR will monitor resignations and terminations for the next 18 months and collect exit interview data for each separation. Reports will be compiled once a quarter.
- The BA team will meet with the department director once a month to review KPIs and customer satisfaction scores.

Recommended Executive Leadership Solution—Hybrid Work Pilot Program

Customer service director:

- Remote work is the top factor currently affecting employee retention, job satisfaction, and the workforce gap. A company-wide needs assessment is recommended to determine the potential risks, benefits, and requirements of remote work options.
- If the company conducts a pilot program for hybrid (or remote) work, the customer service director will allow the department to participate as long as employees meet department process requirements and daily performance standards.

Index

Page numbers followed by *f* refer to figures; page numbers followed by *t* refer to tables.

References and Resources

Ahn, J. 2021. "To Make Better Decisions, Mitigate Bias." *TD*, March 3. td.org/
magazines/td-magazine/to-make-better-decisions-mitigate-bias.

Altschuld, J.W., and B.R. Witkin. 2000. *From Needs Assessment to Action:
Transforming Needs Into Solution Strategies.* Thousand Oaks, CA:
SAGE Publications.

Altschuld, J.W., and R. Watkins. 2014. "A Primer on Needs Assessment: More
Than 40 Years of Research and Practice." *New Directions for Evaluation. Needs
Assessment: Trends and a View Toward the Future* 144: 5–18.

ATD (Association for Talent Development). 2018. *Needs Assessments: Design and
Execution for Success.* Alexandria, VA: ATD Press.

ATD (Association for Talent Development). 2019. *10 Steps to Successful
Presentations*, 2nd ed. Alexandria, VA: ATD Press.

ATD (Association for Talent Development). 2020. Talent Development Body of
Knowledge (TDBoK). Alexandria, VA: ATD Press.

ATD (Association for Talent Development). 2022. *2022 State of the Industry.
Alexandria, VA*: ATD Press.

ATD (Association for Talent Development). 2022. *Succession Planning: Preparing
Organizations for the Future.* Alexandria, VA: ATD Press. td.org/research
-report/succession-planning-preparing-organizations-for-the-future.

Barnes, B.K. 2019. *Building Better Ideas: How Constructive Debate Inspires
Courage, Collaboration and Breakthrough Solutions.* Oakland, CA: Berrett-
Koehler Publishers.

Bennis, W.G., and B. Nanus. 2007. *Leaders: Strategies for Taking Charge.* New York:
HarperBusiness Essentials.

Bergin, T. 2018. *An Introduction to Data Analysis: Quantitative, Qualitative and Mixed Methods.* Thousand Oaks, CA: SAGE Publications.

Bickham, T., ed. 2021. *ATD Talent Management Handbook.* Alexandria, VA: ATD Press.

Biech, E., ed. 2022. *ATD's Handbook for Training and Talent Development,* 3rd ed. Alexandria, VA: ATD Press.

Boller, S., and L. Fletcher. 2020. *Design Thinking for Training and Development: Creating Learning Journeys That Get Results.* Alexandria, VA: ATD Press.

Borton, T. 1970. *Reach, Touch, and Teach: Student Concerns and Process Education.* New York: McGraw-Hill.

Botsman, R. 2012. "The Currency of the New Economy Is Trust." Video. TED, June. ted.com/talks/rachel_botsman_the_currency_of_the_new _economy_is_trust.

Brodo, R. 2018. "Business Acumen Basics for Talent Development." *TD at Work.* Alexandria, VA: ATD Press. td.org/td-at-work/business-acumen-basics -for-talent-development.

Burton, J.K., and P.F. Merrill. 1977. "Needs Assessment: Goals, Needs, and Priorities." In *Instructional Design: Principles and Applications,* edited by L.J. Briggs. Englewood Cliffs, NJ: Educational Technology Publications.

Chalofsky, N. 2001. "How to Conduct Focus Groups," *Infoline.* Alexandria, VA: ATD Press.

Cole, M. 2016. "Surveys From Start to Finish," *TD at Work.* Alexandria, VA: ATD Press.

Covey, S.M.R., and R.R. Merrill. 2018. *The SPEED of Trust: The One Thing That Changes Everything.* New York: Free Press.

Creswell, J.W. 1998. *Qualitative Inquiry and Research Design: Choosing Among Five Traditions.* Thousand Oaks, CA: SAGE Publications.

Driscoll, J., ed. 2007. *Practicing Clinical Supervision: A Reflective Approach for Healthcare Professionals.* Edinburgh: Elsevier.

Duarte, N. 2010. *Resonate: Present Visual Stories That Transform Audiences.* Hoboken, NJ: John Wiley and Sons.

Elliott, P.H., and A.C. Folsom. 2013. *Exemplary Performance: Driving Business Results by Benchmarking Your Star Performers.* San Francisco: Jossey-Bass.

Frei, F. 2018. "How to Build (and Rebuild) Trust." Video. TED, April. ted.com/ talks/frances_frei_how_to_build_and_rebuild_trust/transcript.

Fusch, P.I., and L.R. Ness. 2015. "Are We There Yet? Data Saturation in Qualitative Research." *The Qualitative Report* 20(9): 1408–1416. doi. org/10.46743/2160-3715/2015.2281.

Gary, L. 2021. "Focusing on Alignment and Integration: Practicing What We Teach." ATD Webinar, June 24. webcasts.td.org/webinar/4289.

Glenn, J.C. 1972. "Futurizing Teaching vs Futures Course." *Social Science Record*, Syracuse University, 9(3): 26–29.

Glenn, J.C. 2009. "The Futures Wheel." In *Futures Research Methodology 3.0*, edited by J.C. Glenn and T.J. Gordon. Washington, DC: The Millennium Project.

Griffiths, C. 2019. *The Creative Thinking Handbook: Your Step-by-Step Guide to Problem Solving in Business.* New York: Kogan Page.

Guest, G., A. Bunce, and L. Johnson. 2006. "How Many Interviews Are Enough?: An Experiment With Data Saturation and Variability." *Field Methods* 18(1): 59–82. doi.org/10.1177/1525822X05279903.

Hall, MJ. 2021. "Make Your Data Dance." *TD*, February 19. td.org/magazines/ td-magazine/make-your-data-dance.

Indeed Editorial Team. 2022. "What Is a Needs Assessment? (Plus How to Conduct One)." Indeed Career Guide, October 19. indeed.com/career -advice/career-development/needs-assessment.

Kirpatrick, J.D., and W.K. Kirkpatrick. 2016. *Kirkpatrick's Four Levels of Training Evaluation.* Alexandria, VA: ATD Press.

Knaflic, C.N. 2015. *Storytelling With Data: A Data Visualization Guide for Business Professionals.* Hoboken, NJ: John Wiley and Sons.

Knowles, M.S., E.F. Holton, III, and R.A. Swanson. 2015. *The Adult Learner: The Definitive Classic in Adult Education and Human Resource Development*, 8th ed. New York: Routledge.

Koch, R. 2008. *The 80/20 Principle: The Secret to Achieving More With Less.* New York: Doubleday.

Krueger, R.A., and M.A. Casey. 2009. *Focus Groups: A Practical Guide for Applied Research*, 4th ed. Thousand Oaks, CA: SAGE Publications.

Lareau, A. 2021. *Listening to People: A Practical Guide to Interviewing, Participant Observation, Data Analysis, and Writing It All Up.* Chicago: University of Chicago Press.

McGoldrick, B., and D. Tobey. 2016. *Needs Assessment Basics*, 2nd ed. ATD Training Basics Series. Alexandria, VA: ATD Press.

Meadows, D.H., and D. Wright. 2015. *Thinking in Systems: A Primer*. White River Junction, VT: Chelsea Green Publishing.

Michalko, M. 2006. *Thinkertoys: A Handbook of Creative Thinking Techniques*, 2nd ed. New York: Ten Speed Press.

Michalko, M. 2021. *Cracking Creativity: The Secrets of Creative Genius*. Berkeley, CA: Ten Speed Press.

MindTools. n.d. "Developing Commercial Awareness: Understanding How Businesses Make Money." mindtools.com/pages/article/developing -commercial-awareness.htm.

Newbauer, K. 2023. *Aligning Instructional Design With Business Goals: Make the Case and Deliver Results*. Alexandria, VA: ATD Press.

Nuriddin. H. 2018. "Get the Whole Picture With a Performance Assessment." *TD at Work*. Alexandria, VA: ATD Press.

Oliver, L., and E.A. Nin. 2019. *10 Steps to Successful Budgeting*. Alexandria, VA: ATD Press.

Pangarkar, A., and T. Kirkwood. 2022. "Boost Your Financial IQ." *CTDO*, October 14. td.org/magazines/ctdo-magazine/boost-your-financial-iq.

Parkinson, M. 2018. *A Trainer's Guide to PowerPoint: Best Practices for Master Presenters*. Alexandria, VA: ATD Press.

Prestera, G. 2022. "Get Needs Assessment Right the First Time." *CTDO*, September 14. td.org/magazines/ctdo-magazine/get-needs-assessment -right-the-first-time.

Project Management Institute. 2021. *A Guide to the Project Management Body of Knowledge: (PMBOK® Guide)*, 7th ed. Newtown Square, PA: Project Management Institute.

Robinson, S.B., and K.F. Leonard. 2019. *Designing Quality Survey Questions*. Thousand Oaks, CA: SAGE Publications.

Rubin, H., and I. Rubin. 2012. *Qualitative Interviewing: The Art of Hearing Data*, 3rd ed. Thousand Oaks, CA: SAGE Publications.

Scott, B., and B.K. Barnes. 2021. *Consulting on the Inside: A Practical Guide for Internal Consultants*. Alexandria, VA: ATD Press.

Sleezer, C.M., D.F. Russ-Eft, and K. Gupta. 2014. *A Practical Guide to Needs Assessment*, 3rd ed. San Francisco: Pfeiffer.

Smith, W.K., and M.W. Lewis. 2022. *Both/And Thinking: Embracing Creative Tensions to Solve Your Toughest Problems.* Boston: Harvard Business Review Press.

Sweller, J. 1994. "Cognitive Load Theory, Learning Difficulty, and Instructional Design." *Learning and Instruction* 4(4): 295–312.

Torrance, M. 2023. *Data & Analytics for Instructional Designers.* Alexandria, VA: ATD Press.

Voss, C., and T. Raz. 2016. *Never Split the Difference: Negotiating as if Your Life Depended on It.* New York: Harper Business.

Wiseman, L. 2017. *Multipliers: How the Best Leaders Make Everyone Smarter.* New York: Harper Business.

Witkin, B.R., and J.W. Altschuld. 1995. *Planning and Conducting Needs Assessments: A Practical Guide.* Thousand Oaks, CA: SAGE Publications.

Zorbini, J. 2022. "Be a Planner." *CTDO*, April 15. td.org/magazines/ctdo-magazine/be-a-planner.

About the Authors

 **Kelly L. Jones, PhD,** is a researcher, leader, consultant, and problem solver with expertise in building solutions that help people and organizations learn. She has 20 years of experience in curriculum development, instructional design, needs assessments, learning technologies, and workplace training and development. She holds a PhD in curriculum and instruction from Mercer University, and a CPTD certification from ATD.

 **Jody N. Lumsden, EdD,** is a consultant, speaker, and facilitator with expertise developing and implementing strategy and data-driven performance metrics in the areas of adult and workplace learning, curriculum planning, change management, and leadership coaching. She has 17 years of professional experience as a talent development and graphic design practitioner. She holds a doctorate in curriculum design and instruction from McKendree University.

About ATD

The Association for Talent Development (ATD) is the world's largest association dedicated to those who develop talent in organizations. Serving a global community of members, customers, and international business partners in more than 100 countries, ATD champions the importance of learning and training by setting standards for the talent development profession.

Our customers and members work in public and private organizations in every industry sector. Since ATD was founded in 1943, the talent development field has expanded significantly to meet the needs of global businesses and emerging industries. Through the Talent Development Capability Model, education courses, certifications and credentials, memberships, industry-leading events, research, and publications, we help talent development professionals build their personal, professional, and organizational capabilities to meet new business demands with maximum impact and effectiveness.

One of the cornerstones of ATD's intellectual foundation, ATD Press offers insightful and practical information on talent development, training, and professional growth. ATD Press publications are written by industry thought leaders and offer anyone who works with adult learners the best practices, academic theory, and guidance necessary to move the profession forward.

We invite you to join our community. Learn more at **td.org.**